D1606676

Living on Automatic

Living on Automatic

How Emotional Conditioning Shapes Our Lives and Relationships

Homer B. Martin, MD, and Christine B. L. Adams, MD

Foreword by Mary E. Schwab, MD, MAR

 PRAEGER™

An Imprint of ABC-CLIO, LLC
Santa Barbara, California • Denver, Colorado

Library of Congress Cataloging-in-Publication Data

Names: Martin, Homer B., MD, author. | Adams, Christine B. L., MD, author.
Title: Living on automatic : how emotional conditioning shapes our lives and
   relationships / Homer B. Martin, MD, and Christine B. L. Adams, MD;
   foreword by Mary E. Schwab, MD, MAR.
Description: Santa Barbara : Praeger, [2018] | Includes bibliographical references
   and index.
Identifiers: LCCN 2018012896 (print) | LCCN 2018018529 (ebook) |
   ISBN 9781440865190 (ebook) | ISBN 9781440865183 (hardcopy : alk. paper)
Subjects: LCSH: Emotions. | Interpersonal relations.
Classification: LCC BF511 (ebook) | LCC BF511 .M277 2018 (print) |
   DDC 155.9/24—dc23
LC record available at https://lccn.loc.gov/2018012896

ISBN: 978-1-4408-6518-3 (print)
      978-1-4408-6519-0 (ebook)

22 21 20 19 18   1 2 3 4 5

This book is also available as an eBook.

Praeger
An Imprint of ABC-CLIO, LLC

ABC-CLIO, LLC
130 Cremona Drive, P.O. Box 1911
Santa Barbara, California 93116-1911
www.abc-clio.com

This book is printed on acid-free paper ∞

Manufactured in the United States of America

To our patients for their bravery in seeking self-understanding

"The circumstances of the world are so variable that an irrevocable purpose or opinion is almost synonymous with a foolish one."

—William H. Seward (1801–1872) (Secretary of State, 1861–1869; negotiated 1867 purchase of Alaska; opponent to spread of slavery before the United States' Civil War)

Contents

Foreword   xi
  Mary E. Schwab, MD, MAR

Preface   xiii
  Homer B. Martin, MD

Acknowledgments   xvii

Introduction   xix
  Christine B. L. Adams, MD

Part One   **Understanding Emotional Conditioning**   1

Chapter 1   How We Learn About Relationships   3

Chapter 2   Emotional Conditioning   13

Chapter 3   Seven Effects of Emotional Conditioning   29

Chapter 4   The Omnipotent Personality   43

Chapter 5   The Impotent Personality   60

Part Two   **Relationship Struggles: Miscommunications
and Marriages**   79

Chapter 6   Why We Miscommunicate   81

Chapter 7   Roles within Marriages   104

Chapter 8   Conflicts in Marriage   116

Chapter 9   Getting Divorced and Single Again   132

Part Three   Solutions: Psychotherapy and Deconditioning   149

Chapter 10   Emotional Illness and Therapy:
                  The Deconditioning Process   151

Chapter 11   What You Can Do to Decrease Living on Automatic   164

Notes   173

Suggested Reading and Viewing   175

Index   179

Foreword

Living on Automatic presents a unique and creative way to understand yourself and your relationships with others. This is new thinking, refreshingly presented in everyday language so that we can learn clearly how we were formed and who we are.

Much of our happiness, and our unhappiness, has its center in relationships. It is who we are, and our understanding of others, that defines and controls those relationships.

Dr. Adams has been my colleague in our parallel pathways of training and as therapists in adult, adolescent, and child psychiatry. I am grateful for her eight years of dedication and hard work in bringing to fruition Dr. Martin's new concepts, as expressed in this book. This is a lovely tribute to the importance of mentorship.

Dr. Martin and Dr. Adams are both psychiatrists and well-seasoned observers of the human condition. Their insights are drawn from a combined 80 years of work with hundreds of patients. What we find in their book is truly a new approach to understanding how personality and relationship difficulties cause problems for us.

I regret I never knew Dr. Martin. He had a reputation as a creative thinker and skilled practitioner. We can be grateful for his wisdom in thinking outside conventional psychiatric thought. It was this tension that steered his splendid mind down a new path of human understanding.

I have known Dr. Adams most of my life, personally and professionally. She has written about the suffering and treatment of children. She is highly respected for her clinical talents and her incisive understanding of how personalities impact our lives, particularly the central role of personality in our close relationships.

The beauty of this book is that it goes far deeper than self-help. We are asked to *think*, which is a breath of fresh air, because it helps us dig deeper and reveals how we can live with greater know-how, inner direction, tranquility, and thus improved relationships. Martin and Adams show us how to discover who we are, what people we become attracted to, and why.

They explain what they learned about emotional conditioning, what automatic responding does to us, and how it creates relationship struggles. Importantly, they also give us hope by offering solutions for relationship difficulties. They discuss what relationship problems we have and how to lessen conflicts. They ask us: To what extent do you have knee-jerk, automatic, and unaware reactions to others?

Dr. Adams enriches Dr. Martin's concepts with many fascinating cases that enliven what emotional conditioning is, how it works and how we mesh together, but not always well. Most importantly, it offers insights into how you can understand and actively redirect your approach to the people you care about in your life.

I hope you enjoy as much as I have the rich discoveries this fine book offers.

Mary E. Schwab, MD, MA Religion
Associate Professor, Yale Child Study Center,
Child Psychiatry (Retired)
Yale University
New Haven, CT

Preface

Attempting to understand human nature is a pursuit as ancient as mankind itself, and this task has proven to be arduous and baffling. Both men's and women's thinking and behavior remain enigmatic. Despite centuries of study and research, no single, dependable theory of behavior has been proven scientifically. What we gain through the detailed study of one individual may not apply to the next person. Theories to explain the endless variations among individuals may be useful or instructive, but none are completely successful.

Devising a new approach to understanding human psychology and emotional disorder was the furthest idea from my mind 40 years ago when I began training to be a psychotherapist. At that time, I was concerned with learning the theories in vogue then and applying them to patients. My experience revealed the unpleasant truth that the best theory available provided a limited understanding and little of substance to relieve my patients' torments. For a psychotherapist, theories are only useful if they have therapeutic application. In order to achieve widespread scientific acceptance, a theory must be testable by other objective participants. Had I recognized all these difficulties at the outset, I would have gladly pursued a much simpler task.

A few years of frustration led me to discard those psychological concepts that I found did not lead to improvement for my patients. I listened to people with emotional disturbances for several hours a day, and patterns began to emerge that I had not seen previously described. Over 40 years as a practicing psychiatrist, I developed a new concept of normal and abnormal function. As the pieces fell into place, I became more confident of their validity by corroborating their presence in other patients.

I collaborated closely with Dr. Christine Adams and with several colleagues in psychiatry, psychology, and social work, and I was gratified by their endorsements of my work. Although they initially showed caution in embracing a wholly new idea, my confidence in my new findings grew as my colleagues adopted it for diagnosis and treatment in their own psychotherapeutic practices. Perhaps even more encouraging were the reactions of people who knew very little about psychology. On hearing a brief outline of the personality types I proposed, many recognized these dual personality types in their relatives or themselves.

For this reason, I decided to write this book for a general audience rather than for professionals. It is my hope to reach readers who are curious about why they and their family members and friends think and act as they do. I have avoided technical language as much as possible without sacrificing accuracy, and I do not include footnotes referencing scientific theories since this work is a new approach to the study of personality and conditioning.

I hope *Living on Automatic* will illuminate and clarify previous concepts and theories about personality. This book will have served its purpose if it provides our readers with an accurate and useful way to understand the behavior of others and of themselves.

Considering new information in the face of preconceived ideas can be a difficult task. For one thing, hundreds of different psychotherapeutic approaches are used worldwide, many of which are based on Freud's original work. It is also difficult to understand mental processes due to their unconscious nature. In order to understand other people, we need to have an accurate knowledge of how our own mind functions. Embarking on this search for self-knowledge is like a voyage—vast depths lie unexplored beneath the surface. This book is devoted to exploring these mental depths. It may strike readers as being unreal and improbable at times. This is inevitable when venturing into unknown territory for the first time.

Ultimately, all new ideas are generated by a problem. As a psychotherapist dealing with the common but distressing problems of my patients, I was assailed by many questions but found few satisfactory answers. It became apparent to me that no family could escape having significant conflict and pain. The ideal, loving family exists only in fantasy. I pondered why so many of us make gross miscalculations in judging the people who are most vital to us. Many individuals seem drawn to those who hurt them, rejecting others who might be very supportive and helpful.

Marriage and cohabitation are the principle relationship decisions of life and are fraught with difficulty. No one can ignore the disastrous divorce rate and the challenges in maintaining a mutually positive long-term relationship. Social problems of crime, drug addiction, emotional illness, poverty, and marital problems are so widespread in our society that no one is unaffected. Ingenious scientific advances demonstrate the remarkable capability of the human mind. On the other hand, we continue to settle basic disagreements by murder and warfare with the same barbaric fervor seen in ancient times. Historians are puzzled that we have made such remarkable technological and material progress, yet continue to repeat the same emotional blunders and refuse to learn from experience.

All of the questions arising in psychotherapy relate to people and how they interrelate. There has always been some barrier separating us from the vital information necessary to answer these questions. If this unconscious barrier can be breached, many of the human problems addressed in therapy can be understood better and resolved. Long experience suggests we need a wholly different approach to penetrate this barrier.

I refer to this new approach as *emotional conditioning,* which creates two personality styles—*omnipotent* and *impotent.* I trust that you will not only acquire from this book a clear, definite method for recognizing your own specific psychological makeup, but also learn why this has been impossible in the past. I hope it inspires some curiosity about self-understanding and that you will come to know and appreciate yourself as you are. What we cannot understand cannot be controlled.

In the decades spent developing these ideas, I was brought to a halt many times. To my patients who presented these stimulating opportunities, you have my lasting gratitude for your endurance and tolerant patience. It required real courage on your part to be pioneers in the construction of a new concept and mode of treatment.

I wish to express my sincere appreciation to Dr. Jane Polsky who wrote her doctoral dissertation to see if the two basic character types, omnipotent and impotent, could be shown to exist in the oldest piece of literature available in the Western tradition. Using a portion of the Greek text of Homer's *Iliad,* Dr. Polsky found statistical evidence for the two generic personality types still present in our society today. Likewise, the two character types tend to use certain words and manner of expressing themselves in an exclusive way, which is as true today as it was then, more than 2,700 years ago.

Finally, to my intimate friends and family members who believed in my work, my heartfelt gratitude. In times of discouragement over the problems inherent in plowing new psychological ground, the unfailing support of Drs. Lonnie Howerton and James Lee Fisher was vital to my moving forward, as was the unfailing support of my wife, Jane. I feel your sharing every development in my obsessive labor with *emotional conditioning* should, in all fairness, grant you equal credit for whatever good we have accomplished. My gratitude and affection are given to you all.

Now the time has come for us to rest from the unrelenting task and put the record of our shared endeavor in the hands, and minds, of our readers.

Homer B. Martin, MD

Acknowledgments

It took three decades to write this book. There are many people to thank.

We thank our patients for giving us the opportunity to help diminish their suffering and improve their lives. This is why we became psychiatrists. We thank them for their courage in engaging in the difficult work of psychotherapy. They each took part in our discoveries.

Dr. Martin was grateful for the friendship and counsel of Lonnie Howerton, MD, and James Lee Fisher, PhD. They read early drafts of his manuscripts and encouraged him.

Jane Martin, Dr. Martin's widow, honored me by asking me to be the custodian of his ideas and thoughts and take them to print. I am grateful for the confidence she has in me. There is no finer tribute for me as Dr. Martin's protégée than being asked to bring his work to a widespread audience.

Bringing a new understanding of the human condition from inception to the printed page is a long, challenging journey. Many people helped after Dr. Martin's death in 2007. Family, friends, associates, acquaintances, and strangers extended their minds and hands to read, edit, and discuss the concepts in this book. They are from a variety of professional backgrounds from fire chief to massage therapist, psychologists, counselors, and social workers to attorneys, substance abuse counselors to physicians, psychiatrists to schoolteachers, minister to pharmaceutical representatives, and computer analyst to financial adviser. In alphabetical order they are G. H. Beckmeyer, Jennifer Bell, Carol Clifton, Dale Cummins, Kevin Fall, James Lee Fisher, Todd Gardner, Shannon Head-Cunningham, Ron Higdon, DeWitt Ivins, Barbara Jackson, Rich Jones, Moshe Landsman, Judy Milner, Brenda Pappas, Mary Pinson, Cheri Powell, Homayoun Sadeghi, Mary Schwab, José Manuel Valdes-Cruz, and James Wayne. I am grateful to them all.

I participated in Steve Harrison's Quantum Leap Program. The coaches provided professional direction in completing the book, editing, finding a publisher, and marketing. The book benefits from the professional expertise of Debra Englander, Martha Bullen, and Geoffrey Berwind. I am grateful for their able assistance and enthusiasm.

Editors Heidi Grauel and Martha Bullen brought professional talent and exquisite judgment. They corralled the heady structure and academic language and made sure the writing is accessible for a general readership, which Dr. Martin and I both aspired to do.

We are grateful to Praeger and ABC-CLIO for supporting two psychiatrists with a new idea on how to help people better understand their emotional sufferings in relationships.

Dr. Martin and I could not have brought together this book without the unwavering support and kindness of our spouses, Jane Martin and Barry Chafin. They not only typed the entire manuscript many times but also edited, critiqued, put up with discussing the ideas repeatedly when we needed to do so, and rolled their eyes when we worked on the book during vacations. My dear Barry—a journalist by training—advocated forcefully for less convoluted writing, and sometimes I listened. He also dried my tears and knew when to take me out to dinner or away from book writing for a spell so that I might retain my sanity. We are in the debt of such fine mates.

Introduction

Now, well into the 21st century, humans have accomplished incredible innovation. We sent men to the moon and developed immunizations to guard against disease. Incredibly powerful, increasingly compact technology can fit in a smartphone or a watch. Yet, despite this knowledge and how well we apply it, we still lack self-understanding. We have yet to understand why the divorce rate is high, or why one depressed person goes to bed and shuts the world out while another goes and commits mass homicide. We use legal and illicit drugs to reduce anxiety and turmoil. Many of our internal and external conflicts result in emotional illnesses, soaring divorce rates, and damaged family structures. These are just a few factors that suggest life is stressful and difficult to manage. It seems ironic that the luxuries of modern life often come with overwhelming emotional and interpersonal tensions.

New insight into human behavior is rare. New insight into human understanding is even more rare. This book presents both.

If you are like most people, you have, at times, questioned your understanding of yourself and your behavior and have had frustrating relationships. If you are a parent, you may have scratched your head and wondered how your children could be so different from you. You may be confused about why you are attracted to people who are distant or abusive. You may wonder why you have been divorced. What went wrong? Everything seemed so good at the beginning of the relationship. If you've been married more than once, you may wonder why your spouses share similarities. You are not alone. These relationship difficulties are nothing to be ashamed of.

The ways we relate to each other have changed little over time. The earliest written literature shows people behaving in many of the same ways we do now. *The Iliad* and the stories of both Hebrew and Christian scripture contain stories of love, family, relationships, jealousy, weakness, conflict, and violently cruel behaviors as well as generous and kind behaviors toward others. These stories touch something within us, indicating that these behaviors are still alive in all of us.

Living on Automatic is about the discovery of and assembly of a new concept about people, personalities, and relationships. It traces the development of this new concept and is designed to help you better understand yourself and your relationships with others. This book shares experiences and insights drawn from the authors' combined eight decades of seeking self-understanding and knowledge of how others think and behave. The concepts presented to you here were developed and tested through our work with almost 2,000 people, mostly patients in psychodynamic psychotherapy, and verified by our family members, friends, and colleagues. Psychodynamic psychotherapy explores people's early lives to connect what they learned as a child with how they function now.

Our quests have been to understand what causes emotional distress, problems, and emotional illnesses and learn how to treat these illnesses. Dr. Martin used the term *emotional conditioning*. He observed that people start becoming emotionally conditioned, or shaped, beginning within the first two to three years of life by their parents or caretakers. He also discovered that people are emotionally conditioned into one of two roles that become the basis of their personalities. Dr. Martin called these the *omnipotent* role and the *impotent* role. An omnipotent is emotionally conditioned to believe he or she is all-powerful and can emotionally please and do for others while neglecting himself or herself. An impotent is conditioned to believe he or she is helpless to show care for others and, instead, can only demand constant emotional care and attention from others. We observed that these two personality types relate to others in fixed patterns throughout their lives.

By understanding these two personalities, omnipotent and impotent, you can learn how to observe these roles, see how either applies to you, and improve your own relationships with your children, spouses, siblings, coworkers, and extended family.

The idea that our unconscious mental processes influence every moment of our lives and shape all our relationships seemed very complicated in 1967, when Dr. Martin first became a psychiatrist. He spent every day facing this confusion as he searched for some unifying principles. Psychotic patients are very disorganized in their communications, and their treatment is confined largely to medications and social support. Although sympathetic to their plight, Dr. Martin chose to concentrate on emotional disorders in "ordinary" people who were unlikely to become psychotic even under the most remote and disastrous circumstances.

At first, Dr. Martin tried to utilize treatment methods that were taught in his training. None of the treatments and theories he had learned in his training helped his patients, and this frustrated him. He decided to step away from his formal training, but starting from a clean slate was not easy. He returned to the basic psychiatric skills of listening and asking probing questions. Then, he and his patients mulled things over to see what new thoughts and observations came up. He studied his patients with no assumption that he understood anything about them. He focused on treating individuals with psychodynamic psychotherapy—no couples and no families. He wanted a concentrated and in-depth study of individual patients to focus on the complexities of individual lives and their troubles.

Dr. Martin gathered data over several decades and tested his assumptions by sharing his thoughts about his patients' problems with them. He requested feedback from patients after they had observed themselves and thought about what was discussed during their sessions. This back and forth process helped his patients gain insights and improved their depression, anxiety, obsessions, and relationships. And, it helped Dr. Martin grasp a new idea of why people became emotionally ill. He saw patterns that had not previously been observed.

Our Unique Contributions in *Living on Automatic*

Many people contributed to our understanding of conditioning and the field of behaviorism—notably, Ivan Pavlov (1849–1936), John Watson (1878–1958), Konrad Lorenz (1903–1989), and B. F. Skinner (1904–1990). These experts viewed conditioning as focused on behaviors, not thoughts or emotions.

We offer a new approach to understanding conditioning in this book. Our first contribution is an understanding of "emotional" conditioning, how it impacts and shapes not only our behaviors but also our thinking, the ways we see others and ourselves, and the ways we experience and express our emotions.

Dr. Martin and I did not study animals as many behaviorists did. Instead, we studied people, our patients, in depth and over long periods of time. We wanted to discover not only how they behaved, but also how they felt, thought, and lived in their relationships and how they developed their emotional dysfunctions and illnesses.

We also wanted to help our patients get better and recover from their distress. Historically, behaviorism and conditioning treat problem behaviors with behavior therapy, usually behavior modification. This treatment involves offering punishment or negative reinforcement to extinguish undesirable behaviors and offering a reward or positive reinforcement for desired behaviors. Strict behaviorists do not delve into the mind of a person they are studying. Instead, they focus on external behaviors that can be seen. Behaviorists believe the mind is a "black box," and it is unnecessary to know what goes on in the black box to alter people's behaviors.

Our second contribution lies in the method of treating our patients. We did not just want to change their behaviors. We sought to get inside the "black box" of the mind and discover how our patients thought about themselves and their relationships. In addition, we used techniques found in psychodynamic psychotherapy instead of using behavior modification.

This form of treatment helps people discover that their ways of behaving, thinking, and feeling, which they learned in childhood, may be causing their emotional distress and relationship problems. This treatment has its roots in the early 1900s with Sigmund Freud. Freud and Pavlov were contemporaries who both wanted to understand people's minds but whose approaches were quite different. Pavlov studied dogs in laboratories. Freud studied people in his clinical psychiatric practice.

We discovered that children appear to be emotionally conditioned in their thinking and emotions about themselves, their parents, and the world. Such conditioning is unconscious learning that takes place insidiously, stealthily, and manifests in automatic responses in your relationships.

In treating our patients, we used what we called "deconditioning" psychotherapy techniques with our patients. We uncovered the ways they were conditioned as young children and scrutinized how their conditioning affected their thinking, emotions, relationships, and behaviors.

In the process of studying emotional conditioning, we asked ourselves these questions. If a person can appreciate how he is emotionally conditioned and how this process takes place unconsciously, could he learn to stop his automatic conditioned responses by using conscious thought to override his automatic responses? And, will doing this make him stronger psychologically and remove his symptoms and dysfunctional ways of seeing himself and relating with others? We wrote this book in order to share our answers with a wider readership.

Meeting Homer B. Martin, MD

One year after my medical school graduation from the University of Florida, and a year into my general psychiatry residency training in Louisville, I met Dr. Martin. It was 1977. By lucky chance I was assigned to work with him, and he became my supervisor.

I had wanted to be a child psychiatrist for a long time. In residency, I was interested in how my patients' minds worked. I studied the popular historical and current theories of emotional distress and how to treat these illnesses. I loved doing psychotherapy. One of the first things I noticed was how alike many of my patients were, even though they were from different families. And, their relationships with family members, friends, and coworkers were managed in similar ways. *How could this be?* I wondered.

Fortunately, that is when I met Dr. Martin. He encouraged me to listen and to observe my patients and avoid judging them solely against the theories I had learned in training. He had been practicing this method for 10 years. For the next 30 years, I shared my observations and thoughts while doing psychotherapy with both children and adults and in family therapy. Dr. Martin introduced me to his concept of emotional conditioning and its two roles. Our joint observations led to our work in understanding people from infancy through old age.

Sadly, Dr. Martin died in 2007, leaving an unfinished manuscript. His wife, Jane Martin, surprised and honored me by asking me to complete and add to Dr. Martin's work and carry out his wishes that his book be published to share his findings. Accordingly, I have edited and added to the book what Dr. Martin was not able to finish. I also add a child psychiatrist's perspective from my 40 years of psychotherapeutic work with children and families, in community mental health, private practice, academia, schools, and the legal system.

Going beyond Our Offices

Dr. Martin discovered a way of understanding people, which became an effective tool for emotional and behavioral change and self-awareness in psychotherapy work. But, both of us had wondered, could the concepts be taught to nonpatients and be helpful to them?

After Dr. Martin died, I began teaching classes on emotional conditioning through The Veritas Society of Bellarmine University in Louisville. These classes are for people 55 years and older—many are in their seventies, some in their nineties. I taught Dr. Martin's concepts of impotent and omnipotent personalities. My students had no prior exposure to the notion of emotional conditioning. I wanted to see if people could not only grasp these ideas but also find them useful in their lives. The answer was a resounding yes. My students gained insights into the emotional conditioning of themselves, their children, parents, and grandchildren. They learned to deal with others in a better way than they had before the classes. They were more aware, and the new knowledge stayed with them. Once, during a class, a woman in her sixties stood up and with great excitement said, "Now I get it! I understand why I have married three different men who are all the same. I've never understood this before, even with all the therapy I've had."

The findings included in this book are valuable because they give us a logical and clear way to better understand others and ourselves. It is also a new approach that we want others to evaluate for themselves.

Our Plan for the Book

There is much that you need to know in the first two-thirds of our book before you can begin using the solutions offered in Part Three. Part One introduces the new concept of emotional conditioning, how it was discovered, and what it means for your daily life. Part Two applies this concept to long-term romantic relationships and marriage. You need this background to be able to make changes in your relationships. In Part Three, you will see how you can make changes and live a more fulfilling life. Our advice is to keep reading so you will be able to understand how to put these new ideas into practice.

We begin in Chapter 1 with the importance of early relationships for all of us. Early relationships give us the template and guide by which all our future relationships are conducted. By age two or three, our parents begin to teach us about relationships with great precision. This chapter details how emotional dysfunctions and illnesses take place and how emotional and mental illnesses are different. We describe an ideal well-balanced person who is free of emotional strife and illness, and how difficult it is to achieve this ideal.

In Chapter 2, Dr. Martin tells the story of how, in working with his patients, he uncovered and developed the concept of emotional conditioning and the two roles in which people function, regardless of age, sex, nationality, race, or religious upbringing. We present the first case that caused him to begin asking questions about how these roles are formed. We tell you how emotional conditioning appears to begin early in life before we learn language.

Chapter 3 discusses the reality of what being emotionally conditioned means in our daily lives—the errors people make and their blind spots when acting in their emotionally conditioned roles. We describe seven effects and consider if there might be a better way for us to assess people other than through our lens of emotional conditioning and its distortions. The chapter concludes with a table that summarizes descriptions of the emotionally conditioned roles.

In Chapters 4 and 5, we show you how the omnipotent and impotent roles or personalities develop and what they look like in infancy, preschool, grade school, adolescence, adulthood, and old age. We show how these personalities think and live their lives, the good and the ugly, offering extended case examples.

Chapter 6 explores the reasons we misunderstand and miscommunicate with one another and why we all become frustrated in our relationships. In Chapter 7, the discussion shifts to the most important adult relationship most of us have: marriage and long-term partnerships, whether heterosexual or homosexual. We share what we learned about how and why people choose the partners they do. We discuss courtship and its common role pairings—and uncommon ones—and share our view of love in marriage and the ways emotional conditioning alters its meaning.

Chapter 8 describes the roles that take place in marriage and common marital conflicts that cause arguments and may lead to the end of a marriage such as financial stress, coparenting, and substance abuse. We delve into the emotional difficulties and illnesses that take place in marriages. We also share our observations as to why sexual attraction and extramarital relationships take place and what their function is in marriages.

In Chapter 9 we address marriages gone wrong and discuss how and why divorces take place. We delve into the legal side of divorce and explore the effects on children. How people return to single life after divorce and their interest in remarriage are hot topics at the end of this chapter.

In Chapter 10, we talk about psychotherapy and the deconditioning process that we both practiced with our patients. This process was helpful to patients overcoming relationship and emotional problems. We tell you how emotional illness may begin with physical symptoms, but the fundamental cause resides in relationship problems, and we offer possibilities for preventing emotional illnesses. We found there is no such thing as being "normal." It appears we may all be emotionally conditioned to one degree or another and liable to react to life's personal encounters in a somewhat inappropriate and conditioned way. We describe how the "deconditioned" person functions. And, we include two cases of successful deconditioning therapy, one omnipotent and one impotent.

In Chapter 11, we pose this question: What have you discovered about you? We supply strategies and steps for deconditioning yourself and give examples of people who do not engage in automatic emotional responses to one another. We also make suggestions for how you might teach your children these same techniques.

After reading this book, we hope you will have a better grasp of who you are: your emotionally conditioned role; the problems you'll encounter; the emotional illnesses you are prone to; the pitfalls in forming your relationships; and how to lessen and undo some of your emotional conditioning. Most importantly, we hope you'll learn how to live a less automatic, emotionally conditioned life so you can create a broader, clearer view of yourself, your life, and your relationships.

You will be exposed to many new ideas in this book about how to evaluate people and relationships. When venturing into new territory, it is useful to note the starting point. By the end of your journey, it will be useful to have a marker to measure how far these travels have taken you.

Before beginning to read, write down your personal appraisals of the most significant people in your life. What was your father like? What are your personal judgments about your mother, siblings, and other close relatives? Your closest friends? Romantic partners? Most importantly, list your own positive and less-than-positive traits. Save your record as a bookmark for additions to these descriptions as you read further.

As you progress through this book, we direct you to begin thinking about what kind of emotional conditioning you have received. We do this by giving you questions you can use to increase your self-awareness and work around your automatic emotional reactions in your relationships.

Such new ideas are not for the faint of heart, and a new concept for viewing reality may be difficult to accept. Please evaluate our findings by how well they do or do not relate to your own life. This is especially important for mental health professionals, people who have been involved in counseling or therapy, and those who have read psychology self-help books. Allow these concepts to sink in. See if they make sense as a new way of viewing yourself and others. We hope you enjoy the voyage.

Authors' note: The reader will note that both "he" and "she" are used throughout the book. Females are emotionally conditioned the same way males are. Interchanging "her" for "him" and vice versa in the text does not alter the meaning in any way.

Dr. Martin started writing this book and I finished it. His observations I refer to as "his" or "Dr. Martin's." Our joint observations that we shared I refer to as "we" or "us." And finally, for my experiences and observations I use "I."

Disclaimer

Case studies in the book are amalgams of different people we have known supplemented by our imaginations. They do not represent actual individuals. Instead, they illustrate the omnipotent and impotent roles that are evident in relationships. Background information is included to familiarize the reader with common interactions among the various roles in families. Keep in mind that most families have members in these same roles.

Some cases are more fully developed and demonstrate what people are like in more detail throughout their life span. Others are brief descriptions that illustrate points we are making. They are all intended to illustrate the ways the personalities or roles interact.

Christine B. L. Adams, MD

PART 1

Understanding Emotional Conditioning

CHAPTER ONE

How We Learn About Relationships

Abigail was in her mid-forties when she entered my office with bloodshot eyes puffy from crying, no makeup, and a downcast gaze. Her clothes were rumpled. She burst into tears as she told me she was distraught over learning her husband of 20 years was having an affair with another woman. Abigail said it was her fault because she had begun full-time work outside the home. She said her husband was upset she was gone so much, and he felt he and the children were being neglected.

When I met Briana, in her early fifties, she was impeccably dressed, well groomed, and wore makeup. Her look was stern, almost frowning, with knitted brows. She told me she was angry over learning her wife of 12 years was having an affair with another woman. Briana said she blamed the "other woman" for being so seductive around her wife. She assigned no particular blame to her wife or herself. "My wife just did what anyone would do around a seducer," Briana explained.

Charles, in his early sixties, swept into my office and seated himself in an armchair. He was wearing jeans and a T-shirt, revealing an entire arm of tattoos. He told me he was angry to learn his wife of 22 years was having an affair. Charles explained his wife was "an irresponsible b*****" who didn't give a damn about him and the children. He told her he was going to file for divorce. He did not blame himself or the other man in any way.

All of these people experienced the same profoundly upsetting event, yet they saw their situation, themselves, and their spouses very differently. How could this be? Are people and their relationships infinitely variable, or are there common rules and principles we share that affect how we conduct relationships?

The quest to understand human nature has gone on for millennia. Every thoughtful person throughout the ages ponders this question, ultimately finding that age and time bring only more questions. Even at the end of our lives, we may still feel unable to understand other people and to comprehend ourselves.

Questions like these have been troubling people from ancient times until today:

- What is this life all about?
- Do my loved ones really care for me?
- Why do some people admire me while others despise me?
- What can I do to be loved?
- Why do I have conflicts with my friends, relatives, or mate?
- Why do evil thoughts come to my mind?
- When life overwhelms me, who can I turn to? Gods or spirits? Forces of nature? Myself?

We Do Not Learn Self-Understanding

When reading early works of literature and religious writing, we see remarkable similarities between the ancient characters described and people today. We find identical personalities from ancient to modern times and encounter the same recurring relationship problems and the same perplexing questions about life. We find emotional illnesses described in lucid terms that rival modern psychiatric case histories. These historic texts omit none of humankind's quirks, defects, or strengths that we recognize today.

Yet with all our modern knowledge, we don't seem to be any better at understanding ourselves or our relationships than those who lived long ago. Because of humanity's remarkable resistance to learn new approaches, people today use the same antiquated approaches to manage their relationships as people did centuries ago, and are no nearer to gaining self-understanding and emotional security than our ancestors were. Society has experienced impressive scientific breakthroughs in health, education, travel, business, and technology, but such achievements have not substantially enhanced our personal happiness or emotional welfare.

Those of us who work in the field of analyzing and resolving emotional problems are accustomed to hearing patients blame their stresses on external causes such as losing a job, financial problems, or career disappointments. In the end, however, we find that the cause is almost always a result of an ongoing conflict in interpersonal relationships. OUR SENSE OF WELL-BEING DEPENDS LARGELY ON THE STATUS OF OUR RELATIONSHIPS WITH OTHERS AND HOW WELL WE MANAGE THEM.

Most of us are intensely interested in personal relationships, and we are often unaware of the factors that determine their success or failure, or of the influence relationships have on other aspects of our lives. WE LEARN THE BASICS OF HOW TO RELATE TO OTHERS IN EARLY CHILDHOOD. THE WAY WE DO THAT DOES NOT SEEM TO CHANGE SIGNIFICANTLY THROUGHOUT OUR LIVES. AS LONG AS THE METHOD WE LEARNED ALLOWS US TO FUNCTION FAIRLY WELL, WE HAVE LITTLE REASON TO QUESTION ITS EFFECTIVENESS OR TO CONSIDER OTHER OPTIONS.

Our patients don't search for new ways to deal with problems or seek psychological help unless their methods for relating to others malfunction or fail altogether. Because a person suffering with emotional problems initially doesn't understand what is causing her symptoms, she may not know she even needs to ask for help. She might see outward signs that something is wrong, but have no idea that unconscious issues are directing the course and outcome of her relationships.

OVER THE YEARS, DR. MARTIN AND I OBSERVED THAT MOST RELATIONSHIPS ARE STRAINED AND COMPLICATED TO A SIGNIFICANT EXTENT BY THE COMBINED UNCONSCIOUS PATTERNS OF EACH OF THE PARTICIPANTS. IT'S NO WONDER THAT RELATIONSHIPS DEFY INTERPRETATION. Because we don't perceive any of our own unconscious influences, let alone those that affect others, we cannot fully comprehend our relationships. To achieve the intimate connections and successful relationships that we long to have, we must learn to understand the unconscious and how it acts on others and ourselves.

There is a major difficulty in writing a book on relationships. It is difficult to describe behaviors and emotional issues people struggle with that lie outside of their conscious awareness. Our goal is to help you become more aware of yourself. By reading the book, we hope you will become more familiar with how the unconscious is working in your own and others' lives, and be able to take control of situations that you want to change or improve.

To get started on discovering how we each learned to behave in relationships, we go back to the beginning and look at what happens to us as babies and toddlers.

Children Get Early Emotional Shaping

THE MOST IMPORTANT TASK OF EARLY CHILDHOOD IS TO ESTABLISH A METHOD OF RELATING WITH OTHERS. In infancy, a baby's survival depends on support from his parents or other caretakers. For the rest of his life, this experience of how his caregivers relate to him beginning in the first days, weeks, and months of life will govern his ability to deal with all others. What that baby learns will also affect his emotional health. A young child not only experiences all of his own reactions but will scrutinize his parents in minute detail in the ways they interact with him. These interactions are recorded indelibly during the vital first years of life. **WE NEVER ERASE THIS EARLY LEARNING ABOUT HOW RELATIONSHIPS WORK.**

By the time a child can talk, she begins to grasp the basic principles of social contact with others. In other words, she starts to acquire a foundation of socialization early—in the first two or three years of her life. She is taught how to relate to others by her primary caregivers, usually her parents. New parents often take on this daunting task with the belief that parenting skills come naturally. They rely on their own instincts instead of taking formal parenting classes. So, where do parents get their information on how to teach their children how to relate to others? From their own experiences during their childhood—from the way they were treated when they were children.

Most parents face the challenge of child rearing with determination to teach their children their own approaches for dealing with others. They consciously teach their children principles such as kindness, trust, reliability, and self-reliance. They also provide emotional affection, which affects the way a child will embrace these principles.

If you are a parent, you are likely aware of the values you wish to impress on your children because they are the ones you live your life by. What you are not aware of is that you convey unconscious emotional messages simultaneously with your conscious instructions. You may teach your child how to make her bed, but you will also teach her emotionally how to see bed-making—as a bothersome chore, as something to take pride in, or various other possibilities. These unconscious emotional messages are often different from those given consciously and may even contradict them. You may tell your child not to fight with a sibling, yet encourage him emotionally to settle differences with physical aggression if you strike him for misbehaving.

Because of unconscious emotional instruction we receive as children, our actions are often in conflict with and inconsistent with our ideas of who we are. A young child is extremely sensitive to his parents who make up his entire universe. He learns from the beginning that he can ignore certain verbal communications because another message, an unspoken and unconscious one, takes precedence.

An example is a father who tells his son to stay seated in the grocery cart, but who laughs with delight at his son's attempts to stand up or get out of the seat. This father does not correct his son for doing the opposite of what he instructed. His son gets the unspoken message through his father's emotional reaction of laughter that it's okay to disobey *verbal* directives. The boy recognizes the *real* message, which is his father's laughter, because it is charged emotionally. These emotional experiences establish how the boy sees his relationship with his father.

Now add another layer of complexity by including another parent. Parents send different messages to their child. A relationship with one parent might require a very different reaction than when dealing with the other parent. A child learns that although parents may agree verbally on their expectations, their subtler, unconscious messages often conflict. Taken together, these messages offer a coherent, if sometimes complex, approach toward dealing with other people. Each child learns them well.

Therapists who treat children with emotional disturbances understand that these unconscious emotional instructions govern a child's ultimate strategy of relating to people. The messages are highly consistent, and necessarily so, since they represent parents' ingrained attitudes toward others that make up the habitual patterns in their lives. Their emotional instructions are repeated continuously so that, by reinforcement, they become entrenched in their child's personality.

For instance, a child may be told verbally that she is important and loved, but she may hear a stronger, unconscious message of rejection that says, "You have no significance at all and I wish you'd stay at a distance." Or, on a conscious level, she may be told repeatedly the importance of being pleasant and following rules. On the unconscious level, she may be given the compelling message that she may do as she chooses without regard for others. A child who is being neglected or subtly abused by a parent may receive an unconscious instruction that such treatment is reasonable and that she is wrong to question cruel treatment or stand up for herself. When parents repeatedly send these unconscious messages, a child learns to follow them even if she wants to accept and follow the conscious intellectual messages her parents talk about.

WHAT PARENTS CONVEY TO THEIR CHILDREN AS THEY PREPARE THEM TO PARTICIPATE IN SOCIETY IS THEIR OWN METHOD OF RELATING TO OTHER INDIVIDUALS. A PARENT'S REACTION TO A CHILD'S OWN CLUMSY AND INEXPERIENCED EFFORTS TO BE ACCEPTED MOLDS EACH CHILD IN THE PARENTS' OWN IMAGE. EACH PARENT CAN AND WILL TEACH ONLY WHAT HE OR SHE KNOWS. Parents instill and mold their own standards in their children by these continuous emotional responses to their child's behavior. Unaware of the hidden messages their unconscious sends, parents transmit their values, roles, and standards that rigidly govern their child's characteristic response to any given situation involving other people.

This process governs how a child's personality begins to form in his first years of life. He acquires a method of relating to people that he will carry forward from his parents to his immediate environment, to school, and beyond to the demands of adulthood. A child constantly refines her methods and becomes more skillful and, with experience, can handle increasingly complex interactions. But the foundation bears the clear imprint of her parents' basic emotional instruction throughout life. The enduring nature of personality supports the common belief that the personality does not change. But a child's repeated and reinforced emotional conditioning provides continuous and repetitive training for her emerging personality. Each child's personality is established in a gradual but steady manner, its form depending on the particular child and the way her parents, beginning in her first years of life, shaped her.

Unfortunately, most of this early instruction is incomplete and unbalanced and is based on how parents have themselves been instructed. As already explained, this creates a lot of disharmony between the principles and values we want to teach our children and the emotional instruction we give them that sometimes contradicts these values. These contradictory messages often trigger anxiety, depression, and other emotional disorders and problems that develop in response to some of the ways we have been taught and trained in early childhood. These problems keep us from understanding the people we relate to as well as ourselves and wreak havoc in our interpersonal relationships.

How People Would Behave in an Ideal World

In an ideal society, children would grow up endowed with guidelines of behavior so well balanced and reasonable that they would act appropriately in every situation. They would be unfailingly thoughtful, though not a pushover, and share the same concern for others as for themselves. They would meet life's changes and stressful conditions with composure. In order to meet each situation appropriately, they would demonstrate exquisite sensitivity to others, remain flexible and empathetic to everyone, and be capable of navigating between extremes of behavior in both themselves and others. They would not be threatened by other peoples' beliefs that conflicted with their own and would even find them interesting and stimulating. They would understand themselves so well that they would feel neither superior nor inferior to others.

If we were all such well-balanced human beings, we would be exempt from emotional illnesses and be more valuable members of society. Unfortunately, although some of us have such admirable qualities, we would have difficulty existing in most societies of the world.

Although these ideals are extremely difficult to achieve, we can learn how to become more aware of ourselves so we can attain greater balance and compatibility in our relationships. When we continue functioning as we've been emotionally shaped, somewhat handicapped by the experiences we had as children and the way our parents taught us to relate to others and the world, we subject ourselves to many crippling outcomes such as anxiety, depression, and other emotional disturbances.

Let's take a closer look at these emotional illnesses, how they come about in early childhood, and how they affect our ability to see our relationships and ourselves clearly.

What the Need to Control Anxiety Does to Our Relationships

Our social relations would be chaotic if we didn't know what to expect from the important people in our lives. Since we unconsciously want to do what is expected to keep our social interactions running smoothly, we consistently behave in ways that give us predictable responses from others. In the process, we create our inflexible personalities as a self-imposed liability, and accept this handicap to decrease our anxieties. **WE TEND TO REACT TO OTHERS EMOTIONALLY AND REFLEXIVELY IN THE SAME WAY WHENEVER WE MEET THEM. WE LOSE SIGHT OF THE *CONTEXT* IN WHICH EACH INTERACTION WITH THEM TAKES PLACE.**

We strive to have our basic physical requirements and important emotional needs met. Physical needs lack the complexity and sensitivity of emotional needs. We are interdependent with others, and the emotional support we give one another makes survival worthwhile.

However, although we rely on each other for support, that doesn't mean our relationships are free of conflict. Many people experience significant relationship problems. When conflicts arise, we try to resolve them in the most expedient way to maintain a reasonable balance between the emotional support we give and receive. This is like trying to keep a seesaw balanced. If the stresses from our conflicts exceed our ability to cope, we begin to have emotional symptoms. These symptoms signal a warning to us that we're failing to control our anxiety. When this happens, the seesaw tilts too far up or down as our emotional support becomes unbalanced.

Emotional Overload Creates Emotional Illness

WE CAN DISCOVER HOW TO BE BETTER BALANCED BY INCREASING OUR AWARENESS OF THE LEGACY OF OUR EARLY CHILDHOOD EXPERIENCES. WHEN WE CONTINUE WITH THE EMOTIONALLY CONDITIONED THOUGHTS, BEHAVIORS AND EMOTIONS LEARNED AS CHILDREN, WE FALL PREY TO EMOTIONAL DIFFICULTIES AND ILLNESSES SUCH AS ANXIETY AND DEPRESSION. Let's look at how these emotional illnesses arise.

We observed in our psychotherapy practices that emotional dysfunctions or illnesses arise when stresses from relationship conflicts over a long time surpass our ability to reduce our anxiety. When we have ongoing interpersonal stress, we may have symptoms that totally perplex us. We may have stomachaches, headaches, weight gain or loss, insomnia, acid indigestion, substance abuse, and other symptoms. Our patients often state emphatically that the cause could not be emotional because they haven't experienced any changes in the pressures of everyday life.

Our inability to see the connection between physical symptoms and emotional disturbances results from a lack of awareness of how our mind and emotions operate. We may be unaware of what problems we are reacting to, which conflicts exceed our coping limits to manage anxiety, and our patterns of giving and receiving emotional support. We feel helpless in unraveling the mystery and have no idea how to respond or what actions to take. This often results in anxiety and depression.

Examples of emotional dysfunction or illness include a child who cannot adjust to school or social situations; a teenager who rebels or obsessively overachieves; a young adult who cannot adapt to work or marriage; a middle-aged person faced with a chaotic marriage or infidelity; or an older person who cannot accept aging, poor health, or life itself and plans suicide.

Emotional illness affects almost every family, and one family member's problems impact every other member. Although the toll in emotional impairment is not always apparent to others outside the family, it negatively affects everyone who is close to the person who is suffering.

Emotional Illnesses Are Different from Mental Illnesses

Emotional illnesses are upsetting and can be debilitating, but usually they can be successfully treated. They're different from mental illnesses, and their treatment is different. Major mental illnesses refer to severe dysfunctions of the mind and brain that may create psychotic states. In psychosis, a person's mind is so disturbed that she is unable to differentiate her ideas and fantasies from real events. Mental illnesses appear to come from disturbances of brain metabolism and function. We treat them mainly with medications (although psychotherapy certainly plays a role).

A person's loss of contact with reality and an inability to differentiate fact from fantasy, as in a psychotic break, is common in mental illnesses. But psychosis is neither common nor characteristic of someone who suffers from an emotional illness. Although some emotionally ill people may have some distortions of reality, they are rarely psychotic and have little likelihood of being so.

Although many of us think briefly of seeing a therapist when we are momentarily unhappy, few of us actually do so until our emotional condition seriously impairs our functioning. In many cultures, we still have stigma surrounding emotional illnesses. This stigma is one reason people avoid getting therapy and why it is a last resort. Despite the common misconception that emotional illnesses may be the same as or eventually lead to mental illnesses, this simply isn't so.

Most people who develop emotional illnesses recover spontaneously as they regain control of their coping mechanisms. As people receive increased emotional support from family, friends, or professionals, they usually recover. Some people recover if they leave their situation temporarily and go to a hospital for help. Others recover after taking medications, either self-prescribed or from a medical practitioner. Many health care professionals encourage these briefer treatments. However, none of these methods provides an understanding of the root cause of the problem and leaves people vulnerable to a worsening or repeat occurrence of their emotional illnesses.

If we want to understand how to treat an emotional problem, we must understand that the origin of these illnesses lies where least suspected, in the closest, most intimate family relationships. Only when we take a detailed approach and analyze a problem in an effort to correct old or develop new coping strategies, will we be able to heal our emotional disorders. Dynamic psychotherapy aims to answer the questions of why and how an emotional illness happened and how this understanding can help us change for the better.

In this book, we will help you discover how to create better self-understanding and enjoy improved relationships. In Chapter 2, we'll tell you about our discoveries and how we observed that people become emotionally conditioned into two distinct personalities or roles.

WHAT YOU DISCOVERED IN THIS CHAPTER

- We have not achieved self-understanding in any era, and our self-knowledge has progressed little since the days of our ancestors.
- Our sense of well-being depends on our interpersonal relationships and how well we manage them.
- Most of us begin learning how to relate within the first three years of life and do not significantly change our approach to others throughout our lives.
- Often we cannot identify the causes of our emotional illness, as we do not know what problems we react to, which relationship conflicts exceed our limits, and our patterns of giving and receiving emotional support.

CHAPTER TWO

Emotional Conditioning

Dr. Martin's First Observations

Dr. Martin finished his psychiatry training in 1967. He was filled with the psychological theories he had learned but found that none of these theories adequately described the patients he was seeing. He had much information from psychiatrists who came before him and who seemed confident of their methods and practice. Yet, he did not know how to use the concepts of others to benefit his own patients. His psychiatry training became a ticket to more learning.

DR. MARTIN SOON DISCOVERED THAT THERE ARE MANY PEOPLE WITH ORDINARY LIVES, BUT THERE ARE NO ORDINARY PEOPLE. In 1967, it seemed enormously complicated to grasp that unconscious mental processes influence much of our lives and shape our relationships. For Dr. Martin, as he started his practice, each day was a trip into confusion as he searched for some unifying principles.

We appear to carry our own concept of the world around in our minds—a complex universe exists in each of us. As a psychiatrist, Dr. Martin became fascinated with examining the tiniest details and clues of emotional disorders, the process of intensively treating individuals and examining their thoughts, emotions, and behaviors. His own work in psychotherapy added further insights. In his own therapy his discoveries about himself destroyed the illusion that he functioned differently from his troubled patients.

Dr. Martin's piecing together his new concept was not "a bolt of lightning out of the blue" but more closely resembled hiking through dense jungle. He was at first surrounded with difficult but familiar terrain. Then, some small detail, previously overlooked, pulled him from the beaten path.

Encouraged by this small discovery, he took more steps. With very small advances, he uncovered a fresh perspective, which was exciting but also created the burden of responsibility for affecting or even potentially harming his patients.

Eventually, Dr. Martin hacked out a new trail. He then retraced his steps to where he first began. He was inspired by his adventure and told others of his path into the unfamiliar and unexpected. But, he didn't know if others would dare to take the trip themselves or prefer to remain where they felt more secure.

The first hint of what became Dr. Martin's new concept came when he saw a new patient, a teenage girl. Her parents asked Dr. Martin to evaluate their daughter after her appearance in juvenile court for vandalizing a clothing store. The girl grew up in a religious home. Her concerned mother was an ordained minister and her father a deacon.

Her behavior had been exasperating at times, but her parents had never sought professional advice until this event. She went into a large clothing store and slit expensive clothing with a razor blade while appearing to browse, eventually damaging $10,000 worth of merchandise. Many families tolerate erratic and difficult behaviors until people outside the home become aware of it. In this case, court authorities insisted on an explanation.

The girl's emotional eruption mystified the girl and her parents. She told Dr. Martin that she was angry at her parents for forbidding her to see a boy she was interested in romantically. Her behavior was always normal, and they claimed no relative had ever committed a delinquent act. This mundane case became unique when the father abruptly asked to speak privately with Dr. Martin. With obvious shame, he said when he was the same age as his daughter, he had been rebellious and delinquent and had vandalized several cars and houses. He wondered if his past misbehavior could somehow relate to his daughter's delinquency. "But how could it?" he asked. "It happened long before I met my wife and I never told anybody about it."

Here was the first link in a chain that Dr. Martin assembled over the next four decades. Each new case increased his understanding of the unconscious process of the mind that had all started with that young girl and her family.

The case of the delinquent girl posed many questions. Could the girl have been given an unconscious directive to commit such behaviors? Do such messages, if they exist, affect other parts of a child's behavior? How could the girl know this was not exceptional behavior in her family, even though she didn't know her father's history? Why did she not behave as her parents instructed? She had devout, thoughtful parents who urged their children to act as examples for other children at church and in the community. Why had none of her siblings demonstrated deviant behavior? Do parents somehow suggest such behaviors and give approval without intention or awareness? Do they emotionally shape or condition their children without their knowledge?

Dr. Martin's belief was, and his findings supported, that the girl was emotionally conditioned or shaped to behave delinquently like her father and that she received unconscious messages to do so. We discovered such emotional shaping appears to take place in most people. Such shaping seems to have evolved centuries or millennia ago, perhaps as a way for a simpler society to allocate power. Families, clans, or tribes created harmony by forming groups. One group would maintain the organization to protect the other, more dependent group.

THROUGHOUT LIFE MOST PEOPLE FIND SATISFACTION PLAYING THEIR ROLE AND CONSISTENTLY DOING WHAT THEY ARE "SUPPOSED" TO DO. BUT THIS IS A WEAK SUBSTITUTE FOR REALIZING YOUR FULL POTENTIAL BY EVOLVING INTO A WHOLE PERSON. EMOTIONAL CONDITIONING GETS US THROUGH THE DAY, BUT IT HIDES OTHER, BETTER, OPTIONS.

If we can become aware of the unconscious influences of emotional conditioning, this will allow us to see the hidden realities of our personality makeup and comprehend what drives our thinking and behavior. We could know others and ourselves better, come to know our genuine personalities, and avoid poor relationships and situations. This complex mental mechanism, called personality, is shaped bit by bit in early childhood in countless nonverbal and verbal episodes from parents or care providers. As children, we learn to evaluate reality and behave according to our personality.

Despite the conscious parental messages that we give verbally, a child learns a deeper, unconscious message that he or she must maintain an expected role. At times, verbal input from parents may be difficult to interpret. But, the unchanging and unrecognized messages that serve as the very core of our personalities are consistent, and we interpret them correctly.

Such emotional programming leads to our emotional conditioning. This is not ordinary learning that we can forget. We cannot forget our emotional conditioning. However, Dr. Martin and I discovered that deconditioning is possible, and we explain in Chapter 10 how this works.

Seeing Common Patterns

The next large piece of the puzzle appeared to Dr. Martin several years later when he recognized a pattern common to his patients: the person who came for help was not usually the sickest member of the family. Through detailed patient histories, given over months and years, Dr. Martin realized the person seeking treatment emerged as a designated problem solver for the family. In good times or bad, this person, usually alone, bore responsibility for the entire group. He or she sought psychiatric help when the problem involved significant emotional disturbances in other members of the family.

Other family members, even if urged to seek treatment, often refused or became disruptive to therapy if they did come. Dr. Martin recognized that the person in treatment usually received very little emotional support at home, if any at all. To Dr. Martin it became obvious that many of his patients had family roles in which they acted as if they were all-powerful: *omnipotent*.[1] This required them to attend to the slightest difficulty of the "weaker people": the *impotent*.

For years, Dr. Martin's patients described their dependent, "weaker" family members as less competent, unable to assume great responsibility, and quite limited in their participation in life. As Dr. Martin listened, it occurred to him such people could logically fit into the complimentary role of omnipotents: these people acted helpless, as if impotent. Nothing else would complete a relationship so well as a partnership of a person who can do nothing or only a little bit with one who attempts to do almost everything. The omnipotent would feel powerful and useful by solving all the problems for the helpless impotent. Caring for the impotent makes them feel validated and secure, while the impotent person feels cared for.

This led Dr. Martin to a series of huge questions: Do people have an individuality that makes each person unique? Or do we play roles so we perform a specific *function* rather than appear as our true selves? When do we assume roles, and when do we stop, if ever? How do we become our "authentic" selves? Even the question of individuality presented problems. In our society we romanticize that every human being is unique. We do not like to think we are not one of a kind.

Dr. Martin saw patients who had moved from foreign cultures to the United States and wondered how cultural differences would affect their relationships. Many foreign-born patients had American spouses who had worked overseas. Dr. Martin expected inevitable conflicts when two cultures mixed. This did not happen. The foreign-born partners adjusted to marriage in precisely the same way as their spouses, with all the same "normal" problems.

Dr. Martin saw these same patterns appearing repeatedly: the person playing the omnipotent role does whatever is necessary to establish and maintain family harmony and stability. Surprisingly, Dr. Martin found the sexes evenly divided, with as many women as men in both this omnipotent role and also in the impotent role. Each of these omnipotent people was the sensitive, nurturing person for his or her particular family. Dr. Martin was fascinated that the omnipotent-role patients described themselves as giving emotional and problem-solving support to their dependent, passive relatives.

Such a pair succeeded as long as the omnipotent kept the impotent perfectly comfortable. The world outside this miniuniverse would have little impact on their relationship. This idea suggested to Dr. Martin that people could be emotionally reared and shaped for the impotent role just as their counterparts were trained and molded for the omnipotent role. The next question for Dr. Martin was: Are such roles given to a small segment of the population, or are many people assigned to one of these roles?

Why Two Roles?

If we had to have an original response to every different encounter in our lives, we would be overwhelmed with difficulty. If we have a single, uniform standard, then we have a personal yardstick to apply—the only important variable being whether we are an omnipotent or impotent personality. Because we are comfortable with our standard behavior, we continue to apply it unless we have a very strong reason not to. Every time we display omnipotent or impotent behavior we reinforce our expected role.

THE USE OF EMOTIONAL CONDITIONING SAVES A LOT OF TIME AND EFFORT IN RELATIONSHIPS. WE DON'T HAVE TO THINK ABOUT SITUATIONS. INSTEAD, WE MANAGE OUR RELATIONSHIPS WITH KNEE-JERK REACTIONS, OR GO ON AUTOMATIC PILOT. We don't ask: Who needs support? Who gives support? How much? With emotional conditioning, we revert to roles and perform when the other person and his or her conditioned role triggers a reaction in us. Daily life requires little communication because of its reflex-like nature. Nor do we have to provide explanation since society expects us to maintain these roles.

In this concept, our *belief in omnipotence* is an unconscious psychological aspect of people, not a religious or supernatural idea or a delusional belief. Some people go through life behaving as if they are omnipotent in their thoughts and behaviors. Other people behave as though they are impotent and some other people are omnipotent. It does not matter which face of the coin you are on, impotent or omnipotent. Everyone behaves as though they believe some people can do anything, fix any problem, or care for others at all times and at all costs. But, we did find there is a continuum from mild to severe for each conditioned role of omnipotent and impotent.

Children Learn Two Roles

As we continued to examine families, we gathered information that suggested children knew at an early age to which role they were assigned. Both of us worked with patients who told us about problems in the family, their work, the military, their church, or religious community. Despite their differences, our patients appeared to assume one of these two roles and acted in this way throughout their lives. We found that children copy these roles in their relationships. Neither sex nor gender plays a part. A boy can copy the mother's role or a girl the father's. Either person may occasionally display out-of-character behavior but can never switch entirely from one designated role to the other. **PEOPLE CANNOT CONSISTENTLY BEHAVE IN WAYS THAT ARE INCONSISTENT WITH WHO THEY ARE.**

This strengthened our thinking that most people somehow learn one of these two roles and that they react in the same roles throughout life. The only place in which individuality appeared significant was the degree with which each person pursued his or her role.

How could all this take place? Are all emotional relationships, problems, and disorders unique and complex, as they appear on the surface? Or could they be varied pictures of conflicts that have a common origin? The implications were far-reaching. **THE EVIDENCE DR. MARTIN GATHERED, AND THAT I ADDED TO, SUGGESTED TO US THAT OMNIPOTENT AND IMPOTENT ROLES ARE COMMON AND THAT THERE ARE ONLY TWO ROLES. FURTHERMORE, THE ROLE APPEARS TO BE THE MOLD FOR THE PERSONALITY, AND WHEN WE PLAY OUR ROLE IT REQUIRES US TO LIVE AS IF BY REFLEX ACTION AND NOT AS THINKING, REASONING PEOPLE.**

Here is a case example of role-playing.

Mara and Doug

Mara and Doug, a couple in their late fifties, were distraught and sought my help. Doug had multiple sclerosis. His condition was worsening, and he required help with walking and bathing. He used a wheelchair. He was despondent that he needed so much help to get through each day. Mara was distressed that he required increasingly more help. I had only seen them twice when I received a call from Doug that they would not be returning to therapy. They had arrived at a solution on their own, Doug said. He agreed to move into a nursing home so Mara would not have to care for him. Several months later, I spoke with Doug again. He told me that the week after he went to the nursing home Mara left on an extended international trip with friends. He had not heard from her since.

This couple is a powerful example of the roles they followed due to their emotional conditioning. The omnipotent Doug solved the impotent Mara's problem of wanting to be rid of him rather than care for him. Even very ill, he did not expect her to help meet his needs. Instead, Doug felt he should take care of Mara's need to be free of caring for him.

No One Escapes

The puzzle that Dr. Martin attempted to understand for years, and to which I added my observations about infants and children, began to take form when it became increasingly apparent that many, if not all, families consist of omnipotents and impotents. Children grow up seeing the two roles, one of which they will take on, and undoubtedly learn to copy from their parents or other significant adults in their early lives.

Now, Dr. Martin could see clearly why the omnipotent was the person almost always coming for therapy. The impotent felt unable to participate in any phase of a marriage or relationship that required effort. The roles dictate the choices people make in marriages and in partnerships—both heterosexual and homosexual. Odds strongly favor an attraction between an omnipotent and impotent rather than between two people in the same role. What attraction guides this choice of partners? There might be an occasional omnipotent-omnipotent match or impotent-impotent union but, even here, the couple came from homes where both these roles were obvious and considered normal.

Considering marriage and same-sex partnerships in these two roles sheds light on the historical difficulties of marriage, as well as the divorce rate approximating 50 percent. How could so many people inhabit these roles so clearly and persistently? In all of our cases what emerged was the basic relationship of the omnipotent caretaker staying vigilant to protect his or her totally dependent, impotent partner. Omnipotents do not resent doing the work and solving the problems. Instead, they insist on striving each day to give to impotent others and to reject offers of support to themselves. They have been trained to feel responsible for the problems of impotents and cannot grasp that the obligation can rarely be met, that the situation is like trying to fill a black hole.

For instance, when an omnipotent person learns he cannot cure his impotent spouse's cancer, he keeps seeking a miracle cure. This search is either active in his behaviors or in his own mind, because his unconscious demands omnipotence. On the other hand, if the omnipotent has cancer, the impotent partner remains true to role and acts helpless, regardless of the anguish this causes his suffering spouse and family members. Although an impotent may recognize logically that his omnipotent spouse is in dire need of support in a crisis, he becomes powerless when his emotional inertia takes over and he turns abruptly to some irrelevant personal interest to divert his attention from his spouse's needs.

These emotionally conditioned reflexes appear so ingrained in our unconscious that logic cannot compel us to be more nuanced in our behaviors. We often act inappropriately in spite of ourselves. In reality, no human beings are totally strong or utterly weak, omnipotent or impotent, even if they assume these postures in an automatic way in relationships.

For us to have appropriate and reasonable responses we need to react to the circumstances of the moment, rather than automatically assuming a role. The problem is solved when we see that **WE ARE NOT CAPABLE OF REACTING TO THE NEEDS OF OTHERS BUT, INSTEAD, REACT IN THE ROLE WE HAVE LEARNED.** The ingrained roles demand a lot of us and all too often dominate our relationships.

Omnipotents play the hero to any impotents. They protect impotents, who drain or abuse them and attend to the whims of impotents while neglecting themselves. Metaphorically, when their ship sinks, they encourage the weaker impotents into the lifeboats and give them a cheery farewell before sinking themselves. Impotents, on the other hand, will not exert themselves for omnipotents. They can see loyal omnipotents suffer with little compassion for their plight. They can lose a best friend and experience the loss only to the extent they themselves are affected.

AN OMNIPOTENT BELIEVES SHE MUST SATISFY EVERYONE. AN IMPOTENT BELIEVES EVERYONE MUST CATER TO HER. An omnipotent will deny illness when called to duty, whereas an impotent will assume a helpless posture and avoid duty. An omnipotent shuns a sympathetic audience. An impotent compulsively seeks one.

In other words, **EACH OF OUR BEHAVIORS, EMOTIONS, AND THOUGHTS ARE EMOTIONALLY SHAPED BY WHO WE ARE WITH RATHER THAN REAL-LIFE CIRCUMSTANCES. WE LEARN IN CHILDHOOD TO GIVE A CONDITIONAL RESPONSE BASED ON UNCONSCIOUS EMOTIONAL CUES FROM OTHER PEOPLE. WE USE DIFFERENT APPROACHES AND TECHNIQUES TO RAISE CHILDREN AND TO HANDLE PROBLEMS. ALL OF THIS IS CONSCIOUS. BUT, IN ACTUALITY, WE EMOTIONALLY CONDITION OUR CHILDREN UNCONSCIOUSLY TO PLAY THE SAME ROLES WE PLAY.**

Performance improves as omnipotent children develop and, in exceptional cases, perform far beyond their ages. Like Pavlov's research dogs, an omnipotent child is filled with anxiety and hyperawareness, awaiting cues, especially from an impotent parent. An omnipotent child hones his abilities and builds his strength to meet that parent's needs. The child knows failure is painful and tries to avoid displeasing his impotent parent.

An impotent parent also derives pleasure from an omnipotent child, because the child represents a future protector. Thus, each parent and child is most gratified when assuming his or her role. *An omnipotent assumes a position of control and service whereas an impotent assumes dependency and passivity.* Throughout life this transaction, once learned, repeats. Omnipotents compulsively seek situations where they can provide control for others.

Impotent children appear to get their emotional conditioning cues primarily from their omnipotent parents. These children quickly learn these parents are most pleased when putting out maximal effort to *do for them*. They observe these parents become anxious and apprehensive at the prospect of the children attempting anything on their own. An omnipotent parent wants always to catch you before you fall and never let you fall and see how you manage on your own. As a result, impotents become shaped to seek out situations where others readily attend to their wants and needs.

EMOTIONAL CONDITIONING IS DEHUMANIZING BECAUSE IT REQUIRES US TO STRIVE TO BE SOMETHING OTHER THAN THE FULL HUMAN BEINGS WE ARE. IT FOLLOWS THAT WE WILL TREAT OTHERS IN A DEHUMANIZED WAY AND USE THEM TO FULFILL OUR OWN ROLES. Our lives will be geared to inappropriate expectations and behaviors from the effort to fulfill impossible expectations of others or ourselves at either extreme—omnipotence or impotence.

The reactive or reflexive quality of these roles gives control of our lives to others and creates emotional maladjustment. You might wonder about the impossible role expectations for impotents. Their role is to always act helplessly, be dependent on others, and not show much caring for other people, responsibility for themselves, or independence.

Any long-term study of behavior shows our personalities are remarkably consistent. This idea gives rise to the belief that the personality is permanent and unchanging. Slight changes might occur, but the basic responses last throughout our life spans. Even in childhood, it becomes clear that some of us will be problem solvers and caretakers in society and others will become the emotional dependents of our society, never quite able to care for themselves, much less for others.

We notice future omnipotents when they perform a service for others. They discover a reason to exist by solving the problems of others. They accept that their worth resides in performing and producing. These activities sustain their tenuous self-esteem. Omnipotents redefine perfection as being able to meet the particular desires of an impotent person. This definition links back to what their parent(s) considered perfect. Eventually, omnipotents become obsessed with creating solutions for dependent impotents. They don't pay any attention to the positive or harmful aspects of the interaction.

Impotents can never develop their potential for logical thought either, and their thinking processes are channeled in a different direction. From infancy, their parents attend urgently to their discomforts with lavish or permissive care. Before they can express a problem, their caregivers resolve it. Impotents grow up learning not to think for themselves, resent being put in a position where thinking is required, and resent being asked questions. They may be as intelligent as anyone, but their minds become limited to their basic appetites, and they concentrate much more on fleeting concerns.

Throughout the book we do not make value judgments that one role is "better" than the other. Each role has its set of attributes, problems, and drawbacks, as you will see in Chapters 4 and 5.

Labels Make Us Uncomfortable

Most of us do not like to think of personalities and roles as omnipotent or impotent. Labeling ourselves as either omnipotent or impotent may make us feel uncomfortable. There are several reasons we want to reject these labels. First, the terms *omnipotent* or *omnipotence* may refer to our personal God, and we do not commonly use these terms in a secular or generic sense. Second, if we think we are omnipotent, we might think we are delusional or comparing ourselves with a deity. Finally, if omnipotence is an accepted factor in many (or all) relationships, it loses its uniqueness and we accept it as normal.

We may have difficulty accepting that there may be some glitch in our thinking, emotions, or behaviors. We have yet to find anyone who is comfortable with the tag of either an omnipotent or impotent. Even people who casually hear of the two types become uneasy and say, "Can't you use some other words or labels?" But, if we cannot accurately name it, we cannot understand or correct it. We leave this question to you to help us determine if omnipotent and impotent are a good choice of words. Do they accurately reflect many of the significant behaviors, thoughts, emotions, and relationships in our lives?

How We Become Emotionally Conditioned

Parenting is a unique challenge. We often do not recognize its astonishing implications. Many of us grow up seeing little importance or attention invested in child rearing. Others witness too much and the wrong kind of investment in the form of "helicopter parenting." The number of books about parenting shows just how hard it is. Advice from books or articles has little impact because we already have deeply ingrained procedures for dealing with others before we become parents. The result is each of our children learns to act and perceive reality in ways that we parents impose unconsciously on them. Considering how easily animals can be conditioned to perform complex tasks, for people the emotional conditioning process is an easy undertaking.

We found the greatest numbers of parental couples are in omnipotent-impotent combinations. Each parent selects the other because of his or her complementary personality. We tell you about this in Chapter 7. There-fore, these roles are not only acceptable but considered ideal. As parents we have sincere intentions to give our offspring the best foundation but are unaware of the unconscious roles we will impose on them.

Few young people doubt their parenting ability, at least enough to cause them to wait or not have children. Some young couples lack enthusiasm for parenthood because of traumas they experienced in childhood but believe they would parent well if the need arose. Generally speaking, many people regard parenting as a basic chore that any of us can do.

We devalue child rearing in comparison to a trade or a profession, which require skills worthy of pay. Parenting is underrated because we recall the parenting we received, which provides a sense of familiarity and knowledge. Last, but not least, is our emotional conditioning. If we are impotents, we are unaware of the challenge of child rearing, and if we are omnipotents, we overrate our abilities and accept the task with confidence. As far as parents are concerned, each child's personality appears to evolve from within. Many of us are not conscious of our own role in shaping our children's personalities and behaviors.

As Dr. Martin's evidence mounted for omnipotent and impotent per-sonality types and the emotional conditioning process, the crucial ques-tion arose: How does it work? We both saw patients in our offices, treating people with psychodynamic psychotherapy one to three times a week for 50-minute sessions, some for months, others for decades. This form of treatment helps you discover ways of behaving, thinking, and feeling that you learned in childhood that may still be functioning in your life and causing your emotional distress and relationship problems.

Dr. Martin observed people ranging in age from adolescence to old age, and I worked with all ages, from babies through the adult years. As a child psychiatrist I worked with parents and their children or teenagers. I saw families in my office and also went on home and school visits and to day care centers and nursery schools. By observing how families interacted in various settings beyond my office, I was able to gather more information about how they interacted and what roles they seemed to assume. We pieced together observations made during treatment of almost 2,000 people through the entire life span.

We discovered that parents decide unconsciously on the role designa-tion of each child, even before the baby is born. At some point after con-ception, parents decide whether the child will be a "good" baby who requires minimal attention or one who needs extreme protectiveness and support. We discovered that the current needs and situation of the par-ents and family help shape the decision. These factors might include the parents' age, if one parent is absent, the child's birth order, the role assigned to other children in the family, or unusual circumstances. We did not find the family's economic level to be a factor. Once we parents decide that the child will be strong and competent or weak and needy, our unconscious attitude will launch the baby into that role. We will treat each child based on what we believe he will need and what we believe we can provide.

Once parents agree unconsciously on the approach to each child, they convey the role characteristics by way of projection. A child will be either a good baby who thrives on minimal care, or one who, due to perceived specialness, needs continuous care and attention. In the good baby scenario, we expect the child not to be an inconvenience and to mix into the family easily.

Or, parents may reason that the tiny, helpless child is so delicate as a result of a health condition, sex or gender, being adopted, and so on, that they must give nothing less than hypervigilant, extraordinary care. They are not aware that their interactions with the baby mold their baby's behavioral (and ultimately emotional) responses. Nor are they aware that their interactions begin to shape their child's personality.

A newborn emerges into the world incapable of independent existence. Little else functions in his central nervous system other than reflexes operating through his spinal cord. These reflexes are primitive nerve links that are present in all animals. It takes years to refine essential functions that depend on more mature, higher brain functions. The newborn's pathways to memory storage are unused, and they are unable to see clearly or make sense of sounds.

An infant awaits any hint of personality. Although every infant has certain biological drives and temperamental leanings, his personality is not yet formed. But the baby's immediate family projects onto him and perceives an emerging character in the traits they attribute to him. We perceive babies as recognizing relatives, as being comfortable or in distress, as enjoying or rejecting certain people or conditions, or of wanting certain objects or rejecting them.

Even before the baby becomes aware of her surroundings and long before her thoughts fully function, she is being shaped to respond in a stereotypical manner. For this to be possible, she must distort or dilute certain large areas of her reality as she grows up. Dr. Martin and I observed that each growing child increasingly adopts this "altered reality" as she seeks the emotional reward of acceptance given by her parents for performing unnatural behaviors. This role through reinforcement becomes more rigid and fixed, as a child loses her more natural behavioral traits.

Once the excitement of the newly arrived baby is over, parents apply their decision about how to treat their baby. Based on their earlier unconscious decision, the parents apply either consistent, minimal attention or intense, excessive attention. The parents constantly correct the level of care, in either case, to align with the parent portraying the same role. This means a child shaped to be omnipotent will have the omnipotent parent as his role model and the same process for the impotent child. In order to project this precise standard, the parents' corrections include positive affections and emotions for compliance versus subtle rejection and withdrawal of affection for any deviation from compliance.

The end result is that we subject children to emotional conditioning, rather than raise them in a way that enables their unique individuality. We had many of these insights from working intensively with people of all ages in dynamic psychotherapy, because in therapy every patient produces many examples of parental influence that directly shaped his personality. We saw that these same influences can be followed to current, previous, and subsequent generations—grandparents, siblings, grandchildren, and other relatives. When we examined the unconscious elements behind the superficial, conscious self portrayed to the world, we gained a clearer perspective on the transgenerational transmission of roles.

As she grows, a child accepts family-given directives as not only correct but as the best way to act. She will obey these unconscious rules in the future, however functional or dysfunctional. As she develops, she will share in what is possibly the greatest closeness the family will achieve. As children embrace family standards, they affirm these standards and beliefs to their parents. As this process of emotional conditioning unfolds, parents and children feel very close to one another for a while, and the family feels harmonious.

Then, after a few years, usually in their children's adolescence, parents wonder in amazement at their offspring's unusual achievements or failures. For the first time they may become vaguely aware of how skewed their children's behaviors, thoughts, and emotions have become. They wonder, "Whose child is that?" What is happening is that these same parents fail to recognize anything of themselves in their offspring. Here are some case examples of emotional conditioning in young children.

Elise

Elise, three years old, reached across the table to grab a dinner roll. Her mother yelled at her not to do that and smacked her hand. Elise then began to whimper, and her mother told her, "If you cry one tear, I'll send you to your room without eating!" Her mother also rejected many of Elise's other requests and punished Elise for expressing many of her wants or needs. As a result, Elise was becoming emotionally conditioned not only not to reach for food but also to be fearful of reaching for or requesting other things from her mother. Most often Elise's mother met her requests with anger or dismissal. With her mother, Elise was being conditioned emotionally to not have her wants or needs met. Elise received omnipotent shaping to defer to her mother's wants.

Sara

Heather always said her three-year-old daughter, Sara, was "into everything." She would not follow rules and took delight in doing things her mother did not want her to do. However, Heather did not restrict Sara from anything Sara wanted. She could roam freely and get into everything—the CD collection, Heather's books, and her clothes drawers. She climbed on the furniture, and Heather did nothing to stop her. Heather said she thought Sara was being "cute" when she was disobedient. Sara was receiving emotional conditioning to be impotent. Heather only expected Sara to do what she wanted and did not expect her to abide by rules or have consideration for other people, thus reinforcing this behavior in Sara without being aware of it.

We found that conditioning is not identical from one child to the next in the same family. This variation creates tiny differences and encourages people to believe they are unique even though the real differences are only differences of slight degree. We observed that each type of emotional conditioning takes place on a continuum from mild to moderate to severe. Although we like to believe in free will, we may have to question if this is possible with our minds attuned by our conditioning.

The complexity of our behavior is so diverse that to understand it under a single unifying concept seemed doubtful. We wondered if we were observing something in our patients that was peculiar to people in psychotherapy. We started closely observing other people we knew well. We scrutinized our relatives and asked them lots of questions about their childhoods. We did the same with our close friends. Lastly, we looked at ourselves, asking if we, too, had been emotionally shaped in our childhoods. Unexpectedly, we found similar roles in these other people who were not our patients, and also in us.

We found that with a mechanical predictability emotional conditioning appears to operate in many people, both patients and nonpatients. Our diversity appears to be explained by the differing degrees of emotional conditioning we receive as children. We evaluate other people by outward appearance, conversation, and behaviors. But what if it were possible to figure out accurately whether people are assuming omnipotent or impotent roles? Then we could better observe the workings of our minds in detail and appreciate what others and we are truly like (Table 2.1).

As Dr. Martin and I developed and researched our concept of emotional conditioning, we realized that we are all emotionally maladjusted to some degree. However, this is not a hopeless situation. It is liberating to know that most people are skewed in the ways we see ourselves and relate to

Table 2.1   Emotional Conditioning: Twelve Important Discoveries

1. We appear to be emotionally conditioned in early childhood to react in a highly specific manner through an unconscious program of emotional shaping.

2. We appear to be successively emotionally conditioned through each generation in a continuous process to copy one of two distinct roles, either omnipotent or impotent.

3. We adapt to the requirements of our roles and expect similarly emotionally conditioned people to perform their roles in precisely the same way we do.

4. Although humanity appears to be extremely varied and diverse, most people seem to be restricted through emotional conditioning to one of two unconscious roles, omnipotent or impotent.

5. Both roles are expressed on a continuum from mild to severe, allowing for an infinite number of possibilities in the degree of emotional conditioning.

6. These two separate unconscious roles appear to cause our lasting personality formation.

7. The emotional conditioning process is not limited to our first months or years of life but is repeatedly reinforced in the social environments each of us experiences throughout our lives.

8. We lack a thoughtful, organized approach for perceiving others and ourselves accurately because we have learned an automatic, illogical system with a degree of unreality that corresponds to the severity of our emotional conditioning.

9. Even if we have only the mildest degree of emotional conditioning, our misperceptions may create significant difficulties for ourselves, troublesome conflict in our relationships, and challenging conditions in our larger society.

10. Because emotional conditioning is unconscious and the two roles in society are widely accepted, we ensure transmission of these roles to future generations.

11. We can decrease the negative effects of emotional conditioning and alter our basic personalities through dynamic psychotherapy, which requires a "human deconditioner" (see Chapter 10), or through improved self-understanding (see Chapter 11).

12. We can create successful change through "deconditioning," and this will lead to a reciprocal change in the other people in our lives (see Chapters 10 and 11).

OTHERS. BEFORE, WE WERE IN THE DARK, BLINDLY ACTING OUT ROLES IMPOSED ON US. NOW, CLEAR-EYED, WE CAN ESCAPE OUR AUTOMATIC ROLES AND START LIVING AS OUR AUTHENTIC SELVES.

By becoming aware of the unconscious dynamics of emotional conditioning, we can perceive the underlying realities of personality makeup and the motivations that drive our thinking, emotions, and behavior. If we knew others and ourselves better, we could recognize our genuine personalities and avoid unhealthy relationships and situations.

Historically, there are other concepts of development of children and their personalities that involve temperament, attachment style, developmental phases, object relations, self-psychology, behaviorism, and social learning. Our concept is a supplement to the existing concepts. We want to add on to existing knowledge and not replace anything discovered in the past.

WHAT YOU DISCOVERED IN THIS CHAPTER

- Dr. Martin observed that we assume roles in relationships that appear to transcend culture, gender, or economic situation. *Emotional conditioning* appears to form these roles.
- Dr. Martin observed that we assume two types of roles or personalities. He called these *omnipotent* and *impotent* roles. They appear to exist in many, if not most, families.
- Once we assume a role, we follow it for the duration of our lives, unless there is a process for increased self-understanding.
- In assuming these roles, we live largely by reflex, automatic action, and less as thinking, reasoning people.
- Emotional programming by parents creates emotional conditioning of each child. It is unconscious, and parents are unaware that they transmit these roles to their children.
- Omnipotent and impotent roles vary from mild to severe on the emotional conditioning spectrum.

CHAPTER THREE

Seven Effects of Emotional Conditioning

As revealed in Chapter 2, we found the consequences of emotional conditioning dehumanize us and the emotional conditioning process has many profound effects. In this chapter we explore in detail what emotional conditioning does to us and to our relationships with others. We describe seven effects: short-circuiting thinking, depersonalization, impaired judgment, reducing others to stereotype, symbiosis, different thinking styles, and different reasons for and meanings of emotions (Table 3.1). At the end of this chapter we discuss how to identify the characteristics of the two personalities or roles.

Short-Circuiting Thinking

Conditioning trains a person to react reflexively to a repeated, external stimulus instead of applying independent thought and giving a response that is appropriate to the situation. **NO MATTER HOW INTELLIGENT WE ARE, EMOTIONAL CONDITIONING INDUCES A SHORT CIRCUIT IN OUR THINKING.** First, we receive unconscious cues from other people, which tell us whether we are dealing with an omnipotent or impotent. Then we offer a conditioned, predictable response. When emotional conditioning takes over, we stop thinking and start reacting automatically.

Since an omnipotent has a narrow view of life, focusing on his need to control everyone else's problems, he is often oblivious to large parts of life and focuses on situations where he can perform his role well. By comparison, an impotent views life moment by moment through a pinhole and

Table 3.1	Seven Effects of Emotional Conditioning

1. Short-circuiting thinking
2. Depersonalization
3. Impaired judgment
4. Reducing others to stereotype
5. Symbiosis
6. Different thinking styles
7. Seeing emotions differently

tends to focus on his personal gratification. These distortions lead to relationship problems because we keep reacting to people in the same ways rather than taking the time to think about the best way to respond to a specific situation.

Depersonalization

Depersonalization—the inability to recognize personal or individual aspects of others and of ourselves—is another effect of conditioning. EMOTIONAL CONDITIONING DEPERSONALIZES OTHERS AND US BECAUSE WE ARE UNAWARE OF THE DISTORTIONS IN HOW WE SEE EACH OTHER. THE DISTORTIONS INTERFERE WITH OUR ABILITY TO PERCEIVE PEOPLE IN A REALISTIC WAY.

An omnipotent sees other omnipotents as having no needs, just like herself. She sees impotents as being needy and incapable of meeting others' needs. By contrast, an impotent views omnipotents as able to give her whatever she desires.

Because we ignore personal characteristics and recognize a person's *role* rather than the person, we lack discrimination in evaluating people. We notice a difference only if a person falls into one extreme role or the other. Most people can spot an altruistic omnipotent from a repellent, criminal, or manipulative impotent, but we lose the fine discernment to gauge the vast majority of people lying between those extremes.

Even in the closeness of a small family, we insist that family members play their assigned roles. This makes it very difficult to achieve genuine intimacy with one another. One of the distinguishing elements of true friendship is when both people abandon their roles and bring their whole selves into the relationship. Unfortunately, when an omnipotent strives to maintain a pretense of perfection, he unwittingly sabotages his interpersonal relations because he's not behaving in an authentic way. This is also true for an impotent. He harms his relationships when he consistently puts his own gratification and helplessness as higher priorities than his family members' or friends' needs and desires.

Impaired Judgment

Impaired judgment, or an inability to evaluate others and yourself, creates havoc in the lives of emotionally conditioned people because they react only to the veneer of others. Since the conditioning process in early childhood erases the ability of both omnipotents and impotents to view other people accurately, a child reverts to a role as soon as she receives clear signals from another person. **WHEN THINKING STOPS, JUDGMENT BECOMES IMPOSSIBLE. A PERSON MAY USE CRITICAL INTELLIGENCE IN HER CAREER, BUT MAY MAKE TRAGIC BLUNDERS IN JUDGING HERSELF AND THE PEOPLE SHE RELATES TO.** She may be able to calculate the volume of concrete necessary to build a large sports stadium or decide a color scheme for her office but be unable to evaluate her children or mate.

THE EMOTIONAL CONDITIONING PROCESS APPEARS TO BURDEN US FROM INFANCY ONWARD WITH SUPERFICIAL AND INAPPROPRIATE REACTIONS TO OTHERS. We have a very hard time figuring out with accuracy what we and others are truly like. Often we evaluate people's success by the way they dress, their careers, tastes and interests, possessions, awards, or memberships in prestigious organizations. We assume we understand a whole person by examining only a small part of him or her. Similarly, we often focus on someone's competence or incompetence, social awkwardness, emotional instability, or unusual dress to tell if a person is of dubious character. **WE CREATE CHAOS WHEN WE USE SUPERFICIAL CHARACTERISTICS TO ATTEMPT TO UNDERSTAND A PERSON'S PERSONALITY IN ANY DEPTH BECAUSE SUPERFICIAL TRAITS OFTEN CONCEAL MUCH MORE THAN THEY TELL US.**

As Dr. Martin and I continued observing our patients and their families, we realized we had evidence that emotional conditioning results in impaired judgment to some degree. For example, omnipotents tend to overestimate their own capabilities and underestimate their needs. They also underestimate the strengths of impotents and erroneously attribute to them many admirable traits and motives that impotents do not have.

Omnipotents repeatedly trust the wrong people, accept inconsiderate and abusive treatment, and commit themselves to no-win situations. They may be highly intelligent and accomplished in their professional or intellectual life, yet their personal lives reflect poor judgments imposed by emotional conditioning. Distorted self-images are matched by equally distorted views of the other people in their lives. They are unable to realize their full potential because they are limited by the extent of their conditioning.

Likewise, impotents are also conditioned to operate within strict confines. We discovered that impotents overvalue their worth and importance and discount the significance of others. They often grossly exaggerate the difficult obstacles they encounter in life and blame their difficulties on the omnipotents who care for them. They may be as intelligent as any omnipotent but use their talents to communicate distress signals and arrange support for themselves. Their conditioning does not permit them to harness their intellect in an integrated effort to fully overcome problems or master situations without assistance.

If impotents are forced into a situation where they must rely on their own resources, they may be incapable of thinking through options and creating a logical plan of response. In contrast to omnipotents, whose excessive inner controls and obsession with solving problems weigh them down, impotents may not learn to develop these characteristics. They rely on others to solve problems for them. They make decisions that are based on fleeting whims and are changed at a moment's notice.

When interacting with an omnipotent, both impotents and omnipotents tend to withhold support because omnipotents do not appear to need help from others. On the other hand, impotents are usually seen as needing endless support. When we assess others based on emotional conditioning, this leads to consistently misguided behaviors. An impotent demands extraordinary indulgences, and an omnipotent puts up with an impotent's intrusions and inconsiderate abuses and neglects his own needs.

Omnipotents who came to us for help usually reached a point of desperation before allowing themselves to complain or ask for support. Just about anyone can manipulate or push around an omnipotent, because she equates any complaint about her or retaliation toward her with weakness and imperfection. She fears she will no longer be seen as a strong, worthy person if she shows any weaknesses. Emotional conditioning is so effective that some omnipotents would give up their lives before deserting their roles. Both of us have known people who committed suicide rather than seek changes in untenable situations.

The yardstick by which each person measures herself is based on the emotional conditioning process. Unfortunately, we found this yardstick is not a flexible measure that adjusts easily to the ever-changing circumstances of life. Instead, it is an absolute standard to which a person rigidly adheres, regardless of the situation or the consequences. This yardstick holds true in many relationships, whether romantic, friendships, or with parents and children. An omnipotent adheres to a standard of perfection as if life is a drama and she is the protagonist. An impotent, in contrast, adopts the opposite standard. She pursues the easiest path possible with little variation, clinging to any strong protector who shelters her not only from stress but also from the possibility of personal growth.

If we had the ability to evaluate others accurately, we could use skills from other areas of our lives—the same skills we apply with a thoughtful approach while considering all available information when we are writing a paper, planning a vacation, or researching which appliance to buy. IF WE COULD APPLY OUR LOGICAL THINKING SKILLS TO OUR RELATIONSHIPS, WE WOULD BE ABLE TO PINPOINT THE CAUSE OF RECURRING CONFLICTS AND FIND SOLUTIONS. HOWEVER, UNDER EMOTIONAL CONDITIONING, WE FIND OURSELVES MAKING THE SAME ERRORS OVER AND OVER AGAIN WHEN CHOOSING A ROMANTIC PARTNER OR IN A MARRIAGE AND CAN'T SEE A WAY TO MAKE CHANGES.

Simply put, we are unable to apply those purely intellectual, cognitive skills from other areas of our lives to our relationships. We lack the skill to accurately recognize ourselves or anybody else. As a result, fantastically capable and outstanding omnipotents may picture themselves as hopelessly inept and incapable of any worthwhile achievement. And impotents, who are often arrogant, may perceive themselves as being industrious and capable even in the absence of supporting evidence. Overall, because of emotional conditioning, we lose some of our ability to accurately perceive ourselves and other human beings.

Reducing Others to Stereotype

When we provide emotional knee-jerk responses to others, we fail to look at real individual qualities and reduce every person to a stereotype. For example, an omnipotent may have done a task well, yet decide it is wholly worthless because it contains a slight flaw. He will then feel inadequate and inferior to others. On the other hand, an impotent will feel grandiose after making some small effort. He may feel and act as if he is clearly superior to others who may in fact have accomplished much more. THE SHORTCUT OF STEREOTYPING PREVENTS US FROM MAKING VALID OBSERVATIONS, COLLECTING REAL DATA, AND RESPONDING TO OTHERS WITH APPROPRIATE BEHAVIORS.

Here is an example of stereotyped expectations and behaviors in a relationship.

Mariyah and Samir

Mariyah, 47 years old, was a busy woman who worked at home raising five children. Her husband, Samir, 48 years old, was a physician and busy with his patients. He worked long hours. He had a habit of late afternoon calls to Mariyah to give her a list of things he wanted her to do before he arrived home that evening—run errands, iron clothes, prepare a specific dish for dinner. This always took place at the last minute when Mariyah was preparing dinner or driving carpools for their children or helping with homework. Mariyah usually interrupted her activities to do what Samir asked. She felt stressed and irritated but felt she should comply. She once asked Samir to discuss the issue. He became angry and refused. They both assumed stereotyped roles with one another—one dictating and the other acquiescing regardless of the real circumstances for each.

Creation of Symbiosis

Symbiotic relationships in the animal or plant world usually refer to close relationships where one or both organisms benefit from the other and neither is harmed. The omnipotent-impotent relationship might be beneficial if the two roles were suited to benefit both people in an interactive and cooperative way. But they do not. **THE TWO ROLES APPEAR TO REDUCE BOTH PEOPLE TO A SYMBIOSIS IN WHICH BOTH FEEL INCOMPLETE AND NEED ONE ANOTHER IN ORDER TO CARRY OUT THEIR ROLES.** Although each person may be close to the other, both seem to rigidly follow their roles and sacrifice genuine needs and individuality. Here is a tragic example of inappropriate and stereotyped responses.

Miguel and Elena

Miguel, 80 years old, found himself slowing down. He had difficulty breathing and was often short of breath. Recently he began using oxygen. He realized he could no longer do the bulk of caring for the home he shared with his wife, Elena, who was 75 years old. Miguel had done all the cooking and much of the housework during their long marriage. Now Elena had to do most of the cooking. She had little experience making meals, grumbled, and was often angry over needing to cook. Miguel felt guilty. He felt he was failing to care for Elena. Rather than hire someone to help or discuss Elena's unreasonable anger, Miguel took his own life. He was unable to relinquish his omnipotent role of expecting inordinate performance from himself at all times, regardless of circumstances.

In these examples, we see that each person needs the other to feel whole. An omnipotent assumes responsibilities that often lie far beyond the limits of his expertise. He will assume unrealistic obligations when overstressed or ill. He shuns offers of assistance or support even under the most doubtful odds of success. He only recognizes that he is not omnipotent and reluctantly accepts minimal support when under extreme and desperate circumstances. When he hears a cry for help from an impotent, this triggers his nurturing response.

Impotents also display inappropriate and symbiotic behaviors. An impotent usually lapses into inaction whenever she senses the presence of an omnipotent. Although impotents may be intelligent and strong, they will not display signs of competence if at all avoidable since they expect omnipotents to play that role. Impotents remain inert and passive, even in the face of intense sufferings of their loved ones. They both respond in fixed ways to an emotionally conditioned stimulus rather than analyzing and reacting to the person or situation they are facing.

Different Thinking Styles

We use the word *thinking* in ordinary conversation to describe a broad scope of mental activities. *Thinking* in this book refers to two very different thinking styles.

Unconditioned thinking is a natural and spontaneous assessment of external and internal reality based on a person's innate ability. We accomplish this with an acute alertness and ability to observe, comparing present circumstances to similar situations in the past, organizing this data and, through reasoning, forming a plan in order to respond. We use this ability to offer a creative, specific response to each encounter.

Emotionally conditioned thinking achieves a specific end without concern for subtleties or the realities of the current situation. For example, an impotent uses her mind to identify and seek stimulation and gratification while eliminating the mundane and undesirable. On the other hand, an omnipotent has a remarkable ability for organizing and solving all sorts of problems and an appetite for taking on new tasks and projects. Both omnipotents and impotents expend considerable energy justifying that their thoughts are rational and reasonable, when often they are not.

People in both roles inevitably develop different emotionally conditioned thinking styles. An omnipotent is exquisitely sensitive to any unresolved problem disturbing any of the others who depend on her. When she is aware of a threat, she becomes anxious and hyperalert as she seeks a "perfect" solution. She doesn't find relief until the problem is resolved. Her concentration can be so complete that all her thinking focuses on the eradication of problems, regardless of their magnitude or the sacrifice required. But her unique thinking style and problem-solving talent are her curse as well, as she often excludes all other aspects of life in favor of her single-minded concern with problems.

This obsession with problems occupies an omnipotent constantly. She often stews endlessly over less-than-perfect solutions of the past while anticipating possible future calamities. She concentrates on methods to improve her techniques for handling whatever difficulties may lie ahead and tries to control others with insistent advice and direction. An omnipotent feels a global responsibility for those around her and may lose all awareness of her own needs. Only when alone and isolated from others can she feel free to relax from her emotionally conditioned activity.

The thinking process for an impotent is altogether different. An impotent feels no need to devise solutions. This is unnecessary, since he usually has a relationship with an omnipotent who has taken on this responsibility. An impotent's thoughts are focused on his own welfare, his pleasures and interests, and on maintaining his bonds to omnipotents who provide protection for him. Although an impotent's commitment is primarily to himself, he is aware of others out of self-interest, especially any time someone may jeopardize his connection to his omnipotent partner, friend, or family member.

Overall, an impotent has a transient quality to his thinking, giving attention to his immediate and rapidly changing desires. He neither feels a need to justify his impulsive nature nor show concern for the protector who fulfills his unending desires. **AN IMPOTENT IS BLIND TO SERVING OTHERS, JUST AS AN OMNIPOTENT, PROGRAMMED TO SERVE OTHERS, IS BLIND TO SERVING HIMSELF.**

Since emotional conditioning as a method converts human responses to reflexes, with only minimal organized thinking, it inevitably impairs people's behavior. For example, Pavlov conditioned his dog to secrete saliva and gastric juice in readiness to eat when no food was present. Pavlov was able to bypass the animal's thinking process. If Pavlov's dogs had been using unconditioned thinking, they would have recognized the fact that only the presence of food would create saliva. The reflex action of emotional conditioning is faster, requires almost no effort, and exists outside the realm of thought. Without thought, how can we have rational judgment?

Emotions: Different Reasons and Meanings

Commonly, we assume emotions have identical meanings for all of us. But Dr. Martin and I did not find this to be true. We perceive the same emotions differently, and we have different reasons for experiencing the same emotions—crying, anger, happiness, grief, love, erotic attraction, aggression, generosity, or assertiveness. We misinterpret what other people reveal to us emotionally as a result of how we are emotionally conditioned. Often, we project our emotions onto others who do not feel the same way. Or, we erroneously accept other's emotions as what we should also feel. Here are some examples of how we perceive and interpret emotions differently.

Emma and Laurie

These two young women in their twenties are friends through work. One day, Emma arrives at her job weeping. Laurie is immediately concerned that Emma is sad or upset.

This makes Laurie sad, in an empathetic way, just listening to Emma cry. Laurie asks Emma what the matter is. Emma does not answer and continues to sob. By now Laurie is very upset and almost crying with frustration that she doesn't know how to help Emma.

Emma continues crying for almost an hour, and when she stops sobbing says, "My mom was just diagnosed with cancer. I have to go home and help her with her chemo. I am so upset. I've planned and paid for a great vacation. Now I'll have to cancel it. That really upsets me. Plus, my mom is such a drama queen, she'll want attention from everyone because she's got cancer. I'm really angry."

Laurie is aghast. She thought Emma was crying because she was sad for her mom because of the cancer diagnosis. This was Laurie's projection. Emma's tears were for Emma and the self-pity, anger, and jealousy she felt over her mother's cancer diagnosis and how this would inconvenience her.

Mason and Alex

Mason and Alex are 10 years old. They have been classmates for less than a year. Mason taunts Alex and threatens to punch him if Alex doesn't help him with homework or share his lunch. Mason frequently fights with other boys, always blaming them for bothering him. So far he has not been physically aggressive with Alex.

One day Mason unrelentingly provokes Alex for hours. Alex has no response and stays composed. But near the end of the day, Alex suddenly explodes with anger and aggressively punches Mason. Immediately, Alex is remorseful at his loss of control. He is upset with himself over his aggressive outburst. His explosion is due to his pent-up anger caused by Mason's abusive behavior.

On the other hand, Mason has always resorted easily to aggression and has no guilt or remorse. He readily uses aggression and bullying to get what he wants from others. These two boys exhibit aggression under very different circumstances and with distinctly different motivations and emotional aftermaths.

In summarizing, we can see that emotional conditioning does many things to us. Omnipotents and impotents need the other as a bridge to feel valued and loved. Unfortunately, this bridge cannot provide lasting security any more than the sound of a bell can nourish an animal. Each person in an omnipotent-impotent relationship experiences negative consequences and damage to their emotional and mental well-being. An omnipotent often experiences a growing sense of failure and an impotent an increased ineptness and inertia. An omnipotent cannot ask for nurturing without profound anxiety, while an impotent cannot provide nurturing without subjecting himself to a flood of anxiety at the thought of assuming such responsibility. What could help us avoid the serious limitations imposed by emotional conditioning?

TO SOME EXTENT WE CAN LESSEN THESE EFFECTS OF EMOTIONAL CONDITIONING, BUT FIRST WE MUST BOLSTER OUR ABILITY TO TELL THE DIFFERENCE IN OTHERS AND OURSELVES BETWEEN PEOPLE ASSUMING OMNIPOTENT AND IMPOTENT ROLES.

The remainder of this chapter addresses just that—how you can assess others and how you can tell the difference between these two emotionally conditioned roles.

A New Method for Assessing Others

We believe we can develop a method of assessing people as effective as the way we evaluate the quality of any other object or situation. How can I decide which car is the right choice for our family? Where is the best place for my vacation this year? Because our unconscious is active in evaluating people, we have a unique problem. Through emotional conditioning, omnipotents are taught to accept everyone, to see redeeming features in the least worthy, and to tolerate others almost unconditionally. Impotents are taught only to accept people who feel obligated to provide care for them. So we respond to others according to our perception of their *roles*, rather than as a reasoned response based on *the reality of that particular person at a specific moment in time.*

There has always been enormous confusion about finding a reliable method of assessing other human beings. Few issues have inspired greater interest or could be more useful. We fail to evaluate personality effectively when we attempt to evaluate people by their educational status, social class, race, sex, religious preference, intelligence, or political beliefs. Superficial generalities may be useful as a starting point, but they do not go far or deep enough because they fail to consider individual differences.

COMPLEX CHANGES ARE NEEDED IF WE WANT TO OVERRIDE EMOTIONAL CONDITIONING AND CORRECT ITS MAIN DEFECTS. WE WOULD LOSE THE EASE AND RAPIDITY OF MINDLESS RESPONSES IF WE HAVE A METHOD OF EVALUATING PEOPLE AS INDIVIDUALS RATHER THAN AS STEREOTYPES IN ROLES. WE WOULD HAVE TO OBSERVE OTHERS RATHER THAN USE A ONE-DIMENSIONAL IMPRESSION. AND, WE WOULD NEED TO PUT FORTH MORE EFFORT AND TIME TO OVERRIDE OUR KNEE-JERK REACTIONS.

What would this new approach to evaluating people look like? We would begin by gathering information and data about another person. The next step would be to practice observing ourselves as well as the other person simultaneously in the relationship. We would then focus on creating a response to the other person that fits the needs of the moment and of us both. This response should be based on our individual judgments and actions.

Finally, if we adopt a new method, we would have to relinquish the old way of automatically relating to people. It comes down to a clear choice: we could decide to use new, at first more difficult and unfamiliar methods to evaluate others, or continue our conditioned role and accept its inherent limitations. We hope to help you select better methods of evaluating yourselves and others so you can free yourself from your emotional conditioning. In Chapter 11 we discuss this process in more depth.

How to Tell the Conditioned Roles Apart

Developing a way of evaluating and categorizing individuals is anything but simple. Although the two conditioned roles have distinct and frequently opposite components, which are identifiable to an interested observer, it is challenging to make these assessments when first meeting someone or when time may allow only brief attention to their superficial traits.

It seems remarkable that human intelligence can reach such heights in any external field of study and yet be so unaware of our interior selves. If we were buying a racehorse, we would check for breeding and record of past performance, and make a close observation for any significant defects. Yet most people choose a spouse or romantic partner on the sole basis of our visceral attraction. We are often unaware of treating loved ones who are vital to our lives in an abusive manner. We experience confusion and lack of consideration because of our conditioning.

Dr. Martin and I identified some consistent elements that seem to characterize the two roles. Once we learn to identify which roles other people are playing, that can help us predict their future reactions with a high level of consistency and probability.

ONLY IF WE UNDERSTAND WHETHER WE ARE DEALING WITH AN OMNIPOTENT OR IMPOTENT CAN WE MOVE AWAY FROM A CONDITIONED RESPONSE AND SUBSTITUTE AN APPROPRIATE RESPONSE TO THE OTHER PERSON AS HE EXISTS IN THAT MOMENT. INSTEAD OF RESPONDING TO THE *ROLE* OF THE OTHER PERSON, WE CAN DEVELOP A MORE NUANCED APPROACH BASED ON CIRCUMSTANCES. We may decide to provide needed support to an omnipotent, who is unaware of her stoic, masochistic inability to accept assistance. Or, we may decide to increase the level of support we provide an impotent in keeping with the circumstances, rather than feeling compelled to provide all the support an impotent demands.

In order for us to have better relationships, we must first be able to recognize what kind of person we and the other person are by what roles we are assuming. Table 3.2 sums up our findings on the differences between impotents and omnipotents.

Table 3.2 Differences in Emotionally Conditioned Roles

Omnipotent Characteristics	Factor Observed	Impotent Characteristics
Pride, hubris, smug	*Attitude*	Uncontained arrogance, outrage if questioned
Strives for perfection	*Personal standard*	Expedient, seeks the path of least resistance
Avoids dependency as much as possible	*State of dependency*	Relishes dependency
Devalues self, sees great value in impotents	*Value system*	Self-worth inflated over all else, devalues omnipotents
Has strong problem-solving skills and many methods to control situations	*Mental capacity*	Focus limited to personal desires
Constant reexamination in pursuing perfection	*Reality testing mode*	First impression usually taken for reality
Complex, abstract	*Quality of thought*	Fragmentary, capricious
Seeks thankless relationships, rarely asks for help	*Demands for emotional support*	Insatiable, rarely thankful
Low self-esteem	*Self-esteem*	Inflated self-esteem
Rigid, uncompromising	*Conscience*	Pliable, adjusts to whims
Blames others for one's own imperfections	*Projections*	Blames others for one's own deficiencies
Unconditional, endures beyond "dead" relationships	*Commitment mode*	Conditional, ends over slight disappointments
Exceedingly wide, focus on any observed injustice	*Scope of interests*	Tunnel vision, restricted to personal interests

WHAT YOU DISCOVERED IN THIS CHAPTER

- There are seven profound effects of the emotional conditioning process: short-circuiting thinking, depersonalization, impaired judgment, reducing others to stereotype, symbiosis, different thinking styles, and different reasons for and meanings of emotions.

- There are two styles of thinking: one that realistically appraises external and internal reality of people, and another that is emotionally conditioned and does not consider many realities of a person's circumstance or situation.

- We lack a reliable method of assessing other people. Both impotents and omnipotents make skewed appraisals. We can create a better approach to evaluating one another.

- We can distinguish differences between omnipotents and impotents in the following ways: attitude, personal standard, state of dependency, value system, mental capacity, style of testing reality, quality of thought, demands for emotional support, self-esteem, conscience, what is projected, style of commitment, and scope of interests.

Questions to Ask Yourself

Take some time to look over these questions and reflect on yourself. By doing this you can begin the process of finding out more about who you are and how you might have been emotionally conditioned. Questions like these are scattered throughout the book in hopes you can become better acquainted with your true self and your conditioning.

- What expectations were placed on you in early childhood?
- Were you expected to be a high performer?
- Were you given an unusual amount of support intended to make your life much easier?
- Who are the problem solvers among your relatives?
- Who in the family insists on receiving help in all endeavors of any difficulty?
- Which children receive pampered, overprotective care?
- Which children receive dismissive and inattentive care?
- Which relatives have been most supportive and caring toward you?
- Which relatives have ignored you, been unsupportive, or even abusive to you?
- Do you feel anxious and stressed in dealing with some relatives who are volatile and demanding?
- Do you feel anxious and distressed in dealing with relatives who do not make you the center of attention?
- How do you treat each of your relatives?
- Do you have a priority as to the importance assigned to each family member?
- Do you find you treat some relatives with neglect or a lack of regard without justification?
- What relatives are you most attracted to?

CHAPTER FOUR

The Omnipotent Personality

In the next two chapters we provide descriptions of omnipotent and impotent personalities. This chapter focuses on omnipotents. These chapters provide an overview of typical characteristics and development across the life span of the two roles—from birth to old age. We did not find that the effects of emotional conditioning affect everyone the same way, but they do provide a rigid framework to our personalities. We often think that emotional conditioning is permanent, because, once established, it stays with us throughout our lives. Actually, emotional conditioning is self-reinforcing because we repeatedly affirm our roles through constant reinforcement. Others treat us as omnipotents or impotents over and over as we grow up and throughout adult life, and so we come to see ourselves the same way.

Carolyn

Carolyn was the third of five girls. Her mother, Edith, was a homemaker, formerly an antiques dealer. Her father, Martin, owned an auto parts store. As an infant, she was happy and spunky, little trouble, and adapted easily to her family. As a preschooler, she enjoyed playing with other children and got along well. Edith took care of the five children with little help from Martin. He mostly disengaged.

But when Carolyn was a preschooler, Martin taught her to fish. When she was older he taught her to shoot, hunt small game, and pursue other activities he had enjoyed as a boy. He pushed her to play sports, especially ice hockey and soccer, the sports he liked most. Carolyn was quite agreeable doing what her father wanted. It made her feel happy and close with him.

Carolyn excelled both academically and at sports. She was attentive to Martin and believed he could do no wrong. She occasionally felt unhappy if she failed to please Martin, feeling guilty for not being a good daughter to him.

But toward Edith, Carolyn had a different standard. She was very critical of her mother, believing Edith did not try hard enough to take care of her five daughters. As an adolescent Carolyn grew distant from Edith and became angry and critical that her mother wanted her dad to help out more. Carolyn lacked empathy for her mother's situation and could not see the huge effort her mother made versus the small effort her father made in the day-to-day care of her and her sisters.

Over the years Martin and Edith grew estranged as Martin continued to ignore Edith and evaded most responsibility for raising his daughters. Edith grew depressed because she felt guilty over being unable to solve single-handedly all their daughters' problems. Yet Martin did not take over a parent role or even help. Instead, he filed for divorce. Martin was always a self-absorbed man who liked to hunt game, go to Las Vegas to gamble, and make frequent trips to Nashville for country music events. Edith's depression and her struggles with the children enraged him because Edith was no longer the problem-solving woman he married.

When Edith and Martin divorced, Carolyn continued psychologically supporting her father. She was 13 years old, and she felt sorry for Martin, because her mother "expected too much of him." Carolyn moved into Martin's apartment and rarely saw Edith, nor Edith her. She brought food and prepared meals for Martin, all the while being an honors high school student. Carolyn continued to do well academically, socially, and in sports. In college, she wanted to study archeology. She went on an archeological dig with a group from her church and found it fascinating. But Martin had a different agenda. He wanted her to study business in preparation for working with him at the auto parts store. Carolyn protested but Martin threatened not to pay for college unless she majored in business. Carolyn found funding for her own tuition, but she felt very depressed and eventually gave in to Martin. After graduation she joined Martin at his store, and when Martin retired, she took over.

In her late twenties, Carolyn met a needy law student and they married. Carolyn did most of the work in the relationship, while her husband pursued his hobbies of stock car and horse racing.

Commentary

Carolyn was in a symbiotic relationship with Martin. She complied emotionally with his wants, from pursuing sports activities he wanted to studying business in college to making sure Martin ate and was indulged in his hobbies and travels. Carolyn was in an omnipotent role, and Martin was emotionally impotent. Edith conditioned Carolyn to be in an omnipotent role as she modeled trying in vain to satisfy Martin and care alone for five children. Though overwhelmed, Edith castigated herself for not being a perfect omnipotent caretaker and became depressed. Her self-expectations of omnipotent functioning exceeded her abilities, especially with no help from Martin.

As a young adult, Carolyn continued her role of omnipotent young woman. She fell in love with a bright but emotionally helpless and impotent man, for whom she did most of the work in the relationship. Carolyn also continued to abhor any neediness shown by her mother, Edith. She had an unconscious identification with her mother as a fellow omnipotent. Carolyn had the unconscious idea that "I never need help from others and you shouldn't either." This was her emotional stance toward herself and toward Edith.

Conditioning Begins before Birth

Many, but not all, omnipotents are first-born children, born when parents may be young and inexperienced with child rearing. I have observed and worked with many pregnant couples, who unconsciously expect their child to be a "perfect" child who will achieve academic goals and other endeavors with ease. Such couples, quite unaware, agree to push their child to excel.

Yet they also endow this yet-to-be-born omnipotent with the expectation that he or she can accomplish many things on his or her own. They want their child to have manners and good behaviors. Quite often, they do not plan on cutting back on the adult activities they have been involved in before their child's birth. They expect this child to "fit in" to their environment and do not expect they will need to make many adjustments of their own to accommodate their child. Here is a case example.

Jacob and Alexandra

A couple in their late twenties expected their first child. They were both physicians with active practices and good incomes. She was five months pregnant. In preparing for the baby, this couple planned to clear out a spare bedroom and buy a used crib and chest of drawers. They saw no need to spend money on furnishings or new baby clothes the baby would just outgrow. Jacob and Alexandra enjoyed camping, hiking, and travel abroad. They decided they would take the baby along. "It wouldn't be much of a problem walking trails, riding in cars, buses, or airplanes because babies sleep so much," they agreed. They already seemed to be pigeonholing their baby as an omnipotent, who would require little in the way of special planning, expense, or effort.

Infancy

Omnipotent infants are often initiated into family life without fanfare and with an expectation they will adapt to existing conditions, whatever these may be. Most of the adults who care for them don't rush to meet their needs.

The contrast between the two roles strikes parents later, when they compare raising an omnipotent and impotent child. In retrospect, many parents view the time they spent caring for their omnipotent child as relaxed and comparatively simple. They thought this was so because of their child's character rather than their parenting approach. They only find an omnipotent child challenging if she fails to meet her parents' standards. Parents seem to be determined that omnipotent children will be good-natured and learn quickly.

THE FIRST TWO YEARS OF LIFE START THE BALL ROLLING FOR A PERSON'S EMOTIONAL CONDITIONING. DURING THESE EARLY YEARS IN HIS HOME, HIS PARENTS HAVE BEGUN SHAPING THEIR BABY TO INTERPRET REALITY THE SAME WAY ONE OF HIS PARENTS DOES. THE BABY IS NOT CONSCIOUS OF WHICH PARENT HE IS ASSIGNED TO MIRROR.

Parents enjoy noticing whenever their child learns a new skill, which is shortly followed by increased expectations. They exclaim over her good nature, her ability to amuse herself, how quickly she sleeps through the night, and how interested she is in learning about new objects in her environment. They praise her strength, her intelligence, and how precocious she is. They comment on her ability to be patient and tolerate delays in having her needs met.

The baby being shaped to be an omnipotent child adapts well to a regular schedule, seldom cries, adjusts to schedule changes easily, and travels well. As he begins to develop language skills, parents often tell him, "You don't want to play with that," when drawn to an attractive object. These projections from others start in infancy.

This baby's quick mind grasps ideas, words, and songs quite early, and she may have exceptional coordination. Many parents find pleasure in rearing such a baby who progresses rapidly. Both parents tend to remain unaware that from the start they have been setting high expectations for their baby and projecting their own thoughts onto their child.

PARENTS OFTEN FAIL TO RECOGNIZE—THEN OR LATER—THAT THEIR BABY'S WARM DISPOSITION, EXTREME RESPONSIVENESS TO OTHERS, AND CONFORMITY TO EXPECTATIONS USUALLY MATCH THOSE OF *ONE* OF THE PARENTS. Frequently, parents and other observers comment about this being a "good" baby, who is both lovable and independent. Sometimes parents are astonished that their child "demands so little attention." They are unaware that they give approval and positive emotional reinforcement when he is agreeable and of little bother to anyone.

In the first months of life, newborns have no capacity for judgment and adapt to whatever input, treatment, and expectations their parents expose them to. They learn according to their parents' well-defined expectations and goals. There is little conflict between parents when their child is totally dependent on them. An infant's helpless dependent state is apparent even to the most severely conditioned impotent parent.

But as their baby gains mobility and walks near the end of the first year, his first steps begin to physically remove him from the cocoon in which he has lived. When a child can walk, pick himself up without assistance, and feed himself, his parents withdraw some of their support. They minimize his inevitable bruises and frustrations and respond to his physical hurts with laughter and comments of, "That didn't hurt!"

Parents are likely to impose early toilet training on omnipotents and may do it with such intensity that their child learns she must adjust her bathroom habits so as not to disrupt or inconvenience anyone else. As she approaches two or three years old, she may discover that she is expected to manage her body functions and suppress her spontaneous emotions. She learns that normal bodily products may disgust her caretaker, most often an impotent parent. This parent may go to great lengths to prevent accidents, such as sitting his child on the toilet for long periods or devoting a lot of time and attention to the child's bowel performance, as if it has tremendous importance.

Since a child can recognize this emphasis on bowel hygiene, he may remain concerned all his life that he is highly offensive if he cannot control all of his body odors. As he grows, he may be fastidious, worry about offending others, and become obsessed with cleanliness. He may have an increasing concern over feeling disgraced if he fails to control all body functions. He may also begin to feel he must keep himself tightly controlled and self-contained.

Preschool Age

ANOTHER DOSE OF REALITY TAKES PLACE AROUND THE THIRD YEAR WHEN AN OMNIPOTENT CHILD BEGINS TO RECOGNIZE HE CANNOT SATISFY EVERYONE, REGARDLESS OF EFFORT. For a sensitive child, this is a shattering realization. He moves from being protected and totally dependent to being expected to care for himself and is often flooded with anxiety when his impotent parent devalues him by putting him down or scolding him. At this young age, he begins trying to please many of the people around him, being who they expect him to be, doing what he is "supposed to do," and giving *them* what they want. When he is scolded, he is shocked to learn he might be failing to meet the expectations of these vital people.

By age three or four, a keenly sensitive omnipotent detects a disappointing attitude from her impotent parent. Quite often this parent sees his child as capable of fulfilling her omnipotent role, often chiding her to be more in control of herself, take care of her toys, and share freely. This is a turning point in her development. AS SHE GRADUALLY PAYS LESS ATTENTION TO HER OMNIPOTENT FAMILY MEMBERS AND MORE ATTENTION TO HER IMPOTENT RELATIVES, SHE LEARNS TO DENY HERSELF THINGS SHE WANTS AND EMOTIONS SHE FEELS. This child's predominant concern in life will be to fulfill the ever-increasing expectations of this demanding and exacting impotent parent.

At this age, a preschooler begins to react with anxiety trying to meet the impotent parent's rarely satisfied expectations. The result is that an omnipotent preschooler may develop a growing fixation that it must be possible to perform in some way to ultimately satisfy his impotent parent. He begins to put a lot of energy into winning that parent's approval. A preschooler has no way of realizing that impotents are insatiable. And as he grows up he learns to adopt a value system that an impotent's smallest desire is more urgent and significant than any interest that he or any other omnipotent wants to pursue.

In the emotional conditioning process, parents or caregivers shape children's thoughts, behaviors, and emotions. This begins in infancy and carries over into the preschool years. Parents reinforce some emotions while frowning on others. Omnipotent children frequently feel anxiety, self-devaluation, disappointment, anger, and sadness with themselves when they don't please their impotent parent, and they learn to conceal anger and frustration from impotents. This happens because impotent parents may meet their children's display of strong emotions with their own anger and upset, so children quickly learn to withhold showing their emotions. Over time, many omnipotents lose the ability to even identify their own emotions.

Preschoolers begin acquiring their own standards of behavior and tend to model themselves after their omnipotent parent. Parents often criticize omnipotent preschoolers whenever their behavior falls below either parent's standards and critique their preschoolers' conduct when they have the slightest lapse. When children succeed with expected behaviors, they receive parental approval and acceptance and feel intensely happy at their own success. But, when they fail, they experience disappointment and devaluation by their parents.

When parents devalue their child, the child fears the loss of their affection and of no longer being important to them. She may be afraid her parents will abandon her. Even preschoolers may feel more terrified at this loss of support than at any physical punishment. She quickly learns she can only regain their acceptance by conforming to their expectations once more.

By preschool age, an omnipotent can become overly anxious or depressed. He may have self-deprecating thoughts and sad, angry feelings of being of little value if he is not able to fulfill his role and gratify the high expectations of one or both parents. In these cases, the family may need psychotherapy treatment, even when the child is at this very young age.

School Age

As a child's geographic boundary grows beyond his home to relatives and friends, he learns to practice his role with outsiders. He becomes aware that there are unfamiliar conditions outside his own home, and this may generate anxiety about making mistakes. He may feel most comfortable returning home where his parents made rules and roles clear. School-aged children often learn to idealize their home and the criteria established by their parents, no matter how unrealistic or peculiar they may be. Since many of the values instilled in a child are imprinted just as his memory first becomes formed, he is unable to evaluate whether his family's standards and behavior patterns are reasonable. As a result, these unconsciously learned values and way of operating in relationships become rigidly fixed and are not easily changed later by reason or logic.

In school, an omnipotent performs well, as she does at home. She gravitates toward difficult-to-please teachers and fellow pupils. Her desire to perform also has a secondary benefit. She often becomes a conscientious student and feels increasingly compelled to respond to or please impotents and control problems around them.

An anxious-to-please omnipotent child eagerly seeks signals on how to conduct herself. She will continue this process until her reactions almost duplicate those of her parent of the same role. **A YOUNG SCHOOL-AGE CHILD MAY SURPRISE AND AMUSE HIS PARENTS WHEN HE MAKES A SLIGHT MISTAKE AND BECOMES ANXIOUS AND CRIES INCONSOLABLY. THEY MAY HAVE REGARDED HIS EFFORTS AS MERE CHILD'S PLAY AND BE UNABLE TO RECOGNIZE THAT HE IS ENACTING WHAT THEY HAVE TAUGHT HIM. AN OMNIPOTENT IS OVERLY SERIOUS FOR LIFE.**

By school age, an omnipotent may assume responsibility for whatever goes wrong. At the same time, she will likely develop a perfectionistic, unforgiving conscience that equates the slightest imperfection with *total* failure. Her conscience can make her feel worthless for modest failures. I found that childhood depressions and anxieties can be quite prevalent in this school-aged group.

The school years appear to reinforce the emotional training program of the family. Teachers find high-performing omnipotents useful as models for less diligent students. **OMNIPOTENT CHILDREN SEE GRADES AS A WAY OF GAUGING THEIR OWN PROGRESS IN THEIR QUEST FOR PERFECTION. OMNIPOTENTS OFTEN HAVE INTENSE COMPETITIVENESS WITH OTHER OMNIPOTENTS.** They also may feel fear and worry that if they get too close to others they will reveal their flaws and imagined imperfections, so they keep a distance from other students and appear aloof.

Omnipotents establish a pattern of accountability and self-reliance and receive less attention and input from teachers. Like their parents, their teachers' emotional conditioning compels them to shift their attention to impotent students and leave the omnipotents to fend for themselves. On many occasions, I have seen teachers assign part of their own teaching workload to omnipotent students.

Teachers reinforce family attitudes and approaches to others. When an omnipotent student has an extraordinary achievement, he may receive recognition, and this may encourage a heightened anticipation that he will do even better the next time. As this child performs on a level beyond his age, other people take for granted his exemplary behavior. If he complains that his parents or teacher expect too much of him, they rebuke him as spoiled or lazy.

Omnipotents receive their greatest rewards when they have been very considerate or thoughtful in satisfying an impotent sibling, parent, grandparent, or teacher. A child savors these experiences of delivering perfection and receiving approval from others. This adds to his belief that he can deliver perfection. Often omnipotent children show passive acceptance in the face of intrusions such as bullying or aggressiveness by impotents. Away from the family, a young omnipotent shows attitudes of obedience, amiability, and caring.

Within his tiny universe, his family, the child strives to deliver perfection, which is defined as *what the other person wants*. Others expect a young omnipotent to accommodate all those around her and to be attentive to their desires while appearing to be independent. However, in this situation, she becomes the "dependee" and is not acting independently. She caters to others' dependence and will not accept being dependent in return.

A YOUNG OMNIPOTENT CHILD DEVELOPS PRIDE IN SERVING OTHERS AND REINFORCES THIS EMOTIONALLY CONDITIONED RESPONSE THROUGHOUT LIFE. As she matures, she expands her repertoire of delivering care. She may do so right up to the point of disastrous failure. Here is an example in a young school-age girl.

Sylvia

Eight-year-old Sylvia lived alternate weeks with her mother and father, who were divorced. Her parents agreed to this arrangement during court-ordered mediation. Sylvia and her brother Aaron, age nine, followed this arrangement for three years. Then, six months ago, Aaron went to live full-time with their father. Aaron became very aggressive with his mother and, at one point, assaulted her. For years, he fought constantly with her over her erratic and unpredictable behaviors and lack of rules—not getting him to or from school on time, not helping with homework, and frequently not getting the laundry done so that he wore dirty clothes to school. The court approved Aaron's change in living arrangements.

Since Aaron went to live with their father, Sylvia became more despondent, not sleeping well, and not wanting to play with friends. Her grades fell. She cried a lot. In therapy she said she, too, preferred to live with her dad. She described her mom's strictness and erratic behaviors the same way Aaron did. But, she felt sorry for her mother because Aaron had left, and now she was the only one there to keep mom happy. She feared upsetting her mother if she, too, went to live with her dad and Aaron.

Commentary

Sylvia was willing to sacrifice herself for her mother's need to have Sylvia live with her. Sylvia was emotionally conditioned to be omnipotent for her impotent mother and became overwhelmed and depressed trying to do this. Her inability to please her mother led to her feeling guilty, self-punitive with head banging, and, at one point, suicidal. During two years in therapy, Sylvia grew to appreciate what she was doing to herself. She was then able to tell her mother emphatically she did not want to live with her. She moved on to living with her dad and Aaron full-time, even though her mother took the issue back to court.

When a child begins school, he has already formed his basic unconscious responses to others, and he enters a new stage of learning in which he can apply and practice these techniques. He is triggered by unconscious cues to attempt to deliver perfection to people who are like his impotent parent. The more difficult the challenge, the greater his surge of self-esteem will be. We can compare this with Pavlov's dogs salivating when they see their caretaker who may or may not have food. In either case, both dogs and omnipotent children experience an unconscious gratification—nothing tangible.

Since an omnipotent suffers relatively low self-esteem throughout life and none of his later achievements repair his sense of inadequacy, his inevitable failures to perform perfectly reinforce his conditioning. School-aged children learn to disregard themselves and their fellow omnipotents, and this relegates them collectively to a shared place of a lower worth in society. Often children in elementary school say they feel as if they were servants to the privileged class of impotents.

FROM ALL OF THESE SEPARATE EXPERIENCES AT HOME AND IN SCHOOL, A YOUNG OMNIPOTENT FORMULATES A GENERAL FORMULA OF HOW SHE MUST OPERATE: OTHERS ONLY ACCEPT HER WHEN SHE GIVES THEM WHATEVER THEY WANT AND EXPECTS NOTHING IN RETURN. Her parents only tolerate her when she is being useful. This has been her parents' projected attitude from the beginning, to have a "useful" high-performing child.

By school age, a child learns that relationships consist of a hard-working caretaker providing care to an emotional dependent. He sees this pattern at home, with friends, and at school. An omnipotent child may become a teacher's pet. This approval pleases him, but he discovers he may antagonize many fellow students for being the "pet." Some of his peers, siblings, or cousins may ridicule his compliant behavior, and it worries him if he can't get everyone's approval.

Others label an omnipotent child as an achiever and leader as he progresses through school. School administrators give him special duties because he follows rules, takes pride in protecting other children, and volunteers for unpleasant chores that other students do not want. Teachers will sometimes punish him for allowing other students to copy his homework or for doing assignments for them.

Adolescence

As an omnipotent moves on to adolescence in middle and high school, she broadens her relationships beyond her family. The role she has been learning becomes more established and reinforced as she relates to her peers in her early teen years. These become the years of final practice in operating as an omnipotent in society away from her family. The adolescent period, which may be marked by alienation and conflict, also serves as a child's declaration of independence. Increasingly, adolescents no longer accept parental guidance, because they tentatively and anxiously seek ways of establishing their relationships independently.

Parents may critique her selection of acquaintances and how she deals with them, and be resentful that she is no longer compliant. Steadily, she moves toward separateness, and this move lessens the close family ties and affection of childhood. As family ties lessen, ties to those outside the family intensify. Although a teenager is performing precisely as programmed, parents may be consciously unable to recognize this.

By his mid-teens, an adolescent has replicated the role and standard of his omnipotent parent. He convinces himself of the infallibility of his own thinking, particularly concerning his personal life. He will remain open to useful *ideas* from people he believes are omnipotent, based on a projection of his own omnipotent image. He may accept their information without question, as long as they offer no emotional support. He does not yet comprehend it is an error to believe that any person has "the answer." Two teenage omnipotents may exchange information about their favorite bands, sports teams, and interests, but they do not offer or accept emotional nurturance from each other.

During adolescence, a teen may become critical of his omnipotent parent's perceived defects in performing his or her role, but this is only after he has already acquired these same permanent traits. They become two peas in a pod. When this happens, a teenager grows increasingly protective of the impotent parent and critical of his fellow omnipotent parent, for whom he has little to no sympathy. The young omnipotent gives various explanations for the omnipotent parent's imperfections— bad genes, poor background, lack of education, and so on—and he is determined to do better than his omnipotent parent by eliminating these shortcomings in himself.

A characteristic of adolescence is conformity to fads. **PEER PRESSURE REPLACES PARENTAL PRESSURE AND EMOTIONALLY CONDITIONS THE CHILD TO GET ALONG WITH OTHERS.** Although an adolescent omnipotent may appear differently with her friends and in her social groups, she is still playing her customary role, just with a new group. At times a group of delinquents or a gang will draw in this high achiever, much to the dismay of family and teachers. His role in the gang, or group of whatever type, may be to control situations for the other members and be a protector for delinquent impotents. As he has always learned, he works to gain approval from impotents. He does whatever it takes to receive acceptance.

An omnipotent adolescent may also experiment briefly with drugs, sex, and delinquent acts, but mostly to seek peer acceptance. Around his family and away from the gang, he behaves better. Many adolescent omnipotents avoid the "bad kids" altogether and participate only in school clubs or other organized activities. Quite a few omnipotents may be so intense that they do not socialize or date. Very idealistic adolescents may contemplate a thankless calling or have fantasies of achieving some altruistic benefit for everyone.

AN ADOLESCENT OMNIPOTENT BECOMES INCREASINGLY VULNERABLE TO DEPRESSION AS SHE REACHES THE END OF HER TEENS. She may become disillusioned about attaining lofty goals if she does poorly academically, in sports or in vocational training. She may interpret her failures as insuperable defects, which reduce her self-esteem to a point where she may contemplate suicide.

Many failures that would seem minor to other people can severely discourage brilliant omnipotent achievers. One flaw can condemn the whole effort. By adolescence an omnipotent does not see shades of gray—only the two extremes of black or white, perfection or failure. Taking the long view, omnipotents recall failures painfully but dismiss successes altogether.

For many omnipotents, their high scholastic record often reflects their eagerness to learn. Others may show no outstanding achievements in school and appear quite ordinary in their youth.

By the end of adolescence, omnipotents have learned that they must endure aggression without protest, that aggressive peers will victimize them, and they must not defend themselves. They may be friendly but reserved and always concerned that their perceived imperfections will be loudly obvious to all who know them.

Adult

An omnipotent nearing adulthood is often outwardly affable and ambitious but on a deeper level is a conscientious and serious person with low self-esteem. He frequently thinks he could have been better or done better. His family and friends wonder why he cannot appreciate his own outstanding qualities.

Some omnipotents are eager to display independence and may cut short their education. They often feel compelled to support themselves financially and to end dependency on their family. They also tend to assume work and marital obligations early and become extremely protective of their spouse and children. Others may view their desire to be pleasing and win the approval of an impotent as an expression of love, because of its intensity and single-mindedness. We discuss this in depth in Chapter 7.

The young adult tunes in to any family crisis. Others may expect her to support relatives with financial or other problems. She may take pride in being able to care for many people and is proud of having modest needs of her own. Others notice she works on vacations and may return to work after time off with a sense of relief.

When forming their own families, omnipotents tend to show a characteristic overcommitment, one so consuming that they neglect other pursuits and relationships. People close to an omnipotent may be astonished and perplexed that he lets his impotent partner dominate him.

AN OMNIPOTENT USUALLY BECOMES THE NURTURER, PROBLEM SOLVER, AND RESCUER FOR THE ENTIRE FAMILY, AND DOES THIS INTENSE LABOR QUIETLY AND WITH LITTLE FANFARE. Impotents will deflate her standing in the family by criticizing her when she fails to perform up to some very high expectation. Even later in adult life after her children become adults, she has an undiminished commitment to protect impotents. She remains unaware that she feels little or no commitment to herself.

Coworkers may label him a "workaholic"[1] and assign him extra work, often commenting, "He likes to do it." He may do poorly as a manager since he feels that he, and only he, can do tasks correctly and is reluctant to delegate responsibility to others. He may feel stressed when going to parties and social occasions unrelated to work. He may choose hobbies that are more purposeful than relaxing—building houses or boats or cooking for large groups of people.

As adults, omnipotents seek mastery in their rare leisure pursuits and play games with a vengeance. Beware omnipotents who play tennis, golf, or card games. They most often play to win and take it very seriously. Omnipotents will likely relax somewhat in the company of other omnipotents, since they feel free of the pressures to support them emotionally, as they do impotents. Although omnipotents identify with fellow omnipotents, they may feel defensive and wonder if others discount them because of their past failures.

A group of omnipotents in conversation tend to focus on discussing recent accomplishments or ways of dealing with problems. Although they identify closely with one another, they are also busy assuming each of them is "perfect." This creates a barrier or space that allows companionship but precludes genuine emotional intimacy.

IN THEIR ADULT LIVES, OMNIPOTENTS ARE ENDLESSLY BUSY AND DEVOTE TIME AWAY FROM WORK TO CIVIC, RELIGIOUS, OR COMMUNITY VOLUNTEER WORK. THEY RARELY COMPLAIN, DENY THE NEED FOR TREATMENT DURING ILLNESSES, AND TYPICALLY WORK UNTIL EXHAUSTION. ONLY WHEN COMPLETELY EXHAUSTED, OVERWHELMED, AND SICK WILL THEY SEEK TREATMENT FOR PHYSICAL OR EMOTIONAL PROBLEMS.

Since omnipotents focus their whole lives on their ability to perform, they find failure intolerable, even in the most trivial act. This is one reason they are so busy; they work hard and take on more and more responsibility to avoid any possibility of personal failure.

AN OMNIPOTENT'S MISSION IN LIFE COULD BE SUMMED UP AS FOLLOWS:

"I TAKE PLEASURE IN MASTERING MY WORK AND PERFORMANCE AND IN MEETING THE DEMANDS OF OTHERS. I EXPEND ANY ENERGY AND RESOURCES NEEDED TO SATISFY PEOPLE WHO RELY ON ME. I DO NOT COMPLAIN OR LET ILLNESSES OR HANDICAPS BOTHER ME. I NEVER ASK FOR HELP, FOR OTHERS RESENT ME IF I DO."

People around omnipotents take their high-performance levels for granted. As a result, people place greater and greater expectations on them. This places even more stress on omnipotents.

Old Age

In old age, omnipotents perform as they started learning in infancy. They battle any reduction of their duties at work and at home, and deal poorly with the natural infirmities of aging. They worry years in advance about how their families will manage after their deaths. They may set up trusts and inheritance plans to perpetuate their management of financial affairs even after death.

RETIREMENT IS LIKELY TO BE A TRAUMATIC EXPERIENCE FOR OMNIPOTENTS, SINCE THEY CANNOT TOLERATE NOT BEING "USEFUL." Not only is this declining usefulness difficult, but if he or she is at home after working in an office for decades, this can create an unwelcome inconvenience for their impotent spouses. An impotent devalues an omnipotent anytime she is not performing a useful function. An impotent frequently cannot tolerate an omnipotent's inactivity, even when brought on by physical disability. Regardless of the reasons for, or timing of, retirement, an omnipotent seldom slows down her characteristic constant activity.

Life passes rapidly for them. Many omnipotents have told us that they experience a busy, repetitive routine with little time for reflection or intimacy that often leaves few memorable moments. They typically recall their failures, and these haunt them. In their last years, they wonder why they did not see more of their close relatives and friends.

We found that a typical omnipotent lives through the stages of his life consistently conforming to and reinforcing his emotional conditioning. His efforts to satisfy others bring him to a point where all of life is work, without any real leisure or balance. In some situations, where he pleased others by selfless, sacrificial service, he felt the brief elation of omnipotence. But in continuing to embrace an ideal—perfection—he is doomed never to meet that goal and judges himself harshly.

Here is another case example.

Jared

When Jared was born, he had four older sisters. He was a "surprise" baby who arrived seven years after his next-oldest sister. His mother was an at-home mom, and his father worked in a truck manufacturing plant. Mom was soft-spoken but outgoing. She was full of opinions on people she knew and didn't know and on events and happenings in the wider world. Mom did the household chores and took the children to church. She collected antique dolls. Dad worked long shifts and took care of the yard and cars. He was reserved and barely spoke with his family, preferring in his little free time to read history and biography books.

Beginning as a baby, Jared's sisters cared for him a great deal, at mom's request. They fed, diapered, babysat, and played with him. Later, as a toddler and in grade school, they took him to the park and to baseball and basketball practices. Mom was busy with doll collecting and church activities. Jared played a lot with neighborhood and school friends.

Occasionally dad took Jared to movies, ball games, and went fishing with him. They did not converse much during these outings, but Jared was happy to have any contact with his dad.

By the time Jared was 11, he felt he was on his own as far as figuring out his world and making his own decisions. If he asked his parents for advice about clothes, homework, sports, or other interests, they did not provide many answers or much guidance. Mom criticized him when he made a poor decision but never made suggestions as to how to do better, and dad ignored his questions. Over time Jared quit asking. He felt he was a bother to both of his parents.

By his middle school years, his sisters were grown and gone from home, and he was essentially an only child. Mom and dad did not especially value good grades and were inattentive to Jared's school assignments. Jared was a mediocre student and felt ill at ease, not knowing how to get good grades. He preferred sports and dating girls during high school and did well in both areas.

Jared wanted to attend college to study literature, but neither parent thought college was necessary. Dad believed Jared could have a good job at the truck plant where he worked. Mom just didn't want her "baby" to leave home, as she felt she'd be lonely. Eventually, dad said Jared could go to college, and he'd help him pay some of the costs. But, mom only agreed if Jared would attend a nearby college and live at home. If Jared insisted on leaving town to attend college, she told him they would not pay a dime for him. Dad capitulated to mom. Frustrated and anguished, Jared opted to leave town for college and devise some way to pay the expenses himself. He felt trapped by his mother.

For the last two years of high school, Jared dated Catherine, and they attended the same college. Jared majored in English literature and business. He wanted to be a writer and teacher but also wanted to have some business knowledge, since he hoped to open a bookstore in the future. Catherine worked on a nursing degree. They were both practical and levelheaded, supported one another in academic work, and enjoyed free time together. They rarely squabbled. By the end of their sophomore year, they planned to marry after graduation.

During his junior year of college, Jared injured his shoulder playing intramural football. He dropped out of college and moved back home to heal his shoulder for six months before returning to his studies. Again, his mother pressured him to continue living at home and attend a nearby college.

She enticed him by agreeing to pay his expenses for the last two years of college if he lived at home. Jared had no money to cover college costs and succumbed to his mother's pressure. He was angry and frustrated, but he concealed his emotions. He and Catherine continued to see one another in spite of the distance between them and continued with marriage plans.

One day, Jared's mother introduced him to a young woman she had met at church— Eva. Eva was petite, perky, flirtatious, opinionated and outspoken. Jared was smitten with Eva. He had never known such an outgoing, talkative young woman. In a short time he began dating Eva and broke up with Catherine. Jared and Eva married shortly after Jared's college graduation.

Eva wanted to be a cancer researcher but became pregnant shortly after their marriage and dropped plans for graduate school to stay home with the baby. Jared urged her to continue her studies, but she refused. Jared scrambled to find a job teaching college English but was unsuccessful. He felt the pressure of needing an income and took a job with an insurance agency.

Rather quickly into their marriage Eva became an overpowering person in their relationship. She dictated to Jared what he could and couldn't do, and she complained about everything and everyone. Jared felt cowed and that he should comply with what Eva wanted to keep the peace.

They had three more children before Eva and Jared gradually went their separate ways, although they remained legally married. Jared was angry, fed up, and disillusioned. Nothing he ever did was good enough for Eva. She verbally abused him and some of the children. Jared continued to live with her but focused on his work and on his relationships with friends and colleagues.

At home, Jared had a separate bedroom and kept to one part of the house and away from Eva. Jared visited his grown children on his own without Eva. Each went on separate vacations—Eva with women from church and Jared with men friends on hunting trips.

Jared's life went on like this for decades. He thought of divorce and of having an affair but never took action, fearing what others would think of him. At 87 he entered assisted living with help from two of his children. Eva visited him occasionally and often wound up berating him, causing Jared misery. Jared enjoyed the other residents in his assisted living facility. Many were emotionally warm, friendly, and accepting of him. They shared stories of their lives and went together to movies and theater.

Commentary

As a baby and young boy, Jared's parents showed little attention toward him. They were the opposite of helicopter parents, preferring to be aloof and relatively uninvolved. Jared accepted his omnipotent role of feeling self-sufficient and on his own. When he asked for advice or expressed a desire, dad, an omnipotent parent, ignored him. But mom, an impotent parent, forced her viewpoints and desires on Jared, and he felt he had to surrender his desires and do what she wanted.

He had a mutually supportive relationship with his girlfriend, Catherine, until Eva, an impotent, appeared and swept Jared away into marriage. Jared found Eva emotionally and sexually seductive. He was unaware how like his mother Eva was.

Jared felt trapped in an unfulfilling marriage but did nothing about it, believing he would upset a lot of people if he divorced. He felt it was preferable to live with his own upset rather than risk causing emotional turmoil for Eva and their children. Eva showed no care toward Jared and yelled at and belittled him. We can see how Jared learned the omnipotent role from his parents. His dad modeled the role for him while his mother pushed him into the role to acquiesce to her desires.

Summary of Omnipotent Personality

AN OMNIPOTENT EXPECTS HIMSELF OR HERSELF TO BE CHEERFUL, ALERT, METICULOUS, THOROUGH, TIRELESS, TOLERANT, AND PATIENT, WITH HAPPY EMOTIONS AND RESTRAINED ANGER AND ANIMOSITY. IMPERFECTIONS DISTRESS AND SADDEN HIM, AND HE STRIVES TO CONCEAL THESE "WEAKNESSES" FROM OTHERS. No matter how insignificant the problem disturbing his impotent spouse, he immediately does his best to resolve it.

Over time, others come to rely on her practiced ability to meet difficult situations. She seems to collect chores with glee and thrives on dealing with such troublesome problems. Others increasingly rely on her to take care of existing concerns. Seeing this as completely reasonable, omnipotents assume a caretaker role. When they become parents, they will expect some of their children to assume the same role.

FROM BIRTH, OTHERS TREAT A FUTURE OMNIPOTENT AS IF SHE POSSESSES CAPABILITIES FAR BEYOND THE NORM. SHE REMAINS UNCERTAIN OF THE EXTENT OF HER LIMITATIONS AND WILL ENDEAVOR TO DO THE IMPOSSIBLE. BECAUSE HER PARENTS CONDITION HER TO BE SELF-RELIANT, SHE REMAINS AVERSE TO DEPENDENCY, EVEN WHEN HELP IS OFFERED. SHE DEVELOPS GREAT SENSITIVITY TO WHAT OTHERS WANT WHILE BEING OBLIVIOUS TO HER OWN PERSONAL NEEDS AND DESIRES. When forced to depend on others, she feels a sense of obligation, discomfort, and wrongdoing. Having always lived under the unrealistic expectations of conditioning, her standard becomes one of meeting others' needs perfectly. She is deferential toward others, striving to please all and upset no one. Since she has received little physical or emotional support during her lifetime, she develops a belief beginning in early childhood that she is unworthy and unlovable.

WHAT YOU DISCOVERED IN THIS CHAPTER

- Parents impose abnormally high standards on developing omnipotent children. Infants who are being shaped to be omnipotent adapt well to a routine schedule, seldom cry, travel well, and adjust easily to changes.

- An omnipotent child strives to satisfy an impotent parent and to seek this parent's approval and acceptance. If she fails, she suffers anxiety and devalues herself. She may experience depression and anxiety from pre-school age on.

- By school age, an omnipotent child strives for perfection in academic and social activities. He is competitive with other omnipotents and eager to satisfy impotents. Omnipotents often have low self-esteem in spite of stellar accomplishments.

- An omnipotent expresses few needs and does not expect others to meet his needs. He performs without complaint and does not allow illness or handicap to deter him from performing for others.

- In adolescence, an omnipotent may be involved in delinquent activities, usually in the role of caring for and supporting impotents, who may be delinquent gang members.

- In order to display her independence, an omnipotent may quit school early and assume work and marital obligations early on in life. As an adult, an omnipotent seriously overcommits to the impotents in her life, sacrificing her own leisure interests and other relationships. She is end-lessly busy with civic, religious, community, and family affairs.

- An omnipotent is likely to be a "workaholic." His whole focus is on his ability to perform. People around him raise their expectations of him as he performs so consistently well.

- In old age, an omnipotent has difficulty when removed from work, worries years in advance about how her family will manage after her death, and continues to mull over her past failures to be omnipotent.

CHAPTER FIVE

The Impotent Personality

It's surprising that parents can treat an impotent child so differently from an omnipotent sibling and never be aware of it. If another person points out that an impotent child is receiving special treatment, or if a sibling complains, parents often rationalize why they show a preference to their impotent child. They may justify their actions by saying that special, favored treatment is necessary due to the child having an illness in the past, an overly sensitive nature, or age, size, or gender disadvantages. Often omnipotent siblings will question why they get so little support and attention while their parents lavish attention on their impotent brothers and sisters.

Seth

Jessica worked as a neonatologist and her husband, Peter, was an attorney. They decided in their late thirties to have a child. Jessica wanted to become pregnant earlier, but Peter was opposed to having children because of Jessica's long work hours. He changed his mind after his father died suddenly and prematurely from a heart attack. He adored his father, describing him as a very caring man.

Jessica worked in a hospital's neonatal intensive care unit attending to severely ill babies. She also visited outlying communities, performing well-baby visits and counseling new mothers about their babies' developmental, feeding, and sleeping concerns.

Jessica knew from her work the many pitfalls for premature newborns, so she worried about prematurity and potential health risks her baby might encounter. She was cautious in her approach to her future baby and planned to give him or her a thorough examination to rule out health issues early on in the baby's life, even though a pediatrician would do the same exam at birth.

Their son, Seth, was born full-term and healthy after a problem-free pregnancy. Jessica adjusted her work schedule to part-time. They hired a nanny from Honduras who said she adored little boys. Peter continued to work full-time. Shortly after arriving home with Seth, Jessica became concerned that Seth slept too much, cried too little, and was not as irritable or fussy as she thought he would be. Peter became concerned about Jessica's worry. They consulted their pediatrician who reassured them that Seth was fine and healthy.

Both parents carried Seth in papoose fashion around their bodies so that they could attend to him immediately when he cried or was fussy. As Seth grew in his infancy, he would naturally play briefly, stop, and become fussy or cry. Jessica, Peter, or his nanny would immediately pick him up. They would coo at him and rock him and introduce a new toy, pacifier, or cracker until he calmed. Then the cycle would repeat.

By age two, Seth whimpered and became irritable when anyone delayed the least bit responding to him. He craved constant holding and was almost always held. His speech was delayed, and he communicated by whimpering, crying, grunting, or whining. His parents and nanny attended to him so readily that he did not have to speak to express what he wanted. He didn't learn to walk until he was 20 months old, and only then because their pediatrician adamantly told Jessica to let him walk and stop holding him so much. Seth did not speak in full sentences until age three. He was not toilet trained until almost four, as both parents thought it cruel to have him use his potty when he did not want to.

Seth began kindergarten at age six because Jessica and Peter held him back a year. They rationalized that he was not quite mature enough for kindergarten, but the real reason was they wanted to keep their "baby" home one more year. At school, his teachers saw he did not play well with other children. He cried easily and often when he did not get his way with the children, toys, or food. Occasionally he bit his classmates.

The teacher, Jessica, and Peter differed on the best way to deal with Seth. Jessica and Peter thought he should do what he wanted and that the teacher should reprimand the other children when they interfered with him. The teacher favored "time-out," but Jessica and Peter thought time-out was cruel. Gradually, thanks to Seth's peers, his behaviors found a balance. His classmates occasionally bit or hit him back when he showed inconsiderate and mean behaviors. This had a civilizing effect and caused Seth to share and improve behaviors.

Seth enjoyed school but only on his own terms. Peter and Jessica did not always enforce his coming to the table at mealtimes or having a set bedtime. His parents often allowed him to watch TV or play video games through meals and would cook a meal just for him whenever he was hungry. They also allowed him to fall asleep whenever and wherever he was—the floor, sofa, or his bed.

Seth continued to enjoy learning and was bright intellectually. In fact, he was gifted. But he did not like homework or to have any expectations placed on him. Peter and Jessica cushioned all of life for him, not forcing him to do anything he didn't want to do—meals together, bathing, set bedtimes, homework or assignments, piano or sports practices, or chores. His grades went up and down, depending on his effort and interest.

The results of Seth's early fourth-grade achievement testing surprised his parents, since they thought he would do better. The tests revealed that Seth was only two years above grade level in all subjects but math. In math, he was working at twelfth-grade level. Still, his parents did not have serious concerns as he was still functioning above grade level. And, they did not want to put pressure on him to excel in subjects other than math if he was not interested.

Throughout elementary school, Seth made few friends. Most of his friendships didn't last long since he insisted on deciding what to play, for how long, and at whose house.

Fortunately, at 13, Seth suddenly grew interested in reading about explorers and famous people in history. He devoured information from books and the Internet. In middle school, he joined an academic team and glowed with the admiration of his team members when he knew correct answers. But, he frequently had tantrums when he or his team did not answer correctly or when he guessed randomly and his team forfeited points. He did not get mad at himself but at his teammates or the judge who ruled in the competitions. Seth would storm out of the competition room, requiring a teammate to go after him and plead for him to return to the competition so their team would not have to forfeit the match.

When Seth became interested in girls, he first resorted to physical displays to attract their attention. Once he clobbered a girl with a bat. Seth explained, "I liked her and it was the only way I could think of at the moment to get her to notice me." After that episode and the uproar and anger he created, he shifted to more verbal ways of getting girls' attention—name calling, bragging about his physical strength and high IQ, making silly faces, and grabbing their belongings.

He often paid classmates to do the assignments he had no interest in. He was skilled at manipulating others to get what he desired, and when caught having someone else write an essay for him, he dodged responsibility. In tenth grade, he hired someone to write a 50-page term paper and, when caught, said the person he hired "offered to do it."

He had no interest in part-time jobs during high school, and his parents never insisted he try and find a job. Jessica and Peter gave him whatever money he wanted with no restrictions. As a result, he got all the way through high school and college with no work experience.

When Seth started college, he exerted himself only when he was interested in a particular class or subject. Jessica and Peter hired "organizers" for him, usually other students or recent graduates, who would make sure Seth got up, went to class, did assignments, and prepared for exams. With this kind of external propping up, Seth earned fairly good grades. He graduated with a degree in sociology but foundered in his first jobs in a bookstore, department store, and library. He did not feel the need to arrive at work on time or show up every day. He was fired several times.

As job failures mounted, his parents bailed him out financially and emotionally. They supported his rationalizations about why he lost jobs: "They were mean to me." "They expected way too much." One day, Seth told his parents he wanted a prestigious job where he could earn a lot of money and others' respect. Out of the blue, he announced he wanted to be a physician.

He had been dating a young woman, Sarah, for about a year, and proposed marriage. She accepted. Seth enrolled in premedical courses. With Sarah providing support for him, he managed to get through premed studies and into medical school.

When their first child was born and Sarah's time was spent caring for the baby, he became angry, lashing out verbally at Sarah and resenting their daughter. Sarah became fed up, filed for divorce, and left with the baby. Seth rarely contacted Sarah or visited his daughter.

At that point, at age 24, Seth returned to live with his parents. Jessica took on the role of providing an external structure for Seth. She woke him up on time to be at the hospital, washed his clothes, and set up a daily schedule for him. Jessica quizzed him *before exams and went over difficult patients so he could "shine" during rounds and impress his attending physician professors, although he had done little work. Jessica welcomed helping him and, in fact, saw it as her duty to ensure that he completed medical school.*

Seth had a series of brief romantic affairs but did not have another serious relationship until he was a resident in gastrointestinal medicine. He fell in love with Juanita, a hematology resident from Guatemala, and they married. Juanita was a "do it all" woman. She cared for their two children and hired nannies when she worked as a physician at a clinic. She absolved Seth of any parenting duties.

Seth wasn't interested in his children's activities. He provoked, teased, and ridiculed them, and they responded by giving him a wide berth. His son, also an impotent, butted heads with Seth. They had huge disagreements and verbal sparring over which one of them would have his way. Their children sought out Juanita for affection, support, and daily care.

Over time, Seth made a name for himself in academic medicine. He did research, published professional papers, and was a favored teacher. He had a secretary and a research assistant to do the legwork and keep him organized, and saw patients only one day a week. He was promoted in his job and became a professor, but he was notorious for being demanding, overwhelming to work with, and a hard taskmaster. He preferred to call the shots, sought the limelight, and expected others to handle the day-to-day work. Many employees tried to work with him but left feeling overwhelmed and burned out.

Seth worked as a professor until he was almost 80. When he eventually retired, he made Juanita's life very difficult. He constantly complained and criticized her, and was irritable with their four grandchildren. Many times they would dissolve in tears over grandpa's winning all the games they played, or the brusque, hypercritical way he spoke with them about their looks, their requests, and their attitudes.

With increasing infirmity, at age 89, he went to a nursing home. He terrorized the staff and other residents with name calling, belligerence, and demands. He was only pacified when he met with other retired physicians at the nursing home, and they discussed medicine and reminisced about their careers.

Commentary

Jessica and Peter's approach to rearing Seth emotionally molded Seth's personality. Jessica was an omnipotent mother who very much wanted to "minister" to her son as a baby. She wanted to care for and do for him. As a result, her anxiety grew when he was quietly asleep and required nothing from her. Her anxiety lessened when she could carry out her caretaking of him. Although a neonatologist who knew intellectually that babies normally sleep a great deal and are not necessarily fussy, she could not alter her excessive caregiving behavior, as it was unconscious to her.

Peter was an impotent and identified with his son, seeing Seth as requiring the same tremendous amount of care as himself. As an infant, Seth grew conditioned to the constant attention of his parents and nanny. He did not learn to self-soothe and grew to expect his parents to take action to meet his every want and need. His self-centeredness and lack of empathy for others arose from these early experiences.

Seth's indulgent treatment began at home and escalated with his increasing age. He became plaintive, manipulative, or tyrannical to get care and attention from others. As an adult, he appeared to achieve well academically, but he antagonized peers and could not hold down jobs. He was unable to cope with reasonable expectations placed on him in a daily job routine. As a professor, he fared better, but only because he enjoyed what he did and because other people organized and carried out the work for him.

We can follow Seth's impotent conditioning from infancy through old age and iden-tify his tendency for inertia and having others pick up the slack for him. He had the same role at home with Juanita and with his omnipotent children but often had con-flicts with his impotent son and with his grandchildren.

Conditioning Begins before Birth

Parents unknowingly assign their future child a role from the time of con-ception. In the case of an impotent child, his parents fantasize that he'll be special, precious, and worthy of adoration. While their child is in the womb, parents may fear that his movements indicate some distress. These worries often translate into the expectation that this child will be delicate. Mothers may ask their health care provider for reassurance that the baby is not distressed.

Once the baby is born, his parents see him as unable to handle any delay in care and believe their baby requires every imaginable indulgence. Although these thoughts arise in the parents' minds, they firmly believe that they are divining their baby's thoughts.

Although these babies tend not to be first-born, in some instances they may be. WE FOUND THAT ROLE ASSIGNMENT DEPENDS ON CONDITIONS IN THE FAMILY AT THE TIME OF THE PREGNANCY AND BIRTH, AND BIRTH ORDER IS NOT THE ONLY CONTRIBUTING FACTOR. A family doesn't necessarily pamper their youn-gest child, as many of us believe. Parents can shape last-born and first-born children in either role.

Infancy

From the moment these babies are born, they quickly become the center of attention. Their parents caution family members that their baby's sleep, diet, and possessions are all-important. Family life revolves around them, and parents and grandparents constantly handle them—rocking and jig-gling—to keep them quiet and happy. THE ENTIRE FAMILY'S SCHEDULE OFTEN SHIFTS TO ACCOMMODATE THESE NEWCOMERS AND THEIR NEEDS. IN RETURN, THEIR BABY MAY BECOME OVERSTIMULATED BY THIS EXCESSIVE ATTENTION AND BE EXTREMELY IRRITABLE. PARENTS CAN DOTE ON AND ADORE THIS INFANT SO INTENSELY THAT IT ABSORBS THEM. Other children and former close friends of the parents come to feel excluded as parents have a hyperfocus on their impotent child.

Parents celebrate each tiny accomplishment as exceptional and frequently praise her. Excessive parental concern may lead to many consultations with the baby's doctor. When an ordinary illness occurs, parents often exaggerate its significance. For years, parents may use their memory of the illness to justify more precautions for and attention to their baby. Inevitably, an older omnipotent sibling may question this excessive and unreasonable treatment, but the parents often excuse this double standard with such comments, as "You're jealous! You're just spoiled. Why are you so selfish?"

An impotent baby receives attention and care equal to that demanded by his or her impotent parent. In this way, the standards throughout the family remain consistent: impotents need lots of indulgence and give little in return, and omnipotents are expected to give to others and ask little for themselves.

All of this anxious attendance appears to enclose the baby in an environment of overstimulation and immediate satisfaction of his every desire. IN THESE FIRST MONTHS OF LIFE, AN IMPOTENT BABY IS BEING SHAPED SO THAT EVERY MURMUR OR CRY OF DISTRESS BRINGS IMMEDIATE GRATIFICATION. This is the beginning of the lifelong expectation that other people will respond quickly and on cue.

You might be wondering if impotent parents are willing to do what it takes to care for their children. We found that impotent parents are rarely giving. Only through identification does an impotent parent recognize that babies and children also require special treatment. Childcare is usually left to omnipotent parents, who are expected to meet their children's physical and emotional needs.

By the end of the first year, we may identify that impotent conditioning is falling into place. The infant expresses demands and receives ready support whenever he or she faces a slight challenge. As a result, the baby may have a fleeting attention span. He may want whatever strikes his fancy at one moment, only to lose interest rapidly and switch to wanting something else the next moment.

Babies being shaped to be impotent likely gave rise to the expression "the terrible twos," since the baby's increased mobility often increases her dominance of the household. She follows no rules and seems fearless. She grabs others' belongings and is drawn to anything that is off limits to her. Even at this age he or she seems to lead a charmed life, as few family members ever tell her no.

By age two, an impotent's personality style becomes more obvious. He comes to dominate the adults around him with an imperious attitude that allows for little compromise. When parents ask him to participate with the family, they do so in a pleading and apologetic tone. If he is unhappy because he doesn't get what he wants, his parents regard his behavior as reasonable and often blame someone else. As a result, impotents may go through life perceiving their own behaviors as entirely appropriate and reasonable, and blame their frustrations on people around them.

At this tender age, an impotent toddler increasingly insists on doing whatever he pleases and opposes any attempt to dissuade him. If he meets any resistance, he gets tearful, grumpy, and resentful or has a temper tantrum. Impotent toddlers expect to receive instant attention and compliance whenever they want something.

MANY TIMES IMPOTENT TODDLERS LAG IN BEGINNING TO TALK AND WALK. PARENTS AND SIBLINGS MAY BE SO EAGER TO GRATIFY THEM THAT THESE TODDLERS RARELY HAVE TO SPEAK AND ASK FOR WHAT THEY WANT. Many parents physically carry their toddlers so they do not learn to walk until they are almost two years old.

These toddlers are given great freedom in their toilet training. They are allowed to select their own conditions for moving from diapers to toileting. Many do not make the transition until age three or four when their preschool requires it for admitting them.

Preschool Years

At this age, impotent children show a preference for playmates who appease them and avoid peers who have the same uncompromising self-importance as they do. Also, around age three, an impotent child may discover that not everyone on earth is their adoring servant. By preschool age, a child's demands can reach a level where they may threaten his or her impotent parent. Since an impotent parent cannot tolerate much competition or pressure, she may become angry or blow up at her preschooler. This angry emotion leaves a lasting impression on children who are becoming impotents. They discover that impotent parents will be their allies only if they have common interests that do not create competition between them.

For impotents, the preschool years are a time of continuing overindulgence, although later they may remember their rare disappointments when they didn't always get their way. Family members continue to hover nearby in case impotents experience some discomfort or disappointment. At preschool and at home they continue to have license to intrude into others' space, to take control of others' property, and to feel no sense of wrongdoing or responsibility for their lack of self-restraint. Severely impotent preschoolers resort to aggressive acts of uncontrolled rage, head banging, screaming, hitting, and biting themselves and others. They develop expectations that they should not be thwarted or told "no."

Intimidated parents explain to angry preschool children why they can't comply with their demands. But all the while they hand these preschoolers the forbidden object—allowing television watching instead of enforcing a regular bedtime or giving their child a toy he wants when the parent has already said no.

These preschoolers learn that pleading, unrestrained behavior, and persistence overwhelm their parents every time. They learn that achieving their desires by reasonable means is not nearly as exciting as opposing all rules and being victorious through helplessness without making sacrifices. This is impotence in its purest form.

We discovered that by preschool age, impotents' emotions are shaped and conditioned along with their thoughts and behavioral style. **PEOPLE AROUND IMPOTENTS TOLERATE AND ENCOURAGE THEIR EMOTIONAL DISPLAYS OF ANXIETY, ANGER, RAGE, POUTING, AND FOOT STOMPING, AND MAY REGARD THESE DISPLAYS AS CUTE. AS A RESULT, IMPOTENTS ARE GIVEN WIDE LATITUDE FOR EXPRESSING THEIR EMOTIONS.** Impotent preschoolers learn to use their emotional displays to manipulate others to do what they desire. But, not all impotents are extroverted emotional fireballs. Many impotents manipulate others with their soft-spoken, bashful, quiet, and standoffish styles.

School Age

Entering school can be a traumatic time for an impotent child. School requires responsibility, work, discipline, and interactions with people outside the family. Often, teachers will recognize impotent children's immaturity and suggest holding them back a year. Impotents may show distrust of teachers who fail to recognize their special status and who expect them to give sustained effort, or they may be school phobic and refuse to go to school. Impotent children might perform well as long as the teacher supplies constant encouragement and attention. But without teacher prodding or strong family encouragement, school-age impotents may lose motivation for academic work.

By the time developing impotents reach school age they, for the most part, have led pampered lives. Now they go through school selecting activities that are personally desirable. They try to avoid academic work that requires discipline and effort and choose school activities where they can be the center of attention. Impotents can do well in their chosen activities because their intelligence and inherent abilities are equal to omnipotents. However, their egocentric personality guides their choices, and they take no action unless it advances their self-interest. If they encounter an activity or an academic subject that is extremely enjoyable, they will devote themselves with commitment and endurance as long as it remains pleasurable. Self-reward, rather than giving assistance to others, always dictates their choices.

At school, an impotent is good at shirking group assignments and gets omnipotent group members to do the work. In time, some omnipotents get tired of this and complain to the teacher. Often the teacher urges the children to work it out themselves, as she or he fails to understand what is taking place in the group dynamics.

In school, impotents often find the rules intolerable and set their own. Characteristically, they have rapidly changing attention spans and expect the teachers to amuse them. Impotent children find any repetitious exercises tedious and oppressive. They can believe they have mastered subjects, which they have studied only briefly. An impotent child's difficulty with tolerating direction, or taking tests seriously, sometimes results in his being labeled with ADHD or having some type of learning problem.

The teacher's inability to gain the child's participation often baffles the parents. Parents are unaware that their child has behaved this way at home since he was very young and has only rarely been expected to participate in activities he did not want to do. These young impotents are not without finesse. During these early school years they become masters at studying others to discover how far they can push them. They learn they must not push omnipotent caregivers so far as to alienate them and lose access to their support. Only if a caregiver repeatedly fails to give care, and shows he is no longer useful, will an impotent end the relationship.

In the presence of strangers, an impotent child may be cautious while he gets to know them. But, once comfortable, he will test or break any existing rules. We found he or she interprets restrictions, no matter how slight, as presenting an insufferable environment, inhabited by uncaring people. Since his parents treated him as fragile and weak, they agree with their child's assessment and question why others are so harsh and unaccepting. Parents seldom raise questions about their child's lack of control and judge others as unreasonably intolerant. Impotent youngsters may coerce their parents by threatening to harm themselves or others. When this happens along with anger rages or severe tantrums, many parents decide to seek psychiatric treatment.

DURING THE ELEMENTARY SCHOOL YEARS, PARENTS MAY TEACH IMPOTENTS TO APOLOGIZE FOR AN INJURY OR UPSET TO OTHERS. THE IMPOTENT PERCEIVES "I'M SORRY" AS ADEQUATE RESTITUTION. CHILD IMPOTENTS ARE NOT TAUGHT HOW TO

UNDERSTAND THE EFFECTS OF THEIR IMPULSIVE ACTS ON OTHERS. PARENTS GIVE THEM ALMOST UNLIMITED FREEDOM; THIS MEANS THESE CHILDREN HAVE LITTLE CHANCE TO DEVELOP A CONSCIENCE OF WHAT IS RIGHT, WRONG, FAIR, AND UNFAIR. As a consequence, they grow up lacking inner self-control. Impotent children persist in any behavior they desire so long as they want, unless another person applies external pressure to control them. As they get older, they paradoxically depend on others to monitor and control their unrestrained behaviors, all the while chafing at such control.

Impotent students tend to grasp new concepts quite rapidly, only to lose interest just as quickly. Their intolerance of responsibility can create defiance when teachers expect them to do their homework. This is quite frustrating for teachers when they are dealing with an intelligent child who has flashes of brilliance followed by long lapses of disinterest. Some impotents achieve a brilliant academic record if it brings them family approval and they find their studies easy and pleasurable. When an activity is not enjoyable, an impotent child digs in her heels and tries to avoid it.

As a group, impotents absorb an inordinate amount of teachers' energies due to their frequent demands for support, lack of initiative, and resistance to complete work in subjects they don't like. Impotents have fewer problems in social and recreational activities. They expect admiration and acceptance by all who know them. Often they become pacesetters for styles and introduce popular fads. They may enjoy physical activities more than intellectual pursuits.

During the school years, impotents continue to be self-serving. They may deliberately antagonize teachers or authorities who do not cater to them and can grind away at rules they do not like. OFTEN, IMPOTENTS BAND TOGETHER TO FORM ELITE SOCIAL GROUPS IN ORDER TO DOMINATE LIFE IN SCHOOL—JUST AS THEY DO IN THEIR FAMILY LIVES. An impotent cannot understand why omnipotents work so hard and take school seriously. Sometimes they jealously attack omnipotents for doing homework and obeying school rules. Other times many school-aged impotents become fascinated with omnipotents because of the omnipotents' odd ability to function without self-indulgence.

At this age many impotent patients have told us of wanting to visit with adult relatives during family get-togethers but recall being admonished by their parents to instead "go play." Their parents saw them as not needing serious and mature interactions with older people.

Families experience harmony during this age when interactions with their children reinforce their respective conditioned roles. Two levels form in the family as impotents insist on constant attention, and omnipotents take pride in their ability to fulfill their demands. This harmony may later disintegrate into disenchantment, depression, and disruption of the family if the illusion of omnipotence eventually fails.

Adolescence

As impotents enter adolescence, many downplay the importance of school and use school time poorly or drop out prematurely. They also display adolescent immaturity through their misguided efforts to look and act like adults. Impulsively, they may sample drugs and alcohol, have many sexual encounters, and test limits set by parents and legal authorities. Those who display the least concern about how their behaviors affect others seem to do the most experimenting with drugs and promiscuity. They usually ignore impending problems they are creating until they go beyond parental control. Parents may react as if they had never noticed their child was touchy, noncommunicative, and defiant. They confuse their parents when they ignore curfews and act unpredictably. This confusion happens because adolescent impotents frequently complain their parents *do not trust them.* Still parents continue to appease these adolescents because they are unable to tolerate their children being upset.

Rebellious adolescent impotents show a strong tendency to gravitate toward others who also are defiant of authority and disdainful of social conventions. Such excesses may lead to psychiatric hospitalization or residential treatment. Once there, a typical pattern is that the medical staff evaluates them, describes them as depressed or suffering from low self-esteem, and prescribes medications since they're not aware of the underlying causes of their behavior.

In the teen years, impotents also begin to form clinging relationships to peers as they withdraw from depending on family members. This change may take place when an impotent fails to receive perfect care from a parental figure and develops a negative attitude. When a caretaker isn't catering to their every need, impotents feel disappointed, deceived, and abandoned.

When an impotent moves closer to peers at school, she begins her search for an omnipotent who will devote himself (or herself) to her. Since we condition impotents for pleasurable and unstructured activities, impotents often seek out hard-working, stable people who are omnipotents. Young impotents will likely have friends in both roles but will only consider an omnipotent as a serious candidate for marriage or a long-term relationship.

This fascination with omnipotents shows up early in dating. Impotents find they can identify with fellow impotents, but only an omnipotent generates excitement in an adolescent impotent. This excitement feels familiar because it reminds him or her of the unconditional acceptance and indulgence of his parents, who were patient, tolerant of even abusive behavior, affectionate, and protective of the impotent's right to lead an effortless, easy life. An impotent does not understand consciously this attraction.

Both impotents and omnipotents share the feeling of excitement. Many people feel that this is the necessary basis for a romantic relationship—one that requires little more than "the right chemistry." When he or she becomes romantically serious, an impotent displays an unusual energy in his or her desire to possess the omnipotent. Although omnipotents may find this behavior appealing, it may only be a seductive ploy to capture their attention and loyalty. In Chapter 7 on marriage we discuss how these roles influence us in dating and finding a mate.

IMPOTENTS PROGRESS THROUGH HIGH SCHOOL BY CONTINUING TO FOCUS ON ACTIVITIES THEY ENJOY. OFTEN THEY CHOOSE ATHLETICS, DEBATE, DRAMA, MUSIC, OR ANY AREA OF SCHOOL THAT PERMITS THEIR BEING THE CENTER OF ATTENTION. They have high visibility in school, since they may routinely test the rules. They can be quite vocal in complaining any rule is "unfair" because it interferes with their ability to pursue their desires. They can become resentful rebel leaders who use the omnipotents in their classes as dependable soldiers to carry out battle plans against school authorities.

Nearing college age, impotents may long to go to college to free themselves of family restraints. In college, impotents may demonstrate high aptitude in subjects or sports they find enjoyable. They may decide to pursue a legal or medical degree or another profession because they want to have a job that guarantees prominence and status. They are quite aware that professional positions offer high status and will let them operate without restraints that are intolerable to them.

Adult Years

By their adult years some impotents are adept at conniving and manipulating others. Frequently they are charismatic and can be socially charming and engaging. Other impotents lack social graces and are loud, brutish, and like to bully. Impotents can also be vindictive when thwarted from having their desires met. But, like omnipotents, impotents often continue to live in the same role assignment the rest of their lives. Each day impotents work to increase their emotional support by steadily increasing their demands on omnipotent friends and partners. With each passing year they appear to make less effort in their relationships.

We might think that impotents would endure many hardships during their adult years as a penalty for not having developed mature coping skills. But we did not find this to be true. They became accustomed to receiving imperial treatment and have learned to master the nuances of dominating others from a position of weakness. We can clearly see that they are still reacting according to their emotional conditioning in childhood.

Once impotents form a family of their own, we found an impotent takes on the commanding role. Many impotents point out the failures they perceive in their partner's behaviors as a spouse and parent. From the earliest days of marriage, we observed that a subtle shift takes place in the relationship as omnipotents assume a steadily growing share of responsibility and impotents a declining amount. Impotents accelerate this change if they have a health problem or other impediment that might justify excessive rather than reasonable care.

SOME IMPOTENTS BECOME DISABLED BY MIDDLE AGE WHEN THEIR HELPLESS SELF-CONCEPT BECOMES INCREASINGLY AGGRAVATED BY AN OMNIPOTENT'S COMPULSION TO ASSUME TOTAL RESPONSIBILITY FOR THEM. Over time, impotents may develop a negative attitude and complain when they believe they are receiving inadequate care from others. Some impotents become so disenchanted they become reclusive and drift away from relationships.

Many impotents retire from work early because of their aversion to responsibility, although they can do quite well if they choose a job where they can determine their own working conditions. Just as they operated back in school, they can have gratifying careers if they're able to pressure their coworkers to cater to their exacting demands. Impotents frequently perceive work as an imposition and may complain both at home and at the office about the heavy burdens they bear.

IMPOTENTS MAY ALSO USE WORK AS A REASON TO AVOID UNPLEASANT ACTIVITIES AT HOME. THEY ENJOY THE SOCIAL ASPECTS AT WORK AND TAKE FULL ADVANTAGE OF FRINGE BENEFITS, PROMOTIONS, AND PENSION RIGHTS. They can devote a remarkable proportion of their time to their own interests and comment to their bosses that they are "too busy" to handle more company work. Often, other people accept impotents in the workplace, despite their small contributions and negative attitudes, because families and society condition omnipotents to accept the lackadaisical participation of impotents as equal to their own.

Old Age

IMPOTENTS OFTEN LONG FOR RETIREMENT AND WILL FREQUENTLY RETIRE QUITE EARLY AFTER SHIFTING ALL FINANCIAL AND NONFINANCIAL RESPONSIBILITIES TO THEIR

OMNIPOTENT SPOUSES. Impotents are only willing to remain at work until retirement age if their job is personally gratifying. Once they are retired, their full-time presence at home can create a burden for their spouses, who may look for work or continue working to escape. Impotents maintain their conditioned role by steadily increasing their demands on the family, as the infirmities of aging add to their lifelong sense of impotence.

Impotents continue to focus on every slight condition that offends their supersensitive natures. We often attribute such attitudes to aging, but they are the same attitudes that began in infancy. Impotents demand attention for every grievance they have. Their lifelong self-absorption is obvious, as they remain consumed by their daily comforts with little interest in outside events or people.

If an impotent needs to enter a nursing home, he or she monopolizes all emotional support available. Even after the onset of senility, impotents may persist in aggressive demands.

Here is another case example.

Shauna

Shauna was a six-year-old girl. Since first grade Shauna's problems have exasperated her father, Charles, a 26-year-old single parent. School called daily to complain about Shauna's out-of-control behaviors—hitting other kids, running out of the classroom, throwing books and food in the cafeteria, or spitting on peers and teachers. She was an only child and was in the care of her 48-year-old grandfather, Eugene, while her father worked the day shift as a certified nursing assistant and in the evenings took classes at a junior college.

Charles described Shauna as a "changeable" girl—sweet, calm, and happy one minute and loud, demanding, and pouty whenever something did not bring immediate gratification. Shauna had no history of trauma, no developmental delays, and no medical issues. Shauna's problems had begun in her kindergarten year but, in retrospect, Charles believed they were less intense and less frequent in kindergarten than in first grade.

Charles, Eugene, and Shauna lived together in a two-bedroom apartment. Shauna's mother was never involved with her. She was born unexpectedly, interrupting Charles's college studies. Her mother left home two weeks after Shauna's birth, never returned, and could not be located. Often Charles was tired because he catered to Shauna's every cry as an infant—to pacify her and to get some rest himself.

Grandfather Eugene wanted very much for Charles to finish his studies and become the physical therapist he wanted to be. Eugene did not have a job, due to an on-the-job back injury. He agreed to help with Shauna so that Charles could work and go to school. But Eugene was also tired. He had helped raise five children after his wife died, and he had chronic back pain. Eugene, too, gave Shauna the green light to rule the roost in the household through not setting limits, never telling her "no," and not enforcing rules. Actually, Shauna had no rules whatsoever.

Shauna was a bright, perky, charming child until she didn't get her way. Then, she became hostile, threatening, belligerent, and loud. She explained her behaviors with,

"I just want things to happen when I want them." If she hurt another child during her outbursts of aggression, she showed no remorse and frequently blamed that child for being "in the wrong place" when she [Shauna] "went off."

Although bright intellectually, she disliked schoolwork. She liked only lunch and recess time. Teachers struggled with her. They discovered she would do academic work if they made a game out of it and awarded her a prize for finishing, such as a blue ribbon, candy, or being line leader for lunch. She liked being the center of attention at school, as she was at home. She performed only if recognized by another person, not for any intrinsic value to her.

Throughout elementary school, she barely got by academically or behaviorally and still had aggressive episodes and blowups. By middle school, she became a more subtle bully, making verbal threats rather than physical ones. She became slicker and more manipulative of others to get what she wanted, often cajoling and bribing classmates with empty promises to do their homework or save them a seat at lunch.

She became seductive with boys as she discovered they would do what she wanted—usually shower her with gifts—if she acted sexy and flirtatious with them. She had few friends and alienated many of her peers and spent hours playing video games. In high school, she discovered acting and enjoyed performing in front of an audience. This attention motivated her to memorize lines. Her school put on a musical performance every year, and she discovered she liked to sing for the attention it brought to her. Her father, by now a trained physical therapist, had been able to afford singing lessons for her.

She continued to have tantrums at home with her father and grandfather and with her voice teacher when she did not receive instant gratification or was critiqued or insufficiently praised. Her grades were mediocre except in theater and vocal arts. She obtained a college scholarship for vocal performance and did well. She did not focus on other subjects and did just enough academic work to keep her scholarship. She often manipulated friends to do her academic papers for her.

As a young woman, she liked constant attention from friends. She was socially manipulative and liked to be admired. Frequently, she was irresponsible and sexually promiscuous and did not use contraception. Her father supported her emotionally and financially when she terminated several pregnancies. She developed a career in musical theater and traveled often. Her assistant and manager took endless care of her, ensuring she packed her clothes, did not miss flights, paid her bills, and so on.

In her mid-twenties she met Hank, a stockbroker. Hank was already wealthy, although only in his mid-thirties. He admired Shauna's outspokenness and directness as well as her singing career. Shauna admired Hank's ability to take control of any situation and his ambition at his job. Within 18 months, they were married. Shauna rather quickly abandoned her singing career, preferring to stay home or to accompany Hank on business trips around the world. Reluctantly, she agreed to have two children, but she always had a nanny to do most of the child rearing. She was uninterested in direct contact with her children, preferring her social life with Hank.

Commentary

Charles and Eugene, both omnipotents, were aspiring, hardworking, and goal-oriented people. Yet, they raised Shauna to be an impotent (like her absent mother) by constantly indulging her and putting no limits on her unruly behaviors. She never had time-outs, and Charles and Eugene pacified her, giving her whatever she wanted to quiet her down. She never learned self-control of her behaviors, thoughts, or emotions.

She found one interest in school that she liked—theater. She focused only on this one subject and neglected other academic areas she cared nothing for. After college, when performing in musical theater across the country, she relied on the structure and organization provided by her assistant and manager to meet her needs. Without them she was helpless—unable to make planes or trains on time or even pay her bills.

When she met Hank, an omnipotent, she believed she had met another person who could totally care for her and wrap her once again in the indulgent cocoon of her childhood. Once married, she gave up her singing career in favor of being Hank's wife. They traveled the world and met other wealthy people. She enjoyed these encounters, was the center of attention there as well, and freely offered to provide entertainment with her singing.

Later on, we see Shauna did not like the responsibility of raising children and being a parent, so she relinquished this job to nannies and went on with her social life.

The connections are remarkably consistent between Shauna's early impotent emotional conditioning by her father and grandfather and her later functioning as a helpless and demanding woman who expected indulgence by her husband and children.

Summary of Impotent Personality

TYPICALLY, IMPOTENTS CONCENTRATE ON THOSE PERSONAL INTERESTS THAT GRATIFY THEIR IMMEDIATE NEEDS. THEY SPEND THEIR LIVES SEEKING GRATIFICATION BY OTHERS WHO REQUIRE LITTLE OR NOTHING IN RETURN. THEY PANIC WHEN CONFRONTED WITH EVEN THE SMALLEST PROBLEMS THAT THEY CANNOT TRANSFER TO SOMEONE ELSE TO SOLVE. WHEN PLACED IN AN UNPROTECTED POSITION OR ENVIRONMENT, THEY EXPERIENCE OVERWHELMING ANXIETY AND FEEL UNLOVED AND ABANDONED, FOR THEY CANNOT FUNCTION WITHOUT CONTINUOUS STRONG SUPPORT. COMMONLY, IMPOTENTS SPEND THEIR LIFE DOING WHAT PLEASES THEM AND EXPECT OTHERS TO SPARE THEM THE BURDEN OF RESPONSIBILITY.

IMPOTENTS DO NOT RECOGNIZE OR APPRECIATE THE SUPPORT THEY GET FROM OTHER PEOPLE, AND ARE RARELY HELD ACCOUNTABLE TO ANYONE EXCEPT THEMSELVES. In place of lofty goals, their horizons extend no farther than ensuring their own momentary comfort. Impotents seldom think about tackling new or unfamiliar occurrences of ordinary living. Instead, they view their every need as being the responsibility of the omnipotents in their lives. Impotents show intolerance for the shortcomings of any caretaker. An unquestioned *belief in omnipotence* unites both conditioned roles.

WHAT YOU DISCOVERED IN THIS CHAPTER

- Before the birth of a child who is primed to be an impotent, the parents are busy projecting their fantasies that the infant will be fragile and need constant care.

- As a result of being catered to as if overly delicate, an impotent develops a rapidly shifting attention span, is egocentric, helpless, and demanding.

- In school, impotents select activities that are personally gratifying and where they can be the center of attention. They find rules intolerable and can be rebellious and defiant.

- Impotent children require an inordinate amount of teachers' energies. Impotent adolescents show immaturity and impulsivity, often leading to limit testing, substance abuse, and promiscuity.

- Impotents may excel academically if they find subjects they like. Often they prefer athletics, debate, or drama where they can be the center of attention.

- As adults, impotents seek jobs where they can determine their own working conditions, avoid responsibilities, and put out little effort.

- In old age, impotents can be cantankerous and overly critical of their caretakers.

- Impotents continue to play the role they were conditioned into throughout their lives.

QUESTIONS FOR GETTING TO KNOW YOURSELF

After reading these last two chapters that describe the two roles over the life span, review these questions to help discover your role.

- What was your experience in school?
- Did you enjoy learning and the mastery of new skills?
- What grades were you expected to achieve?
- Did you feel confident of your knowledge?
- Did you think of yourself as intelligent?
- Did you worry that you were hopelessly ignorant?
- Did you feel incapable of significant achievement?
- Did you feel you traveled in the popular social groups?
- Did you suffer a sense of isolation and lack of acceptance by others?
- Did you associate with a group of underachievers?
- Did you associate with other students who took difficult courses?
- Did you look to others constantly for assistance?
- Did you shun the help of others, believing you had to learn on your own?
- Which teachers had the most influence on you, and how were these teachers different from others?
- Have you continued your interest in learning?
- Did you decide long ago you were sufficiently educated?

PART 2

Relationship Struggles: Miscommunications and Marriages

CHAPTER SIX

Why We Miscommunicate

You have learned about omnipotents and impotents and discovered their different characteristics. Most of us live in distinct worlds, and when we attempt to function together we have misunderstandings. **WE EXPERI-ENCE CHAOS IN OUR PERSONAL LIVES, AS WELL AS IN THE WORLD AT LARGE, BECAUSE WE ARE UNABLE TO UNDERSTAND THE PEOPLE AROUND US.** We have difficulty perceiving and interpreting others accurately, and we may interact with people who communicate poorly or deliberately create false impressions. As a result, we know few people well.

In this chapter, we reveal how emotional conditioning creates major barriers to rewarding relationships, produces frustration and confusion, and leads to miscommunication. If you can learn to identify the types of miscommunications you and others make and the reasons for them, you can begin to correct them. We show you the most common types of communication failures: how emotions skew our thinking; failing to observe ourselves and others closely; thinking magically; using projections and rationalizations; having double standards; assuming others think like us; defining words differently; and not being open to others' advice (Table 6.1).

We also experience communication challenges because we know ourselves only partially and imperfectly. Since we treat others based on their defined role in relation to our own, we only recognize the *major* differences among the people we have encountered. We can tell the difference between saintly or heroic people and evil, ruthless people. But the 98 percent between the two extremes endlessly mystifies us.

Because most of us are unable to assess people accurately, we have enormous ups and downs in our relationships caused by our impossible expectations for others and ourselves. These expectations may eventually

Table 6.1   Reasons for Miscommunications

1. Our emotions skew our thinking.
2. We do not observe closely.
3. We use magical thinking.
4. We use projections and rationalizations.
5. We have double standards.
6. We assume others think like us.
7. We define words differently.
8. We are not open to others' advice.

destroy our most valuable relationships. We may support people who show no shred of appreciation and withhold support from others who love us and hold us in high esteem. We may persist in the same destructive methods of building relationships despite repeated failures. We are likely to neglect enriching relationships and seek those that guarantee stress and pain. We often make poor decisions in our choices of friends and marital or business partners.

As we age and gain experience, many of us feel increasingly disillusioned, cynical, and resigned. In order to live more rewarding lives and avoid emotional disasters, we must become more aware of the major factors that create our turmoil.

Our Emotions Skew Our Thinking

Many theories explain the functioning of our minds. Psychologists define the mind as human consciousness found in perception, thought, feeling, memory, will, and imagination. Sigmund Freud had the insight that much of the mind's activities carry on unconsciously, without our awareness. This knowledge presents an opportunity for much greater understanding of how the mind operates.

We store experiences and information in our brain's memory for later recall and use. Then, when we experience similarities between a current situation and an earlier one, the meaningful parcels stored in the brain's memory provide information to help us arrive at a decision or judgment. We also gather knowledge relating to objective data, organize it, file it away in our brain, and then easily recall the information later on. Usually this type of information is factual and elicits little emotional impact.

However, when we exercise our imagination, our will (choosing a course of action), or express our feelings, special chemicals influence these processes in other areas of the brain. These processes follow paths laid down through vital interactions with our parents or caregivers starting in our first years of life. We cannot access them as easily with conscious thought, and they are not objective or emotionally neutral. To the contrary, they are emotionally charged and subjective. As a child acquires pragmatic, rational thinking ability, he will simultaneously incorporate these emotionally laden patterns of feeling and behavior. This emotional material contains distortions to some degree. These unconscious processes affect our rational, intellectual, and cognitive skills. We are not aware that emotionally determined, unconscious impulses dictate most of our personal decisions.

During the early years of life, emotional conditioning begins to dominate over logical reason. Young children develop behavioral and emotional patterns for dealing with people, along with learning factual information to help them understand their surroundings. A growing child learns that his security depends on conforming to precise roles according to the expectations of his parents. In order to feel secure, he learns to ignore certain realities and justifies his emotionally conditioned behavior using rationalizations provided by his parents.

As we described in Chapters 3, 4, and 5, emotional directives overrule reality in both types of emotional conditioning. An omnipotent looks at life and focuses on situations that require control from him and deprive him of personal comfort or support. An impotent focuses on immediate gratification of his whims or caprices and seeks short-lived indulgences.

Why do we restrict the full scope of reality to such a narrow range? We found that at very young ages an impressionable child can detect what creates anxieties within the family. A young omnipotent learns which emotionally conditioned cues an omnipotent parent responds to, and she begins to copy those responses. She also develops a range of emotions to accompany these situations: pleasure when she is in control, anxious when she is partially successful at controlling a situation, excited anticipation when challenged by a difficult assignment, and panic when feeling totally overwhelmed. As she becomes increasingly mature, an omnipotent's thinking shows a capacity for rapid retrieval of relevant information, an ability to organize data in a goal-oriented way and strong problem-solving skills.

Likewise, an impotent is sensitive to the emotional status of his impotent parent mentor and perceives the cues that create a state of total inertia in that parent. He notices his parent's restless, constant shift of focus and insatiable appetite for attention. He feels the pleasure of unlimited care, anticipation of expected gratification, anxiety about satisfaction delayed, and panic when confronted by rather simple roadblocks.

The blind assumption of roles in both conditioned types creates emotions that, once adopted, introduce unconscious, unrealistic distortions into every relationship. Here is an example.

Patrick and Ryan

Eleven-year-old Patrick grew angry and frustrated whenever his nine-year-old brother, Ryan, did not immediately give him a chance to play the video game he wanted. His desire for the game skewed his thinking that he should always get what he wanted from Ryan. He grew angry whenever he needed to be patient. As a baby, his parents gave him items whenever he wanted them. They never expected him to wait or told him "no."

On the other hand, the same parents expected Ryan not to display anger and frustration with Patrick's increasing demands. They urged Ryan to squelch his emotions, and they expected him to regard his emotions as unreasonable. He was often asked to defer to Patrick's emotions and wants. Both boys experienced emotional conditioning that shaped their thinking. The parents reared Patrick as an impotent and Ryan as an omnipotent.

Parents often rear children in these two different roles in the same family, and this creates sibling rivalry. Two impotent siblings can also display rivalry by butting heads over both wanting to have their own way. One is not able to yield to the other.

It is ironic that we may be proud of our logical reasoning abilities, yet repeatedly ignore reason in favor of an emotional decision that offers little chance of fulfillment. Our conscious mind has command of a catalog of vital experiences that we constantly update and that we can scan within seconds when we have a problem. We consider possible solutions simultaneously and consciously compare a series of fantasies. Our fantasies are the ingredients of our imaginations. **AN OMNIPOTENT USES IMAGINATION FOR THE PRIMARY PURPOSE OF SOLVING PROBLEMS. AN IMPOTENT DEVOTES HIS IMAGINATION TO SERVING WHIMSICAL SELF-INTERESTS. EMOTIONS WIN OVER INTELLECT EVERY TIME.**

We Do Not Make Adequate Observations

If we want to see people as they really are, we have to overcome barriers built up in our thinking. Most of us are governed by automatic reactions—we ignore individual characteristics, give a standard response to impotents and an entirely different response to omnipotents. When we maintain the status quo we feel more comfortable than when we try to make changes.

IF WE WANT TO COMPREHEND WHAT IS TAKING PLACE IN ANY RELATIONSHIP, WE NEED TO OBSERVE TWO SEPARATE, SIMULTANEOUS ACTIONS: WHAT WE DO AND WHAT THE OTHER PERSON DOES. Both omnipotents and impotents are equally oblivious to this reality, because their ability to observe others closely is eradicated during their early childhood years. In omnipotent-impotent relationships, omnipotents do not recognize their caretaker roles as they pursue goals and strive to deliver perfection, while impotents serve as their judges. Impotents do not observe their own inertia in relationships because they are accustomed to behaving in accordance with their capricious moods, and reality is always whatever they choose it to be.

Omnipotents and impotents have no superficial characteristics that reliably differentiate them. They speak the same language, dress the same way, and achieve similar status, but they do not consciously or intellectually understand one another. Emotional conditioning is unconscious, illogical, and emotional. We only begin to understand by looking deeper into the personalities of both people to see what lies beneath the surface. Then we can observe the different ways individuals express motivations, judgments, behaviors, and emotions. For this to occur, we must learn to observe one another deeply over a long time period.

From very early on in our lives we have no choice but to submit to our parents' directives. We are taught to ignore reality we perceive and react as our parents expect. As we develop we constantly fine-tune responses and duplicate our parents' conscious and unconscious approach to relationships. In the process, we learn not only to copy our parents' useful techniques but all their deficiencies as well.

One of the skills that we learn is to eliminate observation. We program young children to respond to a situation with little regard for reality and teach children to react to stereotypes. If we are impotent and identify with another impotent, we employ one standard of relating. But if we recognize that another person is in an opposite role, we automatically switch to that standard.

By this programmed system, we fail to make adequate or accurate observations, as they are not only unnecessary but would also complicate things. In order to begin to deal with other people as they are in reality, we must carefully observe the other person's characteristics and, most importantly, observe our own thinking and behavior as objectively as possible.

Most of the time we make assumptions as a substitute for observing and collecting solid evidence about other people. *Making observations is a prerequisite to seeing and understanding reality.* **EACH OF US ASSUMES OUR THINKING IS REASONABLE, THAT OUR PERCEPTIONS ARE VALID, AND THAT OUR JUDGMENTS ARE CORRECT.** Omnipotents think in perfectionistic terms, overrate their own capabilities and those of others, and assume excessive responsibilities. Impotents display poor organization of thought processes, misperceive and distort situations, and reach decisions that defy rational reasoning. Regardless of our conditioned role, none of us takes the time to observe closely.

With omnipotent conditioning, we compulsively undertake to control the problems occurring in our territory without considering reality. We rarely ask ourselves these questions: Whose problem is it? Who is responsible? Is it best to intercede or withhold immediate action? What will be the best approach after considering all options?

Rather than thinking this through, an omnipotent habitually assumes responsibility, trespasses into others' territory, keeps impotents irresponsible, and imposes his notion of perfection onto other omnipotents. An omnipotent doesn't notice when she intrudes into areas where she is not invited. She is self-sacrificing and resolves to help others, yet she may create more problems by her reflex concern with others' interests and neglect of her own. Emotional conditioning is a shortcut that not only excludes observation but also considers real data and information cumbersome and distracting.

This lack of introspection makes an omnipotent blind to the ease with which she or he can be used, exploited, and abused. To the contrary, he or she may wear a halo of pride in delivering care to impotents. If an omnipotent were able to observe the consequences of her actions, she might temper her generosity and see that her role encourages impotents to avoid responsibility. She may realize that she treats herself and other omnipotents in a masochistic way. She may also notice that her façade of perfection cuts her off from the very people who could provide for her neglected human needs.

Impotents are also unable to observe themselves and others. Impotents live in the firm belief that their feelings and desires are more important than anything else. By seeking endless support and relegating their concerns to the omnipotents in their lives, they feel secure. However, in this role they gradually erode any possibility of using their own intelligence and capabilities. Since they have been treated as lacking psychological and emotional strength, impotents feel incapable of supporting others.

It is not easy to awaken dormant observational powers suppressed by emotional conditioning. Our psychotherapy patients are dubious when we first point out major factors in their relationships of which they are unaware. Gradually, they begin to enlarge their stereotyped perceptions of themselves and others as their new observations open new dimensions of reality to them. But it is not an easy journey to abandon the illusions and false security offered by conditioned roles and to face the realities excluded by our emotional conditioning. Here is a case example of problems in observing.

Josh

At age 18 Josh entered college and was away from home for the first extended time. He phoned or texted his parents several times a day, especially his mother, to ask questions about what to do with his unmade bed, dirty laundry, or sleeping through early morning classes. He failed to observe the reality that he was a young man needing to make decisions and act on his own. Nor did he have reasonable expectations of his mother and what she could or could not do from hundreds of miles away. Josh did not face reality or find a way to manage these tasks. Instead, he hired someone to make his bed and do his laundry, and flunked his morning classes until he found someone he could pay to take notes for him. He never learned to observe himself or see other people accurately and did not realize that he asked too much of others and expected too little of himself.

We Use Magical Thinking

Another way we miscommunicate is through the use of *magical thinking*. MAGICAL THINKING IS THE BELIEF THAT NEGATIVE THOUGHTS CAUSE HARM, THAT THINKING OR WISHING SOMETHING MAKES IT HAPPEN, OR THAT WISHING OR THINKING IS THE SAME AS DOING. THIS MEANS THAT ANYTHING IS POSSIBLE WHEN WE USE MAGICAL THINKING. A young omnipotent-to-be has no way to recognize that his emotional conditioning can lead him to think magically and that such thinking is unrealistic. He assumes that his parents know what they are doing since they show no uncertainty and their authority seems limitless.

Parents' ever-increasing expectations keep omnipotent children unsure of the extent of their abilities. If they cannot perform to parental expectations, they must be at fault. When they make every attempt to meet parents' expectations, they are grateful for support and affection, but they despair at any failure. Omnipotents are engaged in continuous effort to reach the ideal standards of their parents. Throughout their lives, they try and exceed their human limits and persist in any undertaking rather than experience failure.

Impotents are also attuned to their parents' expectations. Parents do not expect impotents to suffer frustration or consequences for disobedience. They treat impotents as if their presence is an honor, their behaviors endearing, and any participation with family members is an unexpected bonus. Impotents require parents to support and embrace them in any endeavor they undertake. IMPOTENTS CANNOT HELP BUT ASSUME THEY ARE INCOMPETENT, JUST AS OMNIPOTENTS ASSUME THEY ARE INVINCIBLE. IN THIS WAY MAGICAL THINKING SUBSTITUTES FOR REALITY.

EMOTIONAL CONDITIONING REDUCES COMPLEX HUMAN BEINGS TO ONE DIMENSION. By seeing only the façade, an omnipotent reacts as though impotents are totally helpless even if they are strong and fit. On the other hand, an impotent may see that an omnipotent is ill or feeble but is overruled by his conditioning. This causes him to treat the omnipotent as capable of performing any feat.

Because it is unrealistic to perceive people as limited to their role, magical thinking creates many fantasies. If we direct a child to perform chores far beyond his ability, he will try to accomplish the most challenging tasks. On the other hand, if we condition a child to avoid taking more responsibility with increasing age, a child will comply with that expectation. He will come to believe that others will grant him his wishes and do all the things he desires, wants, and needs, no matter what his actual abilities are. Here are three case examples.

Enrique and Maria

Enrique and Maria married four years ago. They were in their thirties. Enrique was an attorney, while Maria stayed home with their one-year-old son, Javier. Almost every day Maria took Javier to her mother's house so she could go out to lunch and on shopping trips with friends. Maria bought expensive jewelry, home furnishings, and a new car every two years. Although bills poured in and the couple became overextended financially, Enrique believed he could manage these expenses by "putting in a few more hours at work each week." He contributed to these problems by buying expensive clothing for Maria. Enrique thought he could satisfy Maria's every desire and make her happy. Enrique's omnipotent magical thinking led them straight into bankruptcy.

Sara

Sara, six years old, loved kindergarten, but in first grade she cried profusely and refused to get in the car to go to school. Her psychotherapist learned that Sara's mother was diagnosed with cancer the summer between kindergarten and first grade. She felt she must stay home with her mother and nurse her back to health. This little girl used magical thinking through assuming her omnipotent role.

Impotents also exhibit magical thinking, such as believing that others will read their minds and give them what they desire. They also think they can learn or perform work without effort, or that they can live forever and never lose their nurturing parents.

Rodrigo and Angela

Rodrigo, age 26, would soon graduate from medical school. He was a newlywed and heavily in debt from his studies. One day he showed his wife, Angela, a photo of a sports car, telling her how beautiful it was. Several months later when he graduated, he asked Angela where his new sports car was. She had no idea what he was talking about. He flew into a rage, yelling that he had "told" her he wanted a sports car as a graduation present. Rodrigo seemed to think that wanting a car was the same as asking Angela for one.

Magical thinking creates many distortions of reality. Since an omnipotent feels an exaggerated sense of inadequacy with any imperfection, he assumes total responsibility for others' problems. He operates with a magical belief that he knows precisely what others need, and no one else can do the task right. In his zeal for giving care, an omnipotent fails to consider that this excessive support may aggravate an impotent's crippling dependence. Omnipotents also make exaggerated estimates of their own knowledge while exaggerating the helplessness of impotents.

Deep down omnipotents believe they will receive respect and affection for the care they give. They do not foresee that they can never satisfy an impotent's ever-changing, insatiable desires, or that other omnipotents will reject their attempts to help them. Omnipotents believe eventually they will succeed, so they keep repeating their caretaking role.

THE MAGICAL THINKING OF OMNIPOTENTS LEADS THEM TO BELIEVE THEY CAN HAVE A FULFILLING EXISTENCE BY SACRIFICING THEMSELVES FOR OTHERS WITHOUT RETURN SUPPORT. AN OMNIPOTENT'S COMPULSION IN ASSUMING CONTROL IS MUCH LIKE AN ADDICTION WHERE THE ILLUSORY "REWARDS" CONCEAL THE DAMAGE BEING DONE.

Impotents also engage in magical thinking. Although they contribute little effort to their relationships, impotents regard their weak contributions as major ones. Their self-interest motivates them in social interactions so that they may give the *appearance* of empathy and caring. But throughout life, they consistently show much more concern for themselves than for the welfare or misfortunes of others.

Since relationships require two people, impotents absolve themselves of blame if anything should go wrong by shifting responsibility to the other person. Impotents vow to take on significant responsibility, but they do not follow through. Magical thinking accounts for many of these problems in relationships.

We Project onto Others

ANOTHER FORM OF MISCOMMUNICATION TAKES PLACE WHEN WE SUBSTITUTE OUR OWN SUBJECTIVE THOUGHTS FOR THOSE OF THE OTHER PERSON. THIS IS KNOWN AS PROJECTION. WE ACT AS IF WE ARE INFORMED, BUT WE HAVE NO INPUT OR COLLABORATION FROM THE OTHER PERSON. Recall that in the basic emotional conditioning process, parents project their own interpretations onto their infant's gurgling and grimaces. They perceive their child as being happy, intelligent, loving, or fatigued long before a baby can focus her eyes or collect her thoughts.

We convey this program of human emotional conditioning by projection. In the beginning, parents project a role onto each child. This squelches the child's natural abilities to observe and question as she increasingly accepts her parents' emotionally conditioned perceptions as her own. Years later, when each child becomes a parent, she molds her children's grasp of reality in this identical way.

Projection is the term for all variations of this practice of attributing to another person whatever you think or feel. Since no two individuals think exactly alike, projections are unreliable. Inevitably, this creates conflict. We even project our own ideas onto our pets—that they are hungry, angry, or loving—when we have no clue as to how or what our pets think. As children, we made many assumptions of what *all* adults expect of us based on our parents' expectations. As a result, we may have had many inappropriate reactions to other adults who did not share our parents' views.

By projection, we perceive either good qualities or bad ones that simply do not exist. **IF YOU DO NOT QUESTION WHAT THE OTHER PERSON IN A RELATIONSHIP IS ACTUALLY THINKING, THEN YOU ARE BASING YOUR REALITY ON FANTASY AND ON SPECULATION.** Even if you know another person well, you may still err in your assumptions if you base today's interactions on some response or expectation from the past.

We all have faulty beliefs that reflect stereotyped, unquestioned convictions, which cause us to make unreliable assessments of other people. Omnipotents project that the world is full of caring people (like them) while impotents project that the world is filled with self-serving, uncaring masses (like them). At the same time, omnipotents view an omnipotent peer as an unwelcome intruder while impotents generally perceive fellow impotents as being as reasonable as themselves.

Projections reveal the ways we perceive others emotionally, based entirely on our own assumptions. An omnipotent has a stereotyped image of an impotent as being absolutely incapable of withstanding any pressure, however gentle. In reality, no human being is emotionally this fragile. An omnipotent is projecting his or her weaknesses onto the impotent. In dealing with other omnipotents, however, she projects her self-image of someone who needs no care. As a result, an omnipotent may be as uncaring toward other omnipotents as she is toward herself and be totally unaware of the double standard created by her own projection. We can discover much about our thinking processes by observing our own and others' projections.

An impotent reverses this process: she projects her strengths onto omnipotents and psychologically rids herself of all strengths and capabilities. In her conscious mind she exaggerates the small efforts she contributes in maintaining a relationship. An omnipotent, also on a conscious level, mistakenly accepts that the impotent's small participation is greater than it is. By their mutual projections, an omnipotent and impotent perceive one another as people who complete one another.

An impotent individual, relating to other impotents, projects her own image of requiring urgent care in all forms. An impotent will allow no one, not even a peer, to endanger her omnipotent care delivery system. In our experience, impotents' projections are more obvious and much easier to observe than the projections of omnipotents.

THE MOST BASIC PROJECTION OF ALL—AND ONE THAT RESULTS IN ENDLESS CONFU- SION IN RELATIONSHIPS—IS THE BELIEF HELD BY JUST ABOUT EVERY HUMAN BEING ON EARTH THAT HIS OR HER WAY OF PERCEIVING OTHERS IS *NORMAL.* Omnipotents project their belief in perfection by verbally expressing their fundamental philosophy that all good, reasonable people are caring and wish to sup- port their fellow humans. But impotents project a very different basic out- look by viewing others as uncaring, selfish, and totally lacking in ethics.

Imagine small children's confusion when they are exposed to two diverse points of view by one omnipotent and one impotent parent. Children do not recognize that these are projections and accept them as real. They repeatedly experience that their omnipotent parent and relatives accept impotents as well-meaning and intending to care for others, even if they do not do so. Children also accept, without knowing how to question, that their impotent parent might rightfully complain that the omnipotents in the family are inconsiderate, abusive, and showing lack of care. A child hears these projected descriptions and accepts them as reality. In this way, a child will likely build an image of the omnipotent parent as uncaring and inadequate and an image of an inert, uncaring impotent parent as well intentioned and loving.

Each child forms basic attitudes toward himself that distort his self- perceptions due to the parental projections that have shaped his own per- sonality. A child comes to see himself as either a generous care provider who needs no care in return or an insatiable care recipient who must extend no caring to others. For his own sake, a child must accept the family's projections, which were adopted generations before his arrival. The child may learn to suppress his own beliefs and no longer use his own observa- tions to view reality as it is. Later in life when children are separated from parents, they continue to call forth their parents' reactions and behaviors and behave accordingly. The projected role, once taught to us, endures and intensifies through our lifetimes. As adults, we often perform with a belief that "others" expect certain behaviors. This may not be what others expect at all—we project what our parents once expected of us.

Emotional conditioning also shrinks multifaceted ideas into stereotyped images. A growing child assumes all adults are like her parents. Men and women often speak for their biologic or assumed gender as if they are rep- resentative of all those of the same sex, or typecast the opposite sex. We lose individuation, along with losing our reality. We forfeit our appreciation for the remarkable diversity of human beings when we project stereotypes.

We frequently project ideas, images, concepts, or general attitudes onto an individual, group, race, or entire population. As examples, consider these statements often made by omnipotents:

- "It is better to give than to receive."
- "I believe all people try to do what is right."
- "I decided not to tell you because I knew it would upset you."
- "Women are the weaker sex and need men to lean on."
- "You can be anything in life you want to be."

When we encounter these remarks in conversation we rarely question whether the statement is accurate or a projection. We assume that interpreting everyday conversation is a simple task, but it is challenging because of the many ways we project that lead to miscommunication. Interpretation is especially difficult because our emotional conditioning curtails asking questions and thinking. Under these limitations, we almost invariably believe what we are told. Here is a case example.

Amanda

Amanda, 42, has been a librarian for 15 years. She recently had breast cancer and a mastectomy, and has pain in her upper chest and arm whenever she tries to shelve books. A student assistant is assigned to help her but does not because he's on his phone all day with his girlfriend. Amanda does not press him to help. Instead she makes herself available to discuss his girlfriend problems with him. She explains, "It's better to give than to receive."

One day, a young woman student passes by and offers to help Amanda with shelving books. Amanda refuses, saying, "I prefer to do it myself." Amanda assumes an omnipotent role. She is only comfortable giving help and expects nothing in return. She is appalled, angry, and offended when she is offered help: "How dare somebody think I need something." Her thinking is not fully apparent, but her conditioning is. She projects the care and help she needs onto her student assistant. She will not accept help for herself that would make her work easier and less painful.

When we are in either role, we become intolerant of flaws in those we perceive as omnipotent and therefore perfect. Since omnipotents reject relationships that might offer an opportunity for dependency, these projections keep fellow omnipotents at a distance. The same device omnipotents use to maintain an illusion of perfection also helps them appear to be completely independent.

Impotents use projections with great effectiveness to rid themselves of intolerable thoughts and actions. After an impotent offends a close friend, he might say, "But I thought you wanted me to do it." Such projections arise because impotents are unable to bear much responsibility. In any situation in which impotents are asked to account for questionable or irresponsible acts, they immediately project blame onto someone else, absolving themselves at the other person's expense. They usually target omnipotents.

For years omnipotents may receive blame for unhappiness in a relationship and may accept it, believing each instance to result from *their own* personal inadequacies. Assuming all responsibility in a relationship also requires accepting blame for any failure. The following quotations are examples of impotent projections transferring the impotent's own thoughts or actions onto another person:

- "You don't love me and never did."
- "You think you know everything."
- "You don't pay any attention to me."
- "You always want everything your way."

Here is another example of how projections confuse and cause miscommunication.

Matthew and Tina

Twenty-seven-year-old Matthew was in the process of breaking up with his girlfriend of five years, Tina. She initiated the breakup, because she found Matthew erratic and repeatedly insulting. She paid for most of their entertainment, paid their rent, and gave him gas money. Despite that, Matthew called her names in private and in front of friends. Matthew was a businessman and was focused on paying off his student loans. They were testy with one another during their breakup. Matthew projected his anger and overt self-centered behaviors onto Tina. Once, when he was particularly angry, he balled up his fists to Tina, saying, "You'd like to hit me. Wouldn't you?" Later, he blackened his own eye and, in order to gain sympathy, told people that Tina had hit him.

Matthew projected his anger about the breakup onto Tina. He believed it was Tina who was angry with him and wanted to hit him. Actually, Matthew was so angry and upset over her initiating the breakup that he wanted to punch her. He injured his own eye to carry out his projection. His friends were very sympathetic to him over Tina's alleged socking him in the eye.

Our projections are unconscious. If we learn to recognize projections, we can decide who has the specific problem being projected and gain insight into the emotional mechanics behind it. We cannot identify the chaos that results from miscommunicating if we do not know who is projecting what and who is being reasonable or unreasonable. The confusion created by our projections makes interpersonal conflict seem unsolvable. But, if we discover how to identify projections we will devise our own solutions.

We Consciously Rationalize

We create some miscommunications by conscious behaviors, such as rationalizations. **WHEN YOU INVENT A JUSTIFICATION FOR YOUR INAPPROPRIATE BEHAVIORS, YOU FURTHER AVOID DEALING IN THE HERE AND NOW. RATIONALIZATIONS DISGUISE FALSE THINKING.** They are similar to projections in pushing the limits of reality out to the far reaches of our imaginations.

When we ask omnipotents why they work incessantly, they likely answer with the explanation of "I feel better when I'm working." If we ask omnipotents why they do so much work without asking for help, they may respond, "It's easier to do it myself." Inquire of omnipotents about why they neglect routine health care, and they often respond, "I'm never sick." We use rationalizations to allow us to believe that implausible thoughts, emotions, or behaviors are entirely rational. If we do not have one rationalization handy, we are apt to supply another from our repertoire.

An impotent's impulsive behavior patterns can be puzzling to his family and friends. An impotent often uses this phrase, "I just wanted to," in explaining his most aberrant behaviors. Impotents are inclined to act on impulse just to have a new experience. They may only consider the implications of what they did when they must face consequences afterward. Impotents rationalize to omnipotents in markedly childlike and patently illogical ways. Here are two examples.

Roberta

Sixteen-year-old Roberta has been a car thief for three months. When the police caught her and asked why she recently stole another car, she replied, "I just wanted to. It seemed like a way to have fun on a boring summer night." Roberta concocted a "reason" for her delinquent behavior. She knew it was wrong but wanted to justify her inappropriate thievery and evade responsibility. This made her feel she was being rational in her behavior. She wanted to avoid owning up to the reality of the harm she caused.

Allison

Allison, 47, has not had a vacation in four years from her job as a paralegal. When asked why, she replied, "I love my job. Anyway, vacations are a waste of time. There's more work to do to get ready for them and even more when you return from vacation. Who needs it?" Allison is creating a plausible explanation—a rationalization—for why she does not need rest or vacation. She thinks she is being rational in not taking a rest. Allison avoids seeing the reality that working all the time and never vacationing is not good for her. If we can learn to spot rationalizations in our communications we can improve dialogue with one another.

We Do Not Treat Everyone the Same

We do not treat everyone alike, and this leads to miscommunications. This is a basic principle in relationships. Many people are unbelieving and say, "I treat everyone the same. I raise all my children the same way." But for the most part we are unaware that we relate differently to the people with whom we are closest. We can be extremely generous to one person and then turn to another person and be cruelly withholding. Any one of us is capable of moving quickly from cruelty in one relationship to lavish indulgence in another. Our children often see this in how we treat one child differently from a sibling. And, in both instances we feel justified and reasonable.

Since omnipotents spend years grooming themselves to be ultimate caretakers, they are happy when others acknowledge their efforts and when friends describe them as being thoughtful and considerate. They feel confident in their ability to form relationships, and others value their company. They believe they treat everyone quite reasonably.

Omnipotents are not conscious that their abilities are limited to caring for other people. Initially, they attempt to care for everyone they encounter. But once, as if using a radar system, they unconsciously spot another person as an impotent, they gear up and provide unstinting support. However, if omnipotents spot another omnipotent, they hold back care to some degree. They cannot support other omnipotents beyond what they can do for themselves.

Impotents apply their own standard to fellow impotents and a different and opposite measure to omnipotents, once they are unconsciously classified in their minds. Impotents also feel their standard is perfectly reasonable, having held it since early childhood. Since their role is one of complete dependency, they ask nothing of a fellow impotent, as they expect no effort from people like themselves. Then, when turning to an omnipotent, impotents expect perfection and to be cared for. Here is a case example.

Oskar

Oskar and Noelle are in their early forties and have two children. Brittany is six and Werner is seven. Noelle has made their first appointment, worried about Brittany's withdrawal and talk of "being no good." Everyone in the family goes to therapy.

The picture unfolds that Oskar relates very differently with the two children. Oskar enjoys calling the shots and claiming the limelight in the family. He gives Werner the same latitude and indulges Werner's wishes and desires. When Werner wants to go to the park, out for ice cream, or have Oskar play with him, Oskar happily complies. However, when Brittany asks for almost anything, Oskar says no and often berates her for asking: *"You don't need that. I have more important things to do. Quit bothering me. Go ask your mother."*

Oskar unknowingly places Brittany in an omnipotent role. He does not expect her to need his attention or to make requests of him. He believes she is very capable. Instead, he expects her to acquiesce to his needs. Oskar is an impotent and is unaware of what he is doing with the children. He believes he treats both children the same. However, Brittany knows her father treats her differently. She puts herself down because that is what her father does to her. This is why she feels she is "no good."

We Think Others Think Like Us

We have a fixed belief that, since our personal standards and judgment are reasonable, then others must think the same way as we do. This is another major factor frustrating our relationships and causing miscommunication. Every one of us develops personal opinions and presumptions about others. We also devise ways of managing our relationships that guide our actions. However, even with the transmission of our programmed methods of relating via emotional conditioning, we are not perfect copies of one another. In fact, no two people can possibly think exactly alike.

We all have personal standards. In the case of an omnipotent child, his early demonstration of care for an impotent relative teaches him that he will be accepted if he takes on other people's problems. This belief leads an omnipotent to dedicate himself to a life of sacrifice on behalf of others. Omnipotents conclude from their own isolated experiences that there is a *right answer* to life's situations and they must have that answer for the impotents they encounter. They firmly believe in their own omnipotence.

They also witness the actions of relatives in an omnipotent role. In turn, each young omnipotent learns to project his idea onto others. In projecting, omnipotents see society as consisting of people who are selfless, caring, and anxious to control others' problems. Throughout their lives, they assume that others are motivated by the same altruism. However, this emotionally conditioned skew creates constant conflict for all of us.

An impotent, when young, also formulates a set of standards necessary for his survival. He assumes that he holds great importance to others and his emotions and desires should dominate his relationships. Others feel obligated to abandon their own interests and do what an impotent wants. An impotent projects onto others his image of a totally egocentric person so that he sees a world filled with competitors who are insufficiently caring, uncommitted, unfair, revengeful, and parasitic.

WHEN WE ASSUME OTHERS THINK JUST LIKE WE DO, WE FURTHER COMPOUND OUR PROBLEMS BECAUSE WE ALL SEE THINGS DIFFERENTLY. MANY INTERPERSONAL CONFLICTS COME ABOUT BECAUSE EACH PERSON, AFTER A LONG DISCUSSION, REACHES A TOTALLY DIFFERENT IMPRESSION OF WHAT THE OTHER PERSON HAS SAID.

Many of us in long-lasting relationships feel we never quite agree on or understand the other person's viewpoint, even after decades of discussion. Our emotions are pleasant or neutral when they accompany our communications dealing with *informational* exchange between us—the weather, planning an outing to see a movie or a new restaurant in town. But the instant a factual informational exchange becomes personal emotions arise. At this point the emotionally conditioned personality is mobilized, and we perceive the experience from our own particular emotionally conditioned standpoint.

Child and Strange Dog

Different people see the same circumstances in entirely different ways, and this is apparent in our communications. Consider the manner in which an omnipotent views the scene of a child accosted by a strange dog. An omnipotent sees the situation in a panoramic sweep, since he always prepares to solve problems and anticipates possible outcomes. He considers the child's range of possible responses, the dog's possible unpredictable behaviors, other people present, and so on. He will later recall much of the scene in detail but pay little attention to his own personal reactions, since his whole concentrated focus is on the others he feels a responsibility for—the child, dog, and bystanders.

An impotent sees the dog and child situation differently. As a witness, an impotent may fixate on a single point of personal interest. In fact, an impotent might be fixated on a distant object and fail to see the dog and child interaction at all. If an impotent witnesses the interaction, he or she may only note the color of the child's clothes or the decoration on the dog's collar. But, most often, impotents substitute what they felt for what they saw.

In different roles, each observer assimilates the emotional information differently. The differences we have in ways of observing and communicating often lead to conflict between omnipotents and impotents in their emotional responses to any situation.

Suppose the two people in the above example discuss the child/dog incident later. An omnipotent recalls the experience in detail and shares his relief that the dog and child played well together. An impotent, because he often critiques the omnipotent, takes issue with some minor point in the omnipotent's description of the child and dog episode, and accuses him of distorting facts. They have a heated argument, and the impotent demands the omnipotent concede that the impotent's view was correct.

Over the years, many such arguments likely have taken place between them. An omnipotent does not realize that an impotent has a vision limited to unimportant details and to emotions. An impotent becomes increasingly exasperated that an omnipotent collects so much "unnecessary" detail and misses the one important point the impotent sees or feels.

We Define Words Differently

Not only do we *see* things differently in our closest relationships, but we also *hear* and *define* things differently. Our emotional makeup causes us to distort the definitions of identical words. Differently conditioned roles cause us to alter our word definitions. For example, a dictionary definition of the word *help* is to give assistance. Most people agree this is an acceptable meaning. But, when an omnipotent uses the word, he does not mean solely *to assist*. Instead, he attempts to perform a service *completely*, especially for an impotent. And, he will often withhold assistance from another omnipotent, all the while *believing* he is assisting.

When an impotent masquerades as "helpful," he assists only slightly because he expects a greater return from the person he helps. The impotent's offer of help is his projection of an expectation to receive some benefit rather than just giving. Many impotents are aware vaguely of their internal reluctance to help others but feel helpless to change. Frequently they boast about and exaggerate the rare instances in which they offered minimal help.

Although many words can take on personalized meanings, let's consider one further example. The primary definition of *love* in the dictionary is "an intense affectionate concern for another person." Logically, this is a clear, thoughtful definition. Since an omnipotent becomes stirred emotionally to an extreme degree when encountering an attractive impotent, the omnipotent becomes captivated by the impotent's helplessness and lack of concern about solving her own problems. This is such a different operating procedure from the omnipotents' ongoing desire to solve many of life's problems. The omnipotent has no doubt that she has "fallen in love" and idealizes her adored impotent.

Actually, we discovered an omnipotent loves the *role* of an impotent more than the actual person. An omnipotent's excitement is not for an impotent herself. An omnipotent merely gets excited because the omnipotent projects his own perfect traits onto the impotent. This allows the omnipotent to think, "Wow, that new person is just perfect."

This "love" does not meet the definition of true concern for the other person. An omnipotent is merely fulfilling and projecting his own role in discovering an impotent he wants to protect. If the omnipotent were truly concerned for the impotent person, he would not assume *all* the caregiving. Because when he does all caretaking, he creates even more weakness and irresponsibility in an impotent.

These unconscious roles also create a profound effect on impotents. Impotents reciprocate the strong love emotions of omnipotents because impotents feel an overwhelming desire to possess their protectors. They do not doubt they are fulfilling every aspect of love. However, impotents' definition of love is satisfying their needs for devoted care, which means they become almost totally dependent on the omnipotent. In this dependent, needy role they fail to meet the definition of love—a deep concern and affection for another. Instead, impotents only commit themselves to the relationship as *recipients* of care. They wind up feeling affection or "love" for the benefits received from omnipotents' caretaking and not for omnipotents as people.

We're Not Open to Others' Ideas

The ways that two differently conditioned people accept (or don't accept) the ideas of one another creates another major impediment to communication. Omnipotents are open and insatiable for general information that will make them more useful. But, they are often unreadable and out of touch with their own emotions. Omnipotents reason that they always treat others properly and fairly. They will listen to other omnipotents, who may be more knowledgeable on some subjects. But then they reject this more knowledgeable advice as flawed because it disagrees with their own opinions or beliefs. With this same rigidity, they critique other omnipotents' judgments and ideas because they lack sufficient flexibility to recognize and accept ideas superior to their own.

On the other hand, impotents may listen to and solicit others' ideas but eventually do whatever is easiest and gives them the most pleasure. Impotents regard conversation as more of a device. They use it to draw attention away from others and toward themselves. They also use conversation and requests for help to ventilate and not for serious discussions geared toward coming up with new ideas.

In addition, not only are we not open to others' ideas, but we are also unwilling to take advice. Commonly, we believe that each of us could make communication clearer by putting out additional effort. But with this idea we fail to consider the unconscious parts of us. Let's look at a situation where we ask for help with a personal problem and receive thoughtful advice from the points of view of both omnipotents and impotents.

When omnipotents ask for advice, they listen to the advice and often appear to be in agreement with the advice given. But, because omnipotents have an *idée fixe* that they already know the correct advice or perfect answer, they disregard even the best advice and proceed just as they planned all along. In doing psychotherapy we learned that omnipotents disregard our suggestions even when severely distressed. Impotents who request advice respond a different way. After they ask for input concerning urgent problems, impotents usually talk with many people and then do whatever is most convenient and effortless.

In both conditioned roles we flatly ignore advice. This suggests that giving advice is largely a wasted effort. To the credit of omnipotents, they keep other people's advice accessible for later retrieval. Only later when some unhappy life experience repeats frequently enough, they may begin to question the assumption they knew what they were doing. Here is an example.

Jack

At 58, Jack was very upset over his daughter's upcoming marriage. He was so distraught that his wife thought he needed therapy. Jack did not like his daughter's fiancé, believing he was a man who would just take advantage of her, be manipulative and uncaring. Yet while we talked Jack could not give any examples to back up his "gut feeling" about the fiancé. Actually, he described the fiancé as kind, hardworking, and supportive to his daughter. Yet he persisted with his gut feeling.

Jack went on to say he had talked this situation over with several friends and relatives, asking their opinions about what he should do. Most of them had suggested he speak with his daughter about his concerns or else get a therapist. Near the end of his first session Jack announced he wasn't going to listen to any recommendations, nor was he going to begin therapy. He was going to do what he thought was best, easiest, and quickest and what he had thought all along: "I'm going to disinherit her if she marries him. That's it." With that he ended his session and left. He never returned. He was closed off to considering another avenue, did not follow any suggestions from his friends or relatives, and did disinherit his daughter.

Busy Circuits of the Mind

We can see how our minds are occupied continuously with busy circuits carrying countless messages. Some of our circuits operate on a basic level, monitoring conditions in our bodies and automatically managing our physiology. Our conscious thoughts monitor our place in the larger world.

If we are omnipotents, we tend to focus on possible difficulties that might arise and how we would justify ourselves if we were found lacking in some situation—that is, found to be *imperfect*. Omnipotents often overreach their abilities. They may presume knowledge they do not have or assume their answers are correct, pretending they know what everyone else needs. They may take on more responsibility than they can manage. They may become incessantly busy and may be so smug and pious that their minds close to new information that could be helpful to them. They may live their entire lives valuing the control of tasks assigned them and completing all goals. They often fail to enjoy the pleasures of life.

Impotent minds are also busy, but they may have fantasies of endless insecurity during wakeful hours and when alone. Impotents may become highly anxious every time they perceive the least insecurity in their immediate environment. They grow intent on conveying their anxious precariousness to someone nearby who can control it for them. Even impotents with high intelligence who are well off experience insecure feelings of such magnitude that they often demand constant reassurance from someone else that they will be totally protected. Their fixation on personal security impairs their listening ability.

Generally, impotents go through life having mainly one personal interest at a time. They often remain oblivious to happenings around them. They may think and talk only of their appearance, children, hobby, work, illness, and so on. Often they become bored and impatient when a topic is raised that they have no interest in. Thus, mental "busy-ness" hinders communication in both omnipotents and impotents.

Can you clearly spot your emotions turning off your thinking? Can you see times when you do not observe yourself and others closely to see what is taking place? Can you identify your own and others' magical thinking episodes? Can you spot omnipotent and impotent projections and ask questions of the person doing the projecting? Are you able to identify when you and others rationalize your behaviors? Do you recognize when you have two different standards for people you interact with? Can you catch yourself assuming other people think just like you without checking out what they really think? Can you pick out times you see and define things differently? Can you pinpoint times you are closed to advice that could be helpful to you?

It is your turn to work on spotting these forms of miscommunication in your relationships. Once you spot them, see if you can avoid them and improve your communications.

Conclusion

Emotional conditioning creates myriad problems in communication. We mentioned only some of the more apparent ones. The overall significance of communication difficulties, common to all relationships, lies in their constant and cumulative distorting of our reality. Your emotions dominate your intellect. You make inadequate observations of yourself and others. Magical thinking causes even the best educated and well informed, as well as the least educated, to have continual uncertainty about the boundaries of reality. Projections reverse the reality of a situation, making the innocent appear culpable and the guilty seem blameless.

Rationalizations excuse the most questionable behavior without any enlightenment.

Although these types of miscommunication are essential in creating the roles of omnipotence and impotence, our surrender of reality costs us all a great deal. We see the effects everywhere in continuing turmoil in our society, in strife in intimate relationships, and in dysfunctional families. We all pay this toll. But, the good news is now we can stop it because now we know it exists.

What You Have Discovered in This Chapter

- We have chaos in our relationships because of our inability to understand others.

- Emotions dominate over reality. We almost always reject reality in favor of conditioned emotional responses to others.

- We all make snap judgments, engage in magical thinking, and use projections and rationalizations without realizing we are doing it.

- We have double standards, think our viewpoint is reasonable, and believe other people think like us.

- We communicate differently because we see, hear, and define the same emotionally charged circumstance in entirely different ways.

- When emotions are involved, we often are not receptive to others' ideas.

QUESTIONS TO ASK YOURSELF

The most common miscommunication patterns may be easier to spot now that you've read Chapter 6. Focus on these questions for further personal exploration.

- How would you describe your work experience?
- What were your assigned chores at home?
- Did you get an allowance? If so, how did you save or spend it?
- How old were you when you had your first paid job?
- What did you do with the money you earned?
- How did you feel toward work? Challenged? Bored? Resentful?
- What were your reasons for changing jobs?
- What occurred if or when you were fired?
- How do you treat people you supervise or manage?
- Do you have difficulty maintaining discipline among your subordinates?
- Do you have difficulty firing employees who consistently fail to perform well?
- Do you tend to work compulsively and find relaxation difficult?
- Do you have difficulty showing up for work and keeping jobs?

CHAPTER SEVEN

Roles within Marriages

Choosing a Partner

Now that we have shared with you the ways omnipotent and impotent roles contribute to how we miscommunicate with one another, let's shift our focus to the most important one-to-one relationship that most of us have: marriage or long-term cohabiting relationships.

FOR MOST PEOPLE, THE CHOICE OF A MATE IS PROBABLY THE MOST IMPORTANT DECISION IN LIFE. WE ENHANCE OUR QUALITY OF LIFE ENORMOUSLY IF WE CHOOSE A STABLE AND REASONABLE COMPANION FOR A MUTUALLY BENEFICIAL AND ENDURING RELATIONSHIP. THIS HOLDS TRUE WHETHER THE RELATIONSHIP IS HETEROSEXUAL OR HOMOSEXUAL.

In pairing up, our aim is to select a loving, dependable partner who will share the pleasures and problems of life. However, we remain perplexed at the many common problems that plague marriages and long-term cohabiting relationships. Since we can't identify the causes, we are not sure how to resolve relationship issues.

Statistics from around the world reflect marriages' poor success rates. In countries where marriage and divorce are legal, the rate of failed marriages exceeds 50 percent. Even couples who have long-enduring relationships (and who do not divorce or break up) may have grave disappointment in their relationships.

Often such disappointing relationships continue because we find it more desirable to live with our problems than to face the difficulties and stigmas of separation and divorce. By enduring bad marriages, we replace affection with tolerance and fulfillment with resignation and endurance. Although poets, philosophers, novelists, songwriters, and others praise the happiness and satisfaction that come from a loving union, we have found through our work that the actual percentage of couples who find such ful-fillment is small.

Our Definition of Successful Marriage

There are many conflicting definitions of a successful marriage. Many of us believe it is a compatible agreement of role assignments. For exam-ple, one partner is the wage earner, while the other partner is in charge of domestic work and raising children. Others believe any marriage is suc-cessful if we have not terminated it legally. This may be the situation even if the couple has separated physically or emotionally and moved on to other relationships.

Dr. Martin's and my concept of successful marriage is one in which we discard our roles. Each partner presents himself or herself without distortion or subterfuge, and both partners contribute to their fullest abil-ity to whatever joint challenges arise—100 percent contribution by each person. This arrangement has no hierarchy or pecking order; the partners both provide care, labor, and effort because they consider themselves equals. Their children observe the necessity and fairness of sharing, yet without sacrificing each person's individual identity. Ideally, when grown these children will build similar stable relationships, anchored in reality.

But, many children do not have this pattern to emulate. **INSTEAD, CHILDREN ARE LIKELY TO SEE THE IMPACT OF ROLE PLAYING IN THEIR PARENTS' MARRIAGE— ROLES BASED ON BELIEFS IN OMNIPOTENCE AND IMPOTENCE.**

Since children witness their parents' relationships year after year, they learn the parents' standards and roles well. In doing so, they are likely to repeat their parents' errors, often in minute detail. Even if parents advise their children to "do what I say, not what I do," the children will have extreme difficulty adopting new roles and creating new strategies. If we assign a child an omnipotent role, almost inevitably he will seek a partner in the opposite role—an impotent.

On Love

Over the years many people have asked us, "What about love? Doesn't love solve all relationship problems?" Reading our earlier comments on marriage, you might wonder why we place little importance on the power of love. "Love conquers all" and "anything is possible with love" are com-mon platitudes. However, we find great controversy and confusion about the definition of love.

With mutual love and regard for one another, a couple can accomplish more than just one person alone and can survive hardship together. When we hold someone else in high regard, we seek his or her presence and listen and communicate more effectively. We are less inclined to dismiss or consider lightly what he or she says. This high regard contains the elements of what we call love.

IN OUR OPINION, WE DO NOT BASE LOVE ON THE *PERFORMANCE* OF THE OTHER PERSON IN THE RELATIONSHIP. WE SEE LOVE AS RESTING ON HIGH REGARD FOR ANOTHER PERSON. THE LOVER RELATES TO HIS OR HER PARTNER OPENLY, WITH HONESTY AND RESPECT, AND WITH NO ATTEMPT AT PRETENSE OR DECEPTION. SUCH PEOPLE EMBODY A LOVE OF THEMSELVES AND OTHERS BECAUSE THEY PRESENT THEMSELVES AS THEY ARE, NO MORE, NO LESS.

Our ancestors may have misconstrued love as the blind frenzy of emotion that omnipotents and impotents set off when they connect with each other. These two halves of a couple fit in a complementary way into a *merging oneness*. Most omnipotent-impotent pairs describe "falling in love." In such opposite role unions, we have seen that each partner places the other on a pedestal. Actually, both partners love something within themselves and project this image onto the other partner. This leads to a fantasy of security because it creates intense, positive feelings that often peak before the couple knows anything about one another. Such an emotion cannot be love if the two people barely know one another.

Such a rapid experience of falling in love is the opposite of the process creating a genuine bond: slowly learning that another person has admirable characteristics, and developing an appreciation and regard for that person as an individual. **THE PREDICTABLE EMOTIONAL FIREWORKS THAT ACCOMPANY THE PAIRING OF A MUTUALLY ADORING OMNIPOTENT AND IMPOTENT ARE FAR MORE SPECTACULAR THAN THE STABLE, LASTING SENTIMENTS IN A GRADUALLY EVOLVING LOVING RELATIONSHIP IN WHICH TWO PEOPLE GET TO KNOW AND ADMIRE ONE ANOTHER.**

When we love another person for the traits he or she possesses, our affection for that person is specific, not general. We base our admiration on actual characteristics the person has and not on our projections. We also create an emotional commitment to the other person that is not transferable to anyone else. This form of love requires acceptance of another person as a whole person who is free to have his or her own unique way of behaving and thinking. We hold the other person in the relationship by the bonds of our mutual affection. We do not love one another on the condition that we act in destructive or sick ways, as is all too often true of the omnipotent-impotent style of affection.

Since omnipotents feel affection for themselves only when they provide sufficient care for impotents, any impotent could spark this reaction. Only later on in the relationship will omnipotents discover some personal traits in impotents to justify or rationalize their emotions as "love."

By contrast, impotents feel affection for themselves when they are passive and dependent on omnipotents. Most of the time impotents have a tenuous and superficial commitment to their love relationships. Impotents can immediately and easily withdraw from romantic relationships over the slightest—real or perceived—neglect by omnipotents. Impotents base their conditional love on their partners' willingness to complement the missing parts of their own impotent personalities.

In the early stages of a relationship or marriage, we tend to overlook serious conflicts or dismiss them as minor. But we need to consider seriously these discords. When we become bored in a marriage, we should explore this feeling to discover if our relationship has fallen into a deep repetitive rut. If we do not discuss the dissatisfactions we have with our partners, our unresolved problems add up and eventually will erupt.

Couples introduce fatal flaws into their relationships when they fail to establish reasonable priorities in their marriages. An impotent spouse almost always assumes a dominant position in most marriages and long-term relationships. Omnipotents rarely receive a chance to view life from the top position. At the beginning of a relationship, we would be more prudent if we focus on whichever partner has more compelling needs at a particular time. This approach would serve the couple and others in the family much better.

However, it is very difficult to change a rigid pattern, especially when a relationship begins to break down. In order to change our relationships, we must be aware of the cracks in our marriage foundation and have a method to correct them. Unfortunately, we almost guarantee that we will deal inappropriately with our marital problems because of our emotionally conditioned roles. **THE OMNIPOTENT-IMPOTENT RELATIONSHIP IS A HUMAN MADE MISCONCEPTION THAT DOES NOT WORK WELL FOR EITHER PARTNER AS THEIR "LOVE" WREAKS HAVOC ON BOTH.**

We do not want you to despair over our observations. We hope the knowledge we have gained about relationships and marriages will be liberating to you, so that you can better understand the pitfalls in attraction, marriage, and relationships and discover how to make improvements.

Rehearsing for Marriage: Reality Does Not Enter into the Decision

We make the decision of choosing a mate only after years of rehearsal. Since we began learning our role in childhood, we practiced it over and over during the middle and high school years. When we start dating, we become aware that only certain people excite us romantically, and other people hold only minimal interest for us. We assume that the excitement and heightened feelings we have around another person must represent affection or love. Although we are aware of our heightened response, we are unaware of the unconscious factors that dictate our ultimate decision in selecting a romantic partner. Uncontrollable forces that seek gratification within impotents match the unconscious forces drawing the omnipotent to supply gratification. The partnership forms.

REALITY IS NOT THE DECIDING FACTOR IN ATTEMPTING TO UNDERSTAND OUR CHOICE OF A MARRIAGE PARTNER. WHEN STRONG EMOTIONS ARE AROUSED, REALITY BECOMES A SILENT WITNESS TO OUR EMOTIONALLY CONDITIONED BEHAVIORS, THOUGHTS, AND EMOTIONS. When "falling in love," omnipotents, who are usually levelheaded, become mindless slaves in the presence of impotents. Omnipotents perceive a charming, adorable, helpless person who needs support or rescue.

Impotents have an equally huge gulf that distances them from reality. In the presence of omnipotents they lapse into helplessness and inaction, which is wholly inconsistent with their actual intelligence and abilities. SUCH CHOICES IN OTHERS' RELATIONSHIPS MYSTIFY US AS OUTSIDE OBSERVERS. YET WE ALL HAVE DIFFICULTIES IN REALISTICALLY OBSERVING OUR OWN *PERSONAL RELA-TIONSHIPS*. OUR RELATIONSHIPS SHOULD FUNCTION TO MAINTAIN A DESIRED LEVEL OF EMOTIONAL SUPPORT FOR BOTH PEOPLE. OUR MISPERCEPTIONS CAUSED BY CONDI-TIONING HAMPER OUR BEST EFFORTS. THE RESULT IS THAT LIFE AND MARRIAGE BECOME A STRUGGLE.

Conflicts Endanger the Marriage

Let us consider how a typical marriage unravels. An omnipotent expects to provide unstinting support to his dependent, impotent spouse, without requesting support for himself. His self-esteem grows when he tries to control his partner's dissatisfactions and keep her content and satisfied. At these moments both spouses experience high self-regard. The couple's harmony reigns supreme, particularly in the early years of the relationship.

Gradually, an omnipotent becomes emotionally frazzled as a result of ever-increasing responsibilities and impotent's demands. His self-esteem plummets when he fails to completely satisfy his impotent spouse. An omnipotent's once happy mood changes to pessimism and resignation due to his repeated failures to satisfy. The impotent begins to resign herself to living with an imperfect partner. To some degree both people suffer with emotional dysfunctions or illnesses such as anxiety, depression, and anger.

If an omnipotent achieves something outstanding, the old magic may be revived, or the relationship may momentarily appear back on track if an impotent supplies an unexpected bit of support. If this happens, both partners briefly feel more satisfaction, but it does not last. The relationship's return to stagnation may eventually become permanent, with both partners either accepting the status quo or filing for divorce.

IF A MARRIAGE FAILS, IT IS BECAUSE OF THE INTERPLAY OF THE TWO DIFFERENT ROLES AND NOT DUE TO ONE SPOUSE OR THE OTHER. **W**HEN THE SITUATION BECOMES INTOLERABLE TO EITHER SPOUSE AND THE LEVEL OF EMOTIONAL SUPPORT IS INCOMPATIBLE WITH MAINTAINING EVEN MINIMAL SELF-ESTEEM, SEPARATION OR DIVORCE BECOMES INEVITABLE. Here is a case example.

Bob and Katy

Bob and Katy met in college and dated for three years. They were inseparable "soul mates," as they often said. Bob studied architecture and Katy modern dance. They had an irresistible attraction for one another. Before they met they had been in long-standing relationships with other people since their high school years. After they met, they rapidly dropped these relationships. They both said these prior relationships had been shallow by comparison. Bob, usually shy and introverted, abounded with energy upon meeting Katy. He described feeling he had met an invaluable person for whom he would sacrifice anything. He fantasized caring for Katy in any way she wanted. Katy believed she had met Mr. Right, who would do anything in the world for her. She had fantasies of being totally nurtured by Bob. They both appeared transformed by their "love."

Bob became romantic, sending poems and flowers to Katy on a regular basis. Katy, usually laid back and somewhat disorganized, became almost pushy and obsessive in promoting their relationship to her friends and family. She wanted marriage and permanency in their relationship, and she wanted it quickly. Compared to earlier relationships that disappointed her, she believed Bob would provide for her without letting her down.

As time passed, some family and friends pointed out flaws or drawbacks in their attraction. Bob was serious, ambitious, and goal-oriented, and Katy was less ambitious and more the life of the party. At times during social gatherings, she was dismissive of Bob. But the young couple did not listen. They could not comprehend why their friends and parents disapproved of their relationship. The emotional pull of attraction due to Bob and Katy's emotional conditioning outweighed all reality factors. Bob was certain he could provide for Katy and their future family.

Bob and Katy both overlooked the reality of how they interacted while dating. In the excitement of their romantic attraction, they failed to recognize that their reality did not fit with their ideal fantasies. For example, Bob noticed that, at times, Katy was inconsiderate and made plans for social engagements without consulting him. When such plans interfered with Bob's work or travel, Katy never apologized or consulted with Bob beforehand. Instead, she became enraged that Bob could not get out of his work obligations and comply with her desires. Bob dismissed these behaviors as insignificant and assumed they would stop once he married Katy.

Katy, too, noticed small imperfections in Bob's behaviors when they were dating. On Saturday mornings, after long workweeks, Bob liked to sleep in and lounge in bed until late morning. This annoyed Katy because she wanted Bob up early so she could make the bed. She dismissed Bob's Saturday morning habit, believing he would do better once they were wed.

Katy wanted a lavish wedding and Bob went along, but he worried about the high cost and the debt they would incur. Katy dismissed his concerns by calling him an "unnecessary worrier." Bob and Katy settled into married life and relaxed a little after the tense months of wedding preparations. Bob displayed his talents of nurturance and protection with Katy. Katy felt she had achieved a totally secure, dependent state, which reminded her of childhood.

Bob was exhausted from being on guard and anxious during the wedding preparations. He feared that if he displayed a single imperfection he might destroy the relationship. He planned on doing further graduate studies but, with a new wife to care for, he decided to end his formal education and seek a job as an architect so he could make Katy comfortable. Katy also finished her degree in dance and began working part-time.

Initially, Bob and Katy lived in a cocoon, insulating their relationship from the world. They seldom went out with friends or visited their families. They felt they only needed one another. Bob gave up golfing with his coworkers after work to immediately return home to Katy. Katy prepared Bob's favorite dinners every night.

Their ecstatic feelings of anticipation that took place early in the marriage slowly faded. Bob became intensely serious in assuming not only his job as an architect but also household responsibilities—laundry, vacuuming, and yard work—and giving up leisure interests. Katy felt secure in their relationship, cut back on household chores, and cooked less.

Gradually, Bob and Katy realized the high costs of ignoring their earlier and current dissatisfactions with one another. Within two years of marriage they both encountered more examples of what they had seen and dismissed during their dating years. Bob saw more of Katy's inconsiderate treatment, and she often told others about their personal problems. Katy noticed more of Bob's imperfections in satisfying her desires. He didn't always come home immediately after work because he had to entertain clients from out of town. She became increasingly disenchanted. Bob was failing to fulfill her fantasy that he would be all things to her at all times.

Their conflicts escalated as they complained to one another of their disappointments in the relationship. Bob increasingly witnessed Katy's demands, impulsive nature, and her tendency to act without restraint. When he came home from work, she would be gone, out with friends for the evening. She did this without consulting with him. Even when she said she would have dinner waiting for him, she did not. She also quit her part-time job, again without discussing it with Bob. And, even when finances became tight, she demanded, whined, and cajoled more spending money from Bob— money she used to purchase pedicures, manicures, tattoos, and up-to-date kitchen equipment, even though she had mostly stopped cooking.

However irritated Bob was, he accepted Katy's behaviors, firmly believing that giving in and accommodating her would satisfy her and "keep the peace." Katy saw Bob's acceptance of her demands as affirmation that they were reasonable and fair. So, Katy escalated her demands and capricious behaviors. She began to display a terrific temper even when Bob so much as questioned her behaviors.

Both Bob and Katy reached out to their families for support during these conflicts. But their families just reinforced their roles by excusing Katy's irresponsible behaviors and by protecting her. They expected Bob, on his own, to control the marital problems he and Katy were having. "You have made your bed so you must lie in it," their families' answered. This stance only further fixed Katy's and Bob's roles.

Astonishingly, Bob did not resent or resist his life of being totally focused on working, sacrificing and solving the problems brought on by Katy. Instead, he prided himself in working hard to appease Katy. Even when he was being neglected and emotionally abused, he remained committed to her. Increasingly he gave up friends, ball games, and visiting his relatives because Katy wanted him to. Occasionally, he would blow up at Katy, but only when she surpassed his limits. Briefly he would be angry and then feel guilt over this lapse in his usual behavior. He would apologize to Katy and vow to restrain himself from such anger in the future.

As time passed, Katy's interests alone drove the couple's activities. Katy allowed Bob to visit her parents and sister but wouldn't let him join her when she went out with friends. Bob ignored his own pursuits in favor of Katy's desires. They existed in perfect unconscious agreement: whatever Katy expressed an interest in, Bob sought to gratify her wish. Bob became so sensitized to the many services Katy demanded of him that verbal communication became almost unnecessary.

Without Katy's emotional support, Bob increasingly sought support from friends and coworkers. The idea was dawning on him that despite his best efforts, he could not make this relationship viable. Katy was insatiable, and he was exhausted giving to her. He grew disillusioned with himself, his wife, and his marriage. He felt depressed, anxious, and had problems sleeping.

Their marriage lumbered along for years this way, and they had two children. Both worked diligently within their roles. Bob was the breadwinner, and Katy was with the children during the day while Bob worked. They resigned themselves to their roles and no longer had enthusiasm or zeal for each other and no goals for their future together.

They adhered to a double standard with one another. Bob had to perform exceptional feats of giving to receive any acknowledgment from Katy. She often refused to go to his award dinners when he received accolades, promotions, and bonuses for his architectural work. But she was more than content to spend Bob's bonuses on herself. However, Katy wanted constant attention and extraordinary gratitude when she did go to one of Bob's work functions and support him, no matter how small her efforts were.

Their children absorbed these values and roles. Only their genders were different. Their daughter was an omnipotent like Bob, and their son was an impotent like Katy.

Commentary

Bob and Katy had a typical marriage of the opposite personality types described in this book. This type of marriage is common throughout many centuries, appears in many cultures, and may be universal. Omnipotents and impotents share a mutual attraction that appears to transcend social barriers and cultural variations.

We might argue that if one person does all the giving, it is not a true relationship. In our research, Dr. Martin and I found that, depending on the degree of emotional conditioning, impotents may supply 1 to 30 percent of the emotional support, leaving omnipotents to supply 70 to 99 percent. It is not logical for omnipotents to agree to a situation where they would give 90 percent for a 10 percent return. However, logic does not prevail. Omnipotents have an emotional predilection for relationships where they receive little or no support. Reality once again falls victim to idealization and fantasy.

The Small Percentage of Marriages That Are Different

From our vantage point, we found that same-role marriages—omnipotent-omnipotent and impotent-impotent—are much less common than omnipotent-impotent marriages. Choosing a partner of your own role can occur for several reasons. One reason is the dating pool may be limited, causing a lack of choice. Another reason may be that a person will, after a series of failed relationships, chance upon an attractive person who is very different from the previous choices of mates and decide to try someone in a different role.

The problem for omnipotents is that when they are in the company of one another, they frequently become critical and inconsiderate and withhold support. And, when two impotents are together, they both perceive the other one as needing assistance, but neither is capable of giving to the other.

Fewer marriages are omnipotent-omnipotent pairs. In our experience if these marriages do work they have the greatest longevity. In such marriages both people are often quite busy caring for others—volunteering, babysitting, being foster parents, charity supporters—yet they do give some care and attention to one another. Their children wind up having two parents to model the omnipotent role. However, this does not mean the couple will not create impotent children. Since both omnipotent parents are often from backgrounds where they interacted with and cared for impotents during their childhoods, they also have the capability to raise children in impotent roles. (Table 7.1 summarizes the three types of role relationships.)

Omnipotent-Omnipotent Marriage
Lucas and Melanie

Lucas and Melanie began dating as high school classmates. They met when volunteering at a car wash to benefit their school's band. Melanie played the violin in the school orchestra, and Lucas played trombone in the band. Both were honor roll students and involved in sports teams in high school. They were each other's first serious romantic relationship.

In spite of being very involved in school and community activities, both were somewhat shy and uncomfortable around the opposite sex. Lucas was reluctant to approach girls romantically. Melanie didn't like to ask her friends or teachers for help with schoolwork, feeling she had to understand tough academic material on her own. They quickly felt at ease with one another and became confidants. They did lots of school activities together and enjoyed music and movies.

Table 7.1   Three Types of Possible Relationships for Omnipotent and Impotent Personalities

Omnipotent-Impotent Relationships	Initially creates a magnetic attraction for each person.
	Omnipotent gives too much to impotent.
	Impotent demands too much of omnipotent.
	Omnipotent feels guilty when he does not give as much as impotent wants.
	Impotent feels anger and rejection if demands on omnipotent are not met.
	Each person needs the other to carry out his or her role.
	If romantic, at first can be highly sexually charged.
	May end when omnipotent is exhausted and impotent feels angry and slighted.
Impotent-Impotent Relationships	Neither can give much support to the other.
	Can be cordial as long as their focus is on common interests.
	Experience increased animosity, arguing, and friction as each person wants his or her way in the relationship.
	Become jeopardized if one or the other risks losing a supportive omnipotent to the other.
	If romantic, can create sexual frustration.
	May end because of conflict over each wanting to be the top dog.
Omnipotent-Omnipotent Relationships	Both resist giving or accepting much support from the other.
	Can be cordial if focus is on common interests outside the emotional realm of giving and getting support.
	Often cause perfectionistic nitpicking of each other because each thinks she or he has the perfect way of thinking or behaving that is superior to the other.
	Become jeopardized when too much criticizing of each other drives them apart.
	If romantic, may lead to sexual impotence in one or both.
	May end over conflict that the other is not "perfect enough."

While dating, they gradually began to nitpick with one another. Melanie critiqued Lucas's use of a word or the way he loaded the family dishwasher. Lucas complained that Melanie did not wash her hairbrush frequently enough or about the way she had the back seat of her car arranged. Each would approach the other with an attitude of "I know what perfection is and you're not doing it right!"

At times, this led to bickering, which drove them apart in a mutual huff, and they would break up. They dated other people in high school. But, by the time they finished college and married, they never again separated. Over time they lessened the nitpicking, became more empathetic, and supported one another.

Melanie became a paralegal, which required more course work at night and on weekends after doing a full day's work. Lucas learned to cook so he could feed them both and she could study and go to classes. Lucas became the owner of an art gallery. Periodically, he had to travel for weeks at a time. While Lucas was away, Melanie managed their household.

They thought of what the other might need, would mention it and ask questions. "You seem pretty tired lately. Are you? Do you think we should plan a vacation? Would that help you?" Or, "How about I take you out to dinner and dancing this week? Would you enjoy a romantic getaway?" Or, "You mentioned you've had a hard week and had several calls from your sick mother. Is there a way I can help? Can we talk about it?"

Commentary

Melanie and Lucas are both omnipotents. They show a great deal of care for one another to help meet each other's needs. They have trouble pinpointing their own needs, but each one has learned to help the other out with this. And, over time they learned to critique each other less.

Impotent-Impotent Marriage

The smallest number of marital combinations falls into the impotent-impotent category. With both individuals oriented toward pleasurable activities and shunning responsibilities, these marriages tend to be the most unstable. We found that with great support from family and friends, these tumultuous relationships may survive for a few years.

Andrea and Andy

Andrea and Andy, in their late twenties, had been married for two years. They were an attractive couple and accomplished in their careers. Both were tall and slender with well-toned physiques. Andy was a hairdresser and Andrea worked at a bank. They had met at the gym where they both worked out. They both said their main attraction to one another was purely physical and sexual. When first dating they loved partying together with friends late into the night.

In their first year of dating they began to argue over where they would go on dates and what they would do together. Each of them wanted his or her way. Andrea preferred attending women's sporting events, while Andy preferred outdoor activities of camping, hiking, canoeing, and skiing. They found they rarely could compromise. They blew up a lot verbally with one another, and sometimes physically, hitting and slapping one another. More than once they ended up in the emergency room with injuries.

Typically, they would become angry and leave one another in a huff, then go to separate friends and family members, complaining about the other one being "so self-ish." Their friends and families spent a great deal of time consoling them and propping them up emotionally. After a day apart they returned home, had sex, and behaved as if everything was fine. They would not bring up their spat to look at it, discuss, or figure out what their problem was. In time, they erupted again with more conflict.

When asked why they frequently went through this rather than breaking up, they replied, "Because we love one another." "He's so handsome," Andrea exclaimed. And, "She's so hot," Andy beamed.

Commentary

Since Andrea and Andy are both impotents, neither met many of the other's needs except for sex. When upset, they both sought emotional support from outside the marriage. Each wanted to call the shots in the relationship and expected the other to give in. This did not happen and led to constant conflict with arguments, physical aggression, violence, and breakups followed by getting back together. They admired one another as they admired themselves, but each wanted top billing.

WHAT YOU DISCOVERED IN THIS CHAPTER

- Marriages have a low success rate. Failed marriages exceed 50 percent. Even in long-term marriages, the relationships may be disappointing.
- Most marriages are omnipotent-impotent pairs. These opposite roles are drawn to one another with a strong emotional and physical affinity.
- True love is not the blind frenzy of emotion that omnipotents and impotents experience when they describe "falling in love" with one another.
- Love rests on high regard for another person, not on his or her *performance* in a role.
- Couples overlook and dismiss early problems in their courtship and marriage.
- The marriage relationship erodes after a few years because an omnipotent grows exhausted, doing more and more to please an impotent. An impotent escalates his demands and does less and less for his omnipotent spouse.
- Some less common marriages are omnipotent pairs, which may endure longer, and impotent pairs, which may be quite volatile and unstable.

CHAPTER EIGHT

Conflicts in Marriage

In Chapter 7 we explained how omnipotent and impotent partners function within marriage, and how the characteristic deficiencies of each role can lead to boredom, conflict, and eventually separation and divorce. Omnipotent and impotent spouses often continue their relationship without acknowledging the reality of their marital problems and the predicament they are in. In this chapter, we focus on some of the most common obstacles that couples face and need to be able to work on: sex and extramarital affairs, financial conflicts, coparenting struggles, and addiction. These are frequent quandaries in many marriages.

Sex in Marriage

We know that omnipotents have unconscious fantasies of finding a fragile, helpless person to protect. And, we discovered that impotents seek a personal hero who is powerful yet gentle—a protector against all the dragons of life who offers endless caring and loyalty. Both omnipotent and impotent personalities base their attraction to each other on compatibility, experience, appearance, social class, education, and personality. **WHEN OMNIPOTENT-IMPOTENT ATTRACTION BECOMES HIGHLY CHARGED, EACH PERSON ENTERS A STATE OF CONDITIONED, RITUALISTIC RESPONDING, MUCH LIKE A MATING DANCE, WHICH ELIMINATES ALL CONSIDERATION OF REALITY-BASED FACTORS. SEX IS ONE OF THE PRIMARY WAYS COUPLES GIVE AND RECEIVE SUPPORT.** Omnipotents are focused on giving pleasure during sex and may unconsciously see their sex organ as having magical powers to gratify others.

Sex for impotents is quite different. Due to impotents' egocentricity, they seek sex primarily for their own gratification. **FOR IMPOTENTS, SEX REPRESENTS**

AN OPPORTUNITY FOR INSTANT ENJOYMENT. SEX ALSO BECOMES A METHOD FOR IMPO-TENTS TO ATTACH THEMSELVES TO OMNIPOTENTS IN ORDER TO RECEIVE SUPPORT.

When an impotent meets an attractive omnipotent, he or she desires to cling to this strong omnipotent person. Although impotents are usually quite inert, at first they become more attentive and alert and put forth a rare burst of energy. They muster an unusual show of seductive charm sufficient to ensure a secure, permanent relationship with the omnipotent they desire.

At this point, impotents appear superficially like omnipotents, eager and enthusiastic about providing what the omnipotent may want. This is the courtship dance. If impotents remain in their customary inert mode, they would not form the relationship in the first place. Their burst of seemingly supportive behaviors usually subsides rapidly once they secure their bond with omnipotents. This behavior serves a secondary but very useful purpose for both impotents and omnipotents. It confirms that omnipotents, when given only a brief show of support, will repay it with a lifetime commitment to impotents.

Omnipotents often look back on the excited, unforgettable premarital sexual excitement with perplexity and wonder what subsequently changed. Early on in marriage impotents welcomed sexual attention by omnipotents and vice versa. But later in their marriages, impotents may believe their omnipotent partner has a perverse interest in sex. Well into a marriage, impotents may resent the sexual urges of omnipotents if they do not correspond exactly with the impotents' own desires. This is because impotents expect omnipotents to think only of the impotent's sexual needs and have no sexual desires of his or her own.

Frequently, sex becomes a focus of discontent and conflict because, like all other aspects of the relationship, the couple focuses on following the impotents' whims and desires. If omnipotents have different thoughts about sex, this will create conflict. Omnipotents may feel guilty and believe they must be sexually abnormal if they are not on the same mental wavelength as impotents. Omnipotents usually decide to accommodate impotents and provide services to them on demand. Although the couple's sexual activities are almost exclusively dominated by the impotent's wants and needs, the couple may declare they have a "good sexual relationship."

Extramarital Affairs Are Not All About Sex

Extramarital relationships have always occurred, and we cannot disregard this lengthy history in any discussion of marriage. Throughout history, most societies have condemned extramarital affairs. We usually *blame them for creating* problems in marriages. But we have not given much consideration to understanding the nature and ubiquity of adultery. **As WITH DRUG OR ALCOHOL ABUSE, PEOPLE DO NOT RESORT TO ADULTEROUS RELATIONSHIPS BECAUSE THEY DESIRE ITS DESTRUCTIVE EFFECTS. IF WE TRY TO UNDERSTAND *WHY* ADULTERY TAKES PLACE IN A TROUBLED MARRIAGE, WE LEARN MUCH MORE THAN IF WE MERELY CONDEMN IT.**

In the same way that our appetite for food is necessary for our body to sustain life, our sexual needs are also initiated by physiological processes. People from early human history who first created marriage vows had already experienced the problems of infidelity. They hoped to eradicate such problems, so they created vows of eternal fidelity as a required part of all marriage ceremonies.

Many elements make up emotional support, of which sex is but one. Since a marriage's support system tends to become a one-way emotional conduit, this is also true in the sexual relationship. In some marriages, impotents may find sex too exhausting and bothersome and become sexually dysfunctional or unresponsive to their omnipotent spouses. Couples typically consider all sorts of physical causes for this dysfunction, but the cause is often solely emotional. Two things are happening. First, impotents will not provide sex or support of any type to their omnipotent spouses unless it pleases them. And second, impotents discount all the support they receive from their omnipotent spouse as inadequate and constantly demand more support. They also may demand more sexual encounters. Omnipotents come to feel desperate that nothing they do is appreciated or acknowledged. When both individuals become disenchanted, the stage is set for adultery. **SEEKING EXTRAMARITAL RELATIONSHIPS ARE ATTEMPTS BY EITHER SPOUSE TO CORRECT FOR AN UNEQUAL DISTRIBUTION OF EMOTIONAL SUPPORT.** Either spouse may take the initiative.

In the more common omnipotent-impotent marriage, the couple accepts the limits of the roles that give the impotent dominance and the omnipotent a subordinate role. But close friends and acquaintances may see the couple quite differently. Their friends and acquaintances may see a devalued omnipotent—who does nothing correctly, sufficiently, or with the correct frequency from an impotent's viewpoint—as generous, loving, and very desirable. They may also see the insatiable impotent—who may be negative and sexually impotent with the omnipotent spouse at home—as gregarious and sexy.

To their great surprise, omnipotents may find they sexually attract people other than their spouses. But all too often these omnipotents feel obligated to perform as their new sexual partner commands in their adulterous romantic liaisons. Many omnipotents will put themselves in the untenable position of trying to provide simultaneous emotional and sexual support to several impotents. Paradoxically, the omnipotents often picture themselves as preying on others sexually when, in reality, anyone who cares to exploit them can easily seduce them. Sometimes omnipotents are drawn to another omnipotent to find the support they need to counter the lack of support and care they each experience in their respective marriages.

SOME IMPOTENTS IGNORE THEIR SPOUSES' ADULTEROUS RELATIONSHIPS. THIS HAPPENS BECAUSE THEY WANT THEIR OMNIPOTENT SPOUSES TO TAKE THEIR SEXUAL AND EMOTIONAL NEEDS ELSEWHERE. When this does happen, it bolsters the impotent's pretense that the omnipotent's needs do not exist. A married omnipotent receives some support through a covert relationship, and, rejuvenated, returns home to further play the omnipotent role with his or her impotent spouse.

If both omnipotent lovers are married, they often gain enough emotional support to return to their impotent partners and to continue to fulfill their roles. Now the omnipotents will give even more to their impotent spouses, since guilt is added to the omnipotents' problems. ADULTERY IS MUCH LIKE A PAIN-RELIEVING DRUG THAT PERMITS YOU TO ENDURE A BAD SITUATION AND PRO-LONGS THE SUFFERING.

IMPOTENTS SEEK ADULTERY AS A MEANS OF MEETING INSATIABLE NEEDS FOR DEPENDENCY. FOR IMPOTENTS, SEX IS NOT A MUTUALLY SUPPORTIVE EXPERIENCE BUT A MEANS OF MEETING THEIR ENDLESS NEEDS BY BEING PHYSICALLY AND SEXUALLY CON-NECTED TO ANOTHER PERSON. Impotents will not and cannot commit deeply to others because they have learned only to commit in barter for their continuous gratification. However, impotents may ardently want a com-mitment from others and may be extremely seductive around anyone who will be attentive to them to capture their commitment.

Impotents may have a total lack of interest in sex with their omnipo-tent spouse, yet become blatantly sexual and unrestrained with other people outside their marriages. IMPOTENTS ARE MORE EXCITED BY SEDUCTION THAN BY LONG, ENDURING RELATIONSHIPS. THEY MAY LOSE INTEREST IN THEIR DESIRABLE, TREASURED NEW LOVE INTEREST ONCE THEY ACQUIRE A NEW LOVER. Impotents' pursuit of other sex partners and total disinterest in sex within their marriage is consistent with the impotent role that omnipotent spouses have come to expect.

In adulterous relationships, omnipotents can act dependent only as long as their dependence is covert. They require the same nurturance and sup-port as anyone else, but their omnipotent conditioning does not allow them to acknowledge their needs for support from others. They only allow them-selves to seek emotional support on the sly or in brief episodes.

ADULTERY WILL CONTINUE TO PLAGUE MARRIAGES AS LONG AS OUR EMOTION-
ALLY CONDITIONED ROLES GOVERN OUR WAYS OF RELATING TO ONE ANOTHER. THESE
ROLES IMPOSE IMPOSSIBLE STANDARDS IN HOW WE MANAGE EMOTIONAL SUPPORT IN
OUR RELATIONSHIPS.

Extramarital Affairs Change the Flow of Emotional Support

Many of us ignore adultery within our marriages, but we almost never
fail to detect it. The addition of a third party inevitably changes the flow
of emotional support. When omnipotents commit adultery, they expect
even less support from their impotent spouses. When impotents engage
in adultery, they receive an additional boost of emotional support from
their lover. That support makes them noticeably more satisfied and agreeable, and they make fewer demands on their omnipotent spouses. Most of
the time omnipotents feel guilt and shame over meeting their needs for
support in their extramarital relationships. But impotents feel justified in
having their needs met by a paramour. As you might expect, impotents go
to little trouble to conceal their extramarital activity.

WHEN RIGID ROLES GRADUALLY CAUSE THEIR MARRIAGE TO BECOME A TEDIOUS,
REPETITIVE EXERCISE, MANY MARRIED COUPLES WELCOME EXTRAMARITAL RELATION-
SHIPS. One of the spouses finds a new sex partner to transfuse the relationship with new emotional support. Although unfaithful spouses are often
judged for seeking sex outside of marriage, we found their need for emotional support is vastly more important.

Some omnipotents may gladly accept impotents' having a new partner.
They may accept this new person in the same manner as they always have
accommodated the desires of their impotent spouses. Omnipotents do this
with the hope that their spouses, after years of complaining of how unful-
filled they are, will finally feel satisfied. Omnipotents may find their impotent spouses' paramour agreeable and acceptable, since he or she is most
often a fellow omnipotent.

Quite often impotents agree to a third person in the marriage and do not
react as if victimized by a rival. This takes place when the lover assumes
the distasteful aspects of marriage that impotents do not like. Since impotents find it difficult, and even repugnant, to meet the needs of omnipotents,
introducing a new person who will take over these unsavory marital chores
may come as a relief.

THE THREESOME ESTABLISHES A NEW EQUILIBRIUM THAT FEELS BETTER EMOTION-
ALLY THAN THE PRIOR BORING AGONY THE MARRIAGE HAD BECOME. IT IS A BIZARRE
ATTEMPT AT A SOLUTION. HOWEVER, IT ALLOWS ALL THE PARTICIPANTS TO REMAIN
CONSISTENT IN THEIR ROLES AND AVOIDS THE REALITIES AND EFFORT REQUIRED TO
CORRECT A SICK, DYSFUNCTIONAL MARRIAGE.

Adultery Creates Havoc

Most spouses do not welcome adultery, and discovering it causes an eruption in the marriage that has permanent repercussions. Since most marriages exist with both spouses staying locked in their roles, over time communication diminishes as the roles become second nature and rather mindless. Words are almost unnecessary. Then one spouse becomes involved with a lover, which alters the pattern of their accustomed emotional support.

In our practices, omnipotents frequently told us they felt tempted to seek support outside the marriage because they did not feel their impotent spouses were meeting their needs. They thought their only option was to have an extramarital relationship. By taking a new sex partner, omnipotents in effect further relieve their impotent spouses of responsibility in the marriage relationship. Omnipotents also respond to impotents' demands to look elsewhere for their emotional support. But omnipotents will hide their extramarital relationships as much as possible to maintain the façade of omnipotence in the marriage, to their family and to their community.

Impotents may feel quite satisfied in their marriages. But when their omnipotent spouse is absent, even briefly, or when they believe their spouse is not sufficiently attentive, they may look for additional support outside the marriage. In these situations, impotents may conceal the new relationship to avoid jeopardizing the acceptable parts of their marriages. The new lover becomes a spare support system held in reserve for any time an impotent wants it. In addition, impotents who appear indifferent to sex with their omnipotent spouse want to avoid disclosing an erotic interest in a new partner.

WHEN A SPOUSE DISCOVERS AN EXTRAMARITAL RELATIONSHIP, THIS USUALLY CREATES AN INTOLERABLE SITUATION FOR BOTH SPOUSES. OMNIPOTENTS OFTEN REACT WITH SELF-BLAME, FOR THEY BELIEVE THEIR SPOUSES' INFIDELITY IS A RESULT OF THEIR OWN DEFICIENCIES. Omnipotents put little responsibility on impotents, whose straying is often just one of many self-indulgent acts.

When impotents discover their omnipotent spouses in a flirtation or an affair, their reaction usually creates permanent consequences because impotents will mercilessly blame and remind omnipotents for decades of their misbehavior. Omnipotents, who cannot forgive themselves for making mistakes or being dependent on others, feel extraordinary guilt for their adultery. Impotents do not forgive and assume great outrage at such inconsiderate treatment by their omnipotent spouse. Since impotents are unaware of how they deny omnipotents' needs to be independent, they see no reason for omnipotents to need other people. In this situation, omnipotents often feel crucified and guilty for being dependent on a lover and being adulterous.

Adultery Prolongs Many Marriages

Historically, adultery has been condemned for interfering with and ending so many marriages. But adultery also perpetuates many marriages, perhaps more than it ends. Omnipotents who seek support outside the marriage, most often from another omnipotent, remain committed to the marriage. ON THE OTHER HAND, SINCE IMPOTENTS SEEK SELF-INDULGENCE WITH A LOVER, THEY RARELY HAVE ANY INTENTION TO END THEIR MARRIAGE OR TO MAKE A COMMITMENT TO THEIR NEW PARTNER. AS A RESULT, BAD MARRIAGES CONTINUE DESPITE ADULTEROUS AFFAIRS.

From the outset of a new marriage, spouses could use the onset of extramarital attraction as a warning sign of the need for them to have frank and deeper communications. This would make the couple aware that problems exist that they need to figure out and correct if possible. The very real defects in the pattern of emotional support in the marriage might be related to the extramarital attraction. In this way, spouses could tackle the problem objectively and could likely arrive at a solution. Unfortunately, this rarely occurs. Instead, after initial emotional upheaval from learning of a new attraction or an adulterous relationship, married couples revert to their old roles and proceed toward even greater future difficulties. Here is a case example.

Rick and Paolo

Rick and Paolo met when they were in their twenties. They were both ballet dancers. They lived together as a couple and then legally married while in their thirties. They adopted two children as babies, a girl and a boy. Paolo stayed home to raise the children. Rick continued dancing until his early forties, then became a ballet instructor.

Paolo said he was attracted to Rick because he was such a "free spirit." By this, Paolo meant Rick said and did what he wanted, whenever he wanted. Paolo admired this because he had always been quiet and restrained, holding back on voicing his own feelings, thoughts, and opinions. Rick was attracted to Paolo's down-to-earth nature and his simple, domestic style of living. Paolo enjoyed cooking, gardening, interior design, running the household, and caring for the children. Rick cared for none of these more mundane tasks, but he enjoyed that Paolo did. Rick was most interested in his ballet performances and later teaching, especially showing off his prowess in choreography.

Their relationship and marriage lumbered along with Paolo in the omnipotent role and Rick in the impotent role. Eventually, they both grew aware of significant conflicts that began to seriously endanger their marriage and became divided on marital issues. Paolo grew perplexed that Rick provided little support in dealing with the marriage's responsibilities, especially with helping to raise their children. To Paolo, it seemed that Rick deliberately created new problems when unresolved problems were already overwhelming Paolo. For example, Rick insisted everyone uproot themselves every couple of years so he could take new jobs elsewhere, when this was not necessary for either financial or job advancement reasons.

Rick's previous admiration of Paolo's domestic interests, over time, gave way to criticism. He complained Paolo spent too much time on the children and the home and not enough time on nightly social life with their ballet colleagues. Rick felt Paolo was a boring companion. Rick and Paolo each began to resent the qualities that had originally been the other partner's main attraction, and soon Rick began an extramarital affair.

With great agony, Paolo began to realize he could not fulfill Rick's insatiable demands for frequent moves, for little engagement with the children, and for constant social life. Paolo began to devalue himself, feeling responsible for the situation. Rick felt betrayed and abused and blamed Paolo. This only made Paolo feel worse. They endured many emotional traumas and exhausted themselves trying to resolve their difficulties. Over time they grew increasingly wary of any exposure to further rejections and withdrew emotionally from one another.

They tried marriage counseling, but Paolo continued to feel guilty and depressed because he carried all the responsibility for their dysfunction. Rick used the therapy time to complain about Paolo's shortcomings and never took responsibility for his own failures to assume more responsibility in their marriage nor for his extramarital affair. They decided to divorce.

Commentary

In any marriage, either person may initiate separation and divorce. Omnipotents do so only as a last resort, in keeping with their never-say-die personalities. Omnipotents act only when convinced that they can do nothing more that will be satisfactory to impotents. This is what happened to Paolo and Rick. Rick, the impotent, left the marriage, deciding to terminate it after feeling cheated and abused in being denied the perfection he sought from Paolo. Rick chipped away at Paolo, recording Paolo's every imperfection, until nothing remained. Paolo accepted their joint failure as his sole responsibility. Each of them played their role to the point of exhaustion, and they remained oblivious to any other options that may have offered resolution for their conflicts.

RICK AND PAOLO USED MANY RATIONALIZATIONS TO EXPLAIN THEIR DIVORCE. BUT THE ACTUAL REASON WAS AN UNCONSCIOUS MISMANAGEMENT OF EMOTIONAL SUPPORT IN THEIR RELATIONSHIP. As their children grew, they adopted these same defective approaches for living in their own lives. Inevitably, Rick and Paolo developed a variety of emotional problems from the failure of their marriage roles. Let's look at these.

Emotional Illnesses in Marriage

Emotional illnesses in one or both spouses are the most common evidence of troubles threatening a marriage. Emotional support by a spouse outweighs the support from any other relationship by a wide margin. Emotional health is based on internal self-worth as we balance the emotional support we receive against the loss of our emotional support.

Throughout life we experience rises and falls in self-esteem because of swings in the unconscious and intangible balance of emotional support in our relationships. With extreme swings, we may wonder about our mental stability. We may even wonder whether we have bipolar disorder as we experience highs and lows. But, these changes are just the consequences that happen when our partners withhold emotional support. For these reasons, the ebbs and flows in our relationships exert control over the quality of our lives as well as in our day-to-day emotional well-being.

Paolo, acting in the omnipotent role, became susceptible to depression. He was obsessed with performing perfectly and was an ever-busy, meticulous person, even as a boy. Then he married Rick who had his own personal definition of perfection. During the marriage Paolo adjusted to whatever Rick's peculiar individual tastes might be, causing Paolo to devalue himself whenever he could not perform to Rick's desires. Paolo never questioned Rick's demands, but, instead, complied with them in a do-or-die manner.

Concerned about his increasing depression, Paolo consulted with his doctor and with a counselor. Paolo seemed to "have it all"—thriving children, no financial problems, and a breadwinner spouse. But, Paolo felt he had failed at his whole reason for living—to be able to totally satisfy another person and control all the problems for that person. He condemned himself and thought of suicide, wondering whether the world would be a better place without him.

Rick had emotional problems of a different sort. As an impotent, he had an exquisite sensitivity to and intolerance of any discomfort. He found release by complaining to friends and professionals about their marital problems. Rick resented Paolo's reminding him he had a spouse and two children he must help care for. Rick readily provided a litany of ongoing complaints about how difficult his life was. This ploy was effective in mustering support from everyone around him.

Rick also attributed his discontent to a minor physical condition combined with smaller ailments such as acid reflux and stomachaches. He received antireflux and pain medications, the latter intended for intermittent use. Over time, he became addicted to the pain medications. They zoned him out, allowing him to remain inert and not deal with his woes and conflicts with Paolo.

Chronic and excessive use of drugs is a sign of deep emotional troubles (see last case in this chapter). When we self-administer drugs, such as alcohol, prescription, or illegal drugs, we take them in hopes they will alleviate or lessen our emotional suffering. But they do not, and our problems progress unchanged. Actually, resorting to drugs delays our taking any specific action to address our problems, and our underlying problems will be aggravated by the drug habit. We may also have serious drug reactions or overdoses, which have permanent consequences.

REALITY IS AN EROSIVE FORCE. WE CAN CURB IT ONLY SO LONG BEFORE IT BEGINS TO REPLACE THE MAGICAL AND IDEALIZED ILLUSIONS ON WHICH WE PILOT MOST OF OUR MARRIAGES. EVENTUALLY, WE PAY THE PRICE OF SELF-DECEPTION IN

THE COIN OF SUFFERING EMOTIONAL DYSFUNCTIONS, UNHAPPINESS, AND DISILLUSION ABOUT OTHERS AND OURSELVES. IT IS NOT ONLY IN MARRIAGE THAT WE ENACT SUCH ROLES. WE PERFORM THE SAME ROLES IN MANY OF OUR RELATIONSHIPS.

The average marriage lumbers along in a predictable way. Spouses diligently complete their assigned parts and relate to each other within the limits of these roles. An air of surrender or resignation predominates. Enthusiasm and zeal declines both for one another and for their future together. A double standard is almost always apparent. Omnipotents must go above and beyond their usual high standard to be acknowledged by impotents, while impotents receive constant attention and extraordinary appreciation for even the smallest show of support. Their children also learn these roles and values. They recognize unconsciously that their omnipotent parent is subordinate, rarely acknowledged, often critiqued, and always in the shadow of their dominant, impotent parent.

Financial Conflict

Both omnipotents and impotents can be either misers or spendthrifts with money. Most often omnipotents are judicious with family funds, because they conscientiously try to keep money in bank accounts and make sure they pay the bills on time. But omnipotents will give money freely to impotent spouses, even when an impotent spends unreasonable sums on frivolous things. As is true in other aspects of their relationship, impotents gladly spend money on themselves but may be stingy with omnipotent spouses and children. MANY IMPOTENTS ARE IMPULSIVE SPENDERS AND HAVE PROBLEMS WITH OVERSPENDING AND GOING INTO DEBT, WHILE OMNIPOTENTS ROUTINELY HAVE A DIFFICULT TIME SPENDING MONEY ON THEMSELVES. Here is an example.

Carmen and Eugenia

A short time into marriage, many couples discover they have arguments over money— how much to spend or save, what to spend it on or save it for, and who should be the biggest spender and biggest saver. Carmen and Eugenia were no different. They married in their early thirties. Both of their families were Central American immigrants. Both worked full-time and had college degrees. They met at a neighborhood group organized to help young Hispanic gay people get first jobs.

Two years into their marriage, Eugenia began asking Carmen for extra money to make purchases. Eugenia wanted some expensive stereo equipment and a new high-end sports car. Eugenia didn't want to have to make monthly car payments and wanted to pay in full for the car. Carmen reminded her they were saving for a house down payment and told Eugenia her "wants" were too pricey for them at this point in their marriage. They argued. Eugenia told Carmen she was "entitled" to have good things that she wanted. After all, her parents had been relatively impoverished immigrants who did without a lot of things to allow their children to succeed by going to college and getting well-paying jobs. Carmen countered with anger about their need to save if they were going to buy a house and continue retirement savings. Eventually, they wanted to have children and would cut back to only one income. They needed to "plan for this," Carmen yelled at Eugenia.

Financial conflicts escalated for this couple. In this example, Eugenia was in the impotent role and Carmen an omnipotent. Eugenia expected to have her way and have Carmen acquiesce to her monetary wants. They both ignored the reality of what was called for in their situation. Their emotional conditioning, and not their situation, dictated their responses to one another. Over the years, Carmen gave in to Eugenia and allowed Eugenia to spend large sums of money on her expensive desires. They continued to accumulate debt until Carmen filed for divorce.

We found that omnipotents are usually good savers and stingy about spending money on themselves. But, like Carmen, most omnipotents will overspend on impotents and work themselves into debt. We also found that impotents spend freely, sometimes their own money but especially *others'* funds. Impotents can be stingy with spending *their own money*. They may only do so for another impotent, such as an impotent family member, and only briefly, and they will *forever* remind the recipient of their extreme generosity.

Parenting

Many people do not realize that they will encounter conflict over child rearing until after the birth of their children. During dating, partners may have discussed having children or not. But this is as far as most couples go. SINCE RAISING CHILDREN IS ONE OF THOSE LIFE ACTIVITIES THAT TAKES PLACE AUTOMATICALLY ACCORDING TO YOUR EMOTIONAL CONDITIONING, YOU WON'T KNOW HOW YOU WILL PARENT EACH CHILD UNTIL HE OR SHE ARRIVES. EACH COUPLE IS UNAWARE OF HOW THEIR CHOICE OF PARTNER PLAYS INTO THEIR PARENTING. Conflict in parenting your children will come up any time you and your mate face differences in your respective emotional conditionings and the way you unconsciously condition each child in your family.

Either before or just after the birth of each child, most parents go forward without much disagreement about child rearing. They may raise one child to be an impotent, then the next to be an omnipotent, or two in a row to be omnipotents or impotents, and so on. But, for some parents, the *reality* of the existing situation of raising each child becomes paramount and may indicate that parents need to make changes in how they treat their children. Here is an example.

Erica and Jon

Jon and Erica, both in their early thirties, have just given birth to a daughter, Arleen. They decide Erica will keep working, since her salary is higher than Jon's. Jon will stay home and care for Arleen. He takes on his job as parent with gusto, preparing Arleen's bottles and making her food from scratch. He records all of Arleen's milestones in her baby book, regularly takes photos and videos of her as she grows, takes her to the park, reads to her, and plays with her. He also lets her play alone for periods of time when he takes care of housework, cooks, or meets with friends.

Everything goes smoothly for a while until Erica begins to comment to Jon, "You are paying too much attention to Arleen. Let her cry it out sometimes, and let her play by herself more. You don't need to be involved with her all the time. Spend more time with me." Jon protests that Arleen needs the attention he gives her.

When Erica is home on nights and weekends, Jon still does most of Arleen's care, as Erica is not much interested. Arleen does well in her development. Erica spends time on clarinet studies, a longtime undertaking since her teens, and plays in a local volunteer symphony. Although Erica is happy to be less involved with Arleen, she critiques Jon's time with their daughter and often wants Jon's attention diverted to her and away from Arleen.

As Arleen grows, she prefers going to Jon for comfort and for having her needs met. Erica becomes increasingly angry with Arleen for not wanting to be with her more, yells at her and calls her names, putting her down with, "You're a bad girl." Jon yells at Erica for doing this, then Arleen cries and everyone is miserable. Parenting conflict ensues.

Commentary

Jon is an omnipotent who wants to raise Arleen and be the best parent he can be. Erica, an impotent, is not particularly interested in Arleen's daily care. She wanted Arleen to be Jon's primary responsibility. But mostly Erica wants attention for herself.

Their parenting struggles take place because Erica sees Jon and Arleen as omnipotents, who can always meet Erica's needs. But Jon sees Arleen as having real needs for care because she is a baby, so her needs must be put above Erica's wants. Erica's impotent conditioning prevents her from seeing Arleen's real needs as an infant and toddler.

If another child is born in this family and conditioned as an impotent, Erica may become a very different and perhaps more involved parent. She is likely to identify with an impotent child, providing that this new baby does not jeopardize her connection to her omnipotent, Jon. And Jon might be overindulgent of an impotent child.

Substance Abuse

Substance abuse can indicate emotional problems, dysfunctions, and, at times, emotional illnesses. Often, substance abuse is the cause or result of marital relationship difficulties. When couples have marital conflict or disagreements over anything, one or both may resort to alcohol or drugs to dull the distasteful and upsetting emotions, avoid dealing with conflict, and stay in their respective, although ineffective, conditioned roles.

We found that substance abusers are not all the same. With different emotional conditioning the reasons for resorting to substance use are also different. Omnipotents use drugs in an attempt to preserve their omnipotence and to avoid making necessary changes in themselves to lessen their omnipotent roles.

Omnipotents turn to drugs and alcohol as an attempt to deal with depression, social and performance anxiety, low self-esteem and heightened stress, or to escape the tirades of impotents rather than confront them. They are drawn to substance abuse when they are unable to please impotents, rather than say they are already doing enough. They may drink or take drugs as their only form of leisure, at the end of a long day of work, and when they are finally home and know no other way to relax and turn off work. Some omnipotents use substances at the request of impotents who they want to please, even if it means destroying themselves. **MANY OMNIPOTENTS WILL SELF-DESTRUCT THROUGH SUBSTANCE ABUSE RATHER THAN LET IMPOTENTS KNOW THEY ARE QUITTING THE IMPOTENT-PLEASING BUSINESS.**

IMPOTENTS, ON THE OTHER HAND, USE DRUGS AND ALCOHOL TO KEEP THEIR IMPOTENT ROLE INTACT AND AVOID MAKING CHANGES IN THEMSELVES. THEY INDULGE TO ESCAPE RESPONSIBILITIES. THEY ALSO USE DRUGS AS PART OF THEIR IMPULSIVITY, THRILL SEEKING, AND NOVELTY SEEKING RATHER THAN STEP UP, HELP OTHERS, AND PUT OUT MORE EFFORT. Impotent alcoholics may drink first thing in the morning upon arising to avoid the responsibilities of the day. If they become drunk, they will call in sick to work. Here are two case examples.

Caitlyn and Hannah

Caitlyn and Hannah are in their early fifties and have been together for 28 years, the last 6 of them married. Both work full-time and have two daughters in their early twenties. They have had many arguments over how to spend their leisure time since their daughters grew up and moved out of the family home. They decided to marry in hopes that it would decrease their conflict and allow them to grow closer, as they had been years before.

Caitlyn had consistently been the main earner while Hannah stayed home and raised their daughters. When their daughters began college, Hannah returned to work as a nurse, and Caitlyn continued working as a freelance journalist. Caitlyn wanted to travel to Europe and try some adventures in places they had never been. Hannah flatly refused to budge, refusing to travel out of the United States or even out of town.

In past years, Hannah said they had to stay put because of their daughters' schedules at school, in sports, and in band. It became clear Hannah wanted to stay home and not travel anywhere ever. She was busy with activities—volunteering at the library, two book clubs, and water aerobics classes. Hannah was adamant and would not waiver, nor would she compromise with Caitlyn about travel.

Caitlyn sometimes traveled alone or with friends, but she missed having Hannah accompany her. In time, Caitlyn began drinking, at first when out with friends and later alone at bars to avoid going home to Hannah. Caitlyn drank only at night after a full day of work as she always fulfilled her work obligations even though she was hung over. Caitlyn blamed herself for not being able to "fix" the stalemate with Hannah. Over the years, she drank more until she was drinking a fifth of spirits an evening, then stumbling home from a nearby bar and passing out in the guest room or on the sofa. Hannah was angry at Caitlyn for being a drunk but failed to see that she had a role in the problems in their marriage. Hannah thought the problem was Caitlyn's alone.

Commentary

Hannah was in an impotent role and Caitlyn an omnipotent one. Caitlyn was trying desperately to fulfill her omnipotent role by going along with what Hannah wanted about staying home. She drank to numb herself and stay in that role rather than dissolve the relationship or compel Hannah to get therapy with her. Only when Caitlyn developed alcohol-related medical problems did she decide to get professional help for her emotional problems—caused by her relationship problems with Hannah—that led to her drinking. Eventually, Hannah joined her in treatment out of fear of losing Caitlyn, and they were able to improve their relationship and do some traveling together. Caitlyn then stopped drinking.

Sabrina and Henri

This couple was in their late forties. Both worked full-time, Sabrina at a camera store and Henri in a trucking company office. They had two teenagers at home. Recently, Sabrina was promoted to manager. She received a raise and worked longer hours. Henri bristled that Sabrina expected more of him in running the household while she was working. He disliked cooking dinner and picking up the children from sports and music activities.

After Sabrina arrived home in the evening, Henri went out with friends to play pool and drink beer. He came home later and later, more and more drunk. Friends often drove him because he was inebriated. He and Sabrina argued over his drinking. Then he switched to pills—oxycodone and hydrocodone—that he bought off the street. He began to pop pills before work and some days never went in. Eventually he lost his job.

Commentary

Henri was an impotent who became angry when he had to take on more responsibilities due to Sabrina's work schedule and because Sabrina had less time for him. He became a substance abuser to avoid these responsibilities and to maintain his inert impotent role with Sabrina. He wanted to have Sabrina care for him and the children as she had before she received her promotion.

WHAT YOU DISCOVERED IN THIS CHAPTER

- An unconscious mismanagement of emotional support in a marriage can lead to separation and divorce.

- Extramarital relationships are attempts by either spouse to correct the distribution of emotional support within the marriage. Couples can ignore adultery, but it almost never goes undetected within the marriage. Some married couples welcome extramarital relationships because it allows them to remain in their accustomed roles.

- Omnipotents experience stress and devalue themselves due to an impotent spouse's ever-increasing demands, which cannot be fulfilled. They may have emotional illnesses, become depressed, or addicted.

- Impotent spouses become stressed due to not having their demands fulfilled by their omnipotent spouses. They often have emotional illnesses, which are expressed through physical complaints, anger problems, or substance abuse.

- Conflicts over finances revolve around which partner underspends or overspends (or does not save) and who benefits from the spending.

- Many parents agree unconsciously on emotionally conditioned roles for their children. Parenting conflict takes place when reality intrudes and interferes with parents' expected roles.

Questions to Ask Yourself

Did you notice any patterns in your relationships that are similar to the examples given in these chapters? Here are some relationship questions for you to consider:

- When you meet people you may never see again, how do you interact with them?
- Do you notice how you are treated in each brief encounter with another person?
- Do you approach strangers easily and ask for their assistance without hesitation?
- Would your family members and close friends describe you as reasonable, likable, or demanding?
- How do you interact with professionals you consult such as a doctor, dentist, hairdresser, or car mechanic? Do you feel intimidated?
- Do you scrutinize the behavior of professionals, since it may affect the quality of their performance?
- Do you place yourself in their hands with whole-hearted trust?
- Do you think you should also make an effort and participate in your own care?
- How have your relationship choices turned out? When you look back, do you think they indicate good or poor judgment?
- If you have a professional career, do you see each of your patients and clients as individuals? Or, do your clients or patients blur into a group and seem similar to each other?

CHAPTER NINE

Getting Divorced and Single Again

The Decision to Divorce

The institution of marriage is idealized in civilized societies, and divorce is viewed as failure and as evidence of weakness and imperfection. **GENER-ALLY, WE BELIEVE DIVORCE OCCURS BECAUSE OF SOME PERSONAL INADEQUACY. DIVORCE NOT ONLY COMES WITH STIGMA, BUT WE ALSO REGARD IT AS JUSTIFIABLE** *ONLY* **IF INTOLERABLE PRESSURES COMPEL IT.**

Our tendency to condemn divorced people has softened somewhat in recent decades, as we have seen the number of failed marriages increase to a point that almost all families are affected. We have become increasingly more aware of divorce and its impact on our entire families. Over the years, couples have tried many alternatives to both marriage and divorce—cohabitation without marriage, coparenting while living separately, living separately alternating with periods of living together, episodic flings with rotating partners or with more than one partner at a time—but without significantly improved results for their relationships.

Each generation appears to have the illusion of being more enlightened than preceding generations. In turn, each younger generation believes it can profit from its forebears' naiveté in devising improved solutions for marriage. Yet, since ancient times little has changed concerning our attitudes toward marriage and divorce. Even in the third century, Romans were concerned about the high divorce rate. We constantly chase fads that give us an illusion of innovation and progress as we try out new ways of relating.

ALTHOUGH MANY OF US CONDEMN DIVORCE, FEELING WE RESORT TO IT TOO EASILY, WE DOUBT THOSE WHO EXPERIENCE DIVORCE WOULD AGREE. For most people, divorce is a last resort, when living with the other spouse becomes intolerable. Each spouse experiences a personal rejection and sense of failure at being unable to control conflicts within their relationship. Each will face the loneliness of separation and the need to reconstruct his or her life, without fully understanding what forces created the rift.

Our deep-seated fear of being alone significantly inhibits the desire to divorce. Many married people delay separation, questioning their ability to thrive if they leave a familiar relationship. This is especially true for omnipotents who express feelings of worthlessness when they lose an impotent to care for. After all, omnipotents have lived to support others and base their self-worth on their services to impotents. Omnipotents prefer not to live alone. Loss of their impotent partner is an emotional experience, which may feel like they have lost their reason to live.

For impotents who consider divorce, their characteristic arrogance and heightened self-importance persuades them they will do quite well on their own. They wonder if their subordinate and devalued omnipotent spouse can function in their absence. Since this viewpoint is a projection of impotents, separation and divorce may lead to an unexpectedly good adjustment for omnipotents but may not turn out well for impotents. Impotents may be unable to manage their finances, have trouble setting up life on their own, and feel lonely. The loneliness of impotents has a definite direction and purpose, as they long for the return of a caring protector that they rarely, if ever, have gone without since childhood.

Each Mate Continues to Act in the Same Role during Divorce as in the Marriage

When we finally accept the inevitability of separation and divorce, the first steps we take are to act on our decision. During divorce and afterward, we found that separating couples continue in the same roles as in the marriage. Nothing really changes in the spousal roles. Omnipotents continue to bear all responsibility, being more concerned with impotents' postdivorce welfare than with their own.

Characteristically, omnipotents surrender many tangible assets from the marriage and may also surrender custody of the children when and if demanded by their impotent spouses. Most often in the divorce process omnipotents are left with overwhelming responsibilities and debt because they continue to expect themselves to cater to impotents and ask for nothing in return. For years after divorce, omnipotents often find they are unable to turn to new relationships, as they remain financially and psychologically committed to their impotent ex-spouses. Here is an example.

Marcus

Marcus appeared to be an upbeat 62-year-old man. After three divorces, he had been dating a woman for 18 months. Marcus explained, "She seems very different from my ex-wives. She is friendly, enjoys getting out and doing things—concerts, travel, visiting grandkids—and she's kind to me. She wants to get married, but I'm not so sure. I have a bad track record with women and marriage."

Marcus paid spousal support to all three ex-wives. Whenever any of them called with a problem, whether a leaky toilet or conflict with children or grandchildren, he would attempt to solve it. He feared upsetting his ex-wives if he said no to them, and he feared they would all be destitute if he asked the court for relief on the spousal payments.

Marcus was overextended financially and emotionally, still wrapped up in his omnipotent married role for his three ex-wives. He had nothing left for a new wife, even for one who appeared to be a "different woman," and who would perhaps be less draining emotionally, and he had nothing left for himself.

Friends and acquaintances often involve themselves in every aspect of divorce. The divorcing person receives comments from both still married and divorced friends. Both groups believe their personal experience equips them to discuss matters with a friend in the throes of divorce. They inevitably ask this question to open the discussion: "What happened?"

By and large, friends react in a consistent fashion. They tend to critique omnipotents about their apparent abandonment of duty. Friends may be skeptical and assume that omnipotents' actions are all self-serving. On the other hand, friends usually offer impotents great sympathy and solicitude at their being deserted and exposed to the pressures of daily life.

A FRIEND'S DIVORCE CREATES ANXIETY AMONG THE MARRIED COUPLES OF THE DIVORCING COUPLES' SOCIAL SET. These couples also react according to their marital roles. Omnipotents may judge their omnipotent divorcing friends because they have failed to keep their marriage vows. And, impotents of both sexes join ranks to support divorcing impotents. The result is that impotents receive a burst of support while omnipotents are criticized and receive diminished support during their divorce crisis.

Going to Court

The courts and legal system often share the same confusion about divorce as the general public. In today's civil legal proceedings, we expect judges not only to know law but to also know about marriage. Judges learn about law in law school. But they learn about relationships and marriages in the same manner as the couples for whom they make decisions. They learn about the marriage relationship from *their parents.* **THE JUDGES IN ANY COURT HAVE UNDERGONE THE SAME EMOTIONAL CONDITIONING PROCESS AS THEIR CLIENTS—EITHER TO BE IMPOTENT OR OMNIPOTENT IN A RANGE FROM MILD TO MODERATE TO SEVERE. THE EMOTIONAL CONDITIONING OF JUDGES AND MEDIATORS AFFECTS THE DIVORCING COUPLE.**

In divorce, many omnipotents will simply give everything to impotents, all the assets, child support, maintenance, and even the children. This is in keeping with their characteristic conditioned roles. Even if their attorney objects to the unfair division of property and assets, omnipotent clients often insist on sacrificing themselves. Omnipotents are incurably trusting, and they follow the basic inviolable rule that omnipotents look after impotents. Omnipotents expect themselves to manage on their own, which can lead them straight into bankruptcy.

UNDER MANY CONDITIONS, DIVORCING IMPOTENTS RECEIVE TREMENDOUS SYMPATHY FROM NEARLY EVERYONE—RELATIVES, FRIENDS, AND THEIR DEPARTING SPOUSES. Without their protective omnipotent spouses, impotents feel totally defenseless, since they are accustomed to receiving most of the emotional support within the family. Nothing changes during divorce except impotents receive even more support as both impotents and omnipotents rally to support them. They receive support from impotents because they respond positively to one another, and they receive inordinate support from omnipotents because of omnipotents' unlimited sense of responsibility and need to barge in whenever they hear an impotent's cry of distress.

We have frequently seen these conditioned psychological factors operating and creating profound effects during the legal process of divorce.

Effects of Divorce on Children

The children of divorcing parents withstand the same intense pressures of the parents' conflicts, even when parents try to contain the emotional warfare. Parents who are careful to argue in private underestimate their children's sensitivities. Children are experts in perceiving parents' tensions and moods. They also have good memories and remember conversations in which one parent confides in them and expresses criticism of the other parent.

We found that opposing teams develop in many families, and the scenario for opposing camps often follows a pattern. Impotent parents appeal for increased family support to replace the support previously supplied by their omnipotent spouses and share a natural affinity to rely on their omnipotent children. Omnipotent parents tend to pair off with impotent children so that they, once again, feel good in performing their caretaking job. These two family groups intensify family conflicts and hasten the marriage's decline. During divorce, and for years afterward, some children describe having felt close to one parent and alienated from the other due to the presence of these two groups.

Parents will often say they did not seek divorce sooner because they worried about the effects on their children. DESPITE THE SEVERITY OF PARENTAL DIS-CORD, PARENTS OFTEN FEEL THEIR CHILDREN ARE DOING WELL AND SHOULD STAY IN THE SECURITY OF THEIR HOME WITH MARRIED PARENTS. PARENTS BASE SUCH THINKING ON THEIR ASSUMPTION THAT THEY'RE MAINTAINING A STABLE ENVIRONMENT FOR THEIR CHILDREN. IN REALITY, CHILDREN WITNESS THEIR PARENTS' UNWORKABLE RELATIONSHIP FOR A LONGER PERIOD OF TIME. Since the children began learning their roles in early childhood, they may fare better if their parents model a more reasonable way to navigate parental conflicts, even if they choose to divorce. WHEN PARENTS KEEP CHILDREN IN A STATE OF FALSE SECURITY, THIS SERVES THE NEEDS OF THE PARENTS MORE THAN IT BENEFITS THE DECEIVED CHILDREN.

People often blame divorce for a multitude of problems that show up later in life for children of divorcing parents. Many of us have the idea that being from a broken home explains misfortunes that occur years later. Believing this, we make divorce a convenient scapegoat. But, we have found that problems in marriages, including problems in child rearing, began long before the marital breakdown and dissolution. Instead, it appears that children's early emotional conditioning plants the seeds for emotional illnesses, alcohol and drug abuse, difficult relationships, and other ills. These outcomes are not the result of divorce. Since children learn to manage relationships just as their parents have, they adopt methods that may be effective or defective, as they have been taught to do. Unpleasant experiences in life traumatize some children, while difficulties in life strengthen other children.

While under legal and court scrutiny during divorce, both parents treat children in unnatural ways, and children may feel like pawns. With the marriage breakup under court scrutiny, omnipotent parents, who most often feel increased anxiety, increase their support to their children. They fear their children will reject them for their failure to keep the family intact.

Under conditions of critical examination by the court—custody evaluations and mediation—impotents may show an increased burst of interest in being parents. Their performance is designed to convince the court and others that they have been caring and loving parents to their children all along. In reality, they often left the child rearing to their omnipotent spouses or raised their children in a way that met their own needs to be seen as involved parents.

Custody Battles

In many divorces, bitter custody battles erupt, and the children may wonder whether they are being used as ammunition. Omnipotent spouses are often inclined to share custody with impotent parents. They also urge their children to agree to joint custody and coparenting. But, we have found that impotent parents often have a different strategy. Impotent parents are very aware that omnipotent parents greatly value the relationship with their children. **So, impotents may be determined to deprive omnipotents of custody of their children. This is an impotent's final punishment to an omnipotent spouse, a punishment for creating the marital breakdown that led to their divorce.**

Although some impotent parents may have felt parenting as a burden, they perceive themselves as good parents. They can be oblivious that they are being punitive to their divorcing spouses and are depriving the children of emotional support by the omnipotent parent in a time of crisis. After all, only omnipotent parents offer a good deal of support to the children. Impotent spouses' intent on revenge is foremost on their agendas. Revenge is more important than whether their children are harmed during divorce combat. Many impotents want custody for the total control it gives them over their children's lives.

Often under such circumstances parental alienation takes place. Impotent parents project their alienation onto their omnipotent ex-spouses by brainwashing the children that their omnipotent parents are bad parents and do not love them. In this way impotents strive to alienate their offspring from the omnipotent parent. Children often pick up an impotent parent's projection and follow their lead in denigrating their omnipotent parent. Richard Gardner, MD, called this the *parental alienation syndrome*.[1]

Despite the chaos and upheaval of protracted divorce, family equilibrium returns. As the passions of the custody battle subside and the participants tire of or are exhausted by the strife, the family regroups. Omnipotent children tend to cluster around the impotent parent to give their support. "We feel sorry for dad (or mom)," they often explain. Impotent children, initially outraged at the omnipotent parent's failure to keep everyone happy, drift back to the omnipotent parent for care.

In many divorces, if not the majority, parents, mediators, and judges decide an arrangement for joint or shared custody for the children. Often this translates to parents having each child with them for 50 percent of the time. Some have their children switch over to the other parent's household for half the week, every other week, every other month, every six months, and every variation in between.

Joint custody, with a 50 percent time split for each parent, has been coming more into vogue as a standard custody arrangement. The judiciary likes these joint custody arrangements because they often decrease parents' friction with one another and lessen repeat court appearances. In joint or split physical custody children may switch from the more organized or disciplined environment of their omnipotent parent's home to the unstructured, disorganized, or rigid home of their impotent parent.

We found that children who go back and forth and spend half of their time with each parent suffer quite a bit of emotional upheaval with these arrangements. Omnipotent children can become overwhelmed and suffer emotional problems from attempting to care for their impotent parents. Impotent children may be in constant conflict with their impotent parents due to their role similarities. We have seen that eventually, impotent children may flee their impotent parent to return to their omnipotent parent for caretaking and more structure in their daily lives. Omnipotent parents are more likely to find children's socks, put their homework in their backpack, and make sure they have lunch money.

Children may have a difficult time adapting to the new single lives of their divorced parents. With strong bonds to both parents, children commonly harbor the fantasy their parents will overcome their differences and reconcile. Children may feel increased stress when their parents begin dating, as this scene is incompatible with their idealized memories of mom and dad together. Prior to divorce, omnipotent children believed they had perfect families, while impotent children had memories of being in perfectly secure and protected environments. Both types of youngsters thought their circumstances would last forever. We found that children's personalities play a significant role in any future marriages of their divorced parents.

LIKE KING SOLOMON'S DILEMMA, THESE SPLIT CUSTODY ARRANGEMENTS ARE MEANT TO BE FAIR TO THE PARENTS, ALLOWING EACH EQUAL TIME WITH THEIR CHILDREN. PARENTS, ATTORNEYS, MEDIATORS, AND JUDGES FEEL GOOD ABOUT THESE DECISIONS, BUT WHAT HAPPENS TO THE CHILDREN? DOES EQUAL TIME MEAN CHILDREN WILL BE CARED FOR EQUALLY BY BOTH PARENTS? What we found may surprise you. Others of you will say you've known it all along, based on your experiences with joint or split custody.

In our experience, these joint custody arrangements do not work well. As long as parents are married and together under the same roof, children do not notice the differences between their parents. They regard them as a "generic parent duo." BUT, WHEN PARENTS DIVORCE AND CHILDREN BECOME EXPOSED TO EACH PARENT LIVING SEPARATELY, THE CHILDREN SEE MORE EASILY WHAT EACH PARENT IS LIKE—THEIR QUIRKS, THEIR SUCCESSES AND FAILURES, AND WHAT THEY DO AND DON'T DO FOR THEM.

Due to opposite emotional conditioning of each spouse in most marriages, children in joint physical custody often go between an omnipotent's house and an impotent's home. The two houses usually have vastly different parenting styles. Here is a case example.

Arnie and Briana

Arnie and Briana, in their late forties, divorced after 18 years of marriage. They have a 10-year-old son, Bruce, and a 13-year-old daughter, Rachel, who are still at home. Their 17-year-old daughter lives in another state attending college. Arnie and Briana agree on joint custody with a schedule of alternating Bruce and Rachel every 10 days between their households. The children change households together. Prior to divorcing, both parents worked outside the home. Bruce and Rachel were in day care together when they were younger. Since Rachel turned 13, she was responsible for caring for Bruce after school.

For the first six months of joint custody, the main problems involve adjusting to the new routines, with forgotten belongings left at each parent's home, transportation mix ups causing missed music and sports practices, and the children forgetting to tell friends at which parent's home they could be found.

Within the first year, Rachel's grades dropped, and she grew increasingly irritable and short-tempered. She frequently fought with her dad. She thought Arnie was too strict with rules about which friends she could visit and how late she could talk or text on her phone. In therapy, she said she wanted one place to live and did not want to go back and forth between her parents. She preferred to live with Briana, because her mom rarely enforced rules.

Arnie reluctantly agreed to allow Rachel to live with Briana for eight days in a row and then visit him for two days. They decided to try this for six months. Briana also agreed but was unsure of how this would work, as she liked the 10 days off from parenting that their prior arrangement gave her. Briana had recently started dating and wanted time to see how the new relationship would work out. Arnie and Briana did not formalize anything legally. They both regarded this as a trial period.

A few months into the new arrangement, Rachel complained to her therapist that her mother was "never home" and rarely made supper. Rachel was left to microwave something for herself and Bruce, or mom told her to call her dad and have him bring food over. Mom either got home late from work or was out on a date. When her therapist asked, Rachel recalled that when her parents were married, her dad had made most evening meals and that her mother never had much interest in cooking.

Living full time at Briana's house, Rachel realized she was lonely and forced to do far more for herself than when she was living with her dad. Rachel and Briana fought frequently over these issues of Rachel wanting her mother to "act more like mother and care for me."

When six months were up, Rachel decided to return to her dad's house. She wanted to live full-time with him and only visit with her mom. Dad agreed to this new arrangement but Mom did not. Arnie and Briana tried to resolve the issue in family therapy, but Briana held firm that she was "entitled to have Rachel with her 50 percent of the time."

In the meantime, what was happening to 10-year-old Bruce? Bruce was more placid and compliant with changing households every 10 days. He seemed to be doing okay with the shared joint custody, but then he began sleeping poorly, cried a lot, and his grades fell. When Rachel began seeing a therapist, Bruce, who was now 11, said he wanted to see a therapist.

Bruce told his therapist he also wanted to live with their dad full-time. He described how his dad did lots of things with him—played games, read books, helped with home-work, did his laundry, and cooked. But at mom's, it was a different story. Frequently, she "forgot" to do laundry, rarely cooked, didn't get him to school on time, and almost never helped with homework. She also left him and Rachel home alone a lot. He and his therapist explored more about whether these behaviors were unusual for mom or whether she had always been like this. Bruce remembered dad had always done a better job of being a parent than mom. But, Bruce quickly added he "felt sorry for mom." "She seems so lonely without dad. I feel like I should be there for her. I don't want to upset her by telling her I want to live with dad. It's not like I don't want to see her. I just want to live with dad."

Arnie reopened their case in court and explained what Rachel and Bruce wanted, but Briana held firm on requiring the original custody and time-sharing plan. Both Rachel and Bruce continued to struggle with the 50-50 custody arrangement.

When Rachel was 15, she started running away from Briana's house to Arnie's. Bri-ana would call the police to pick her up. At age 13, Bruce became suicidal over being forced to continue living half-time with Briana. For a second time, Arnie went back to court to get help from the legal system to change the custody arrangement. This time, the court system appreciated the seriousness of the children's distress and adjusted the custody arrangement so both Rachel and Bruce lived with Arnie and visited with Briana. Both children regained their emotional health and continued relationships with both parents.

Commentary

Clearly, sharing custody and spending 50 percent of the time with each parent did not work well for these children. Arnie was an omnipotent and had many caregiving skills in his parenting repertoire. Briana was an impotent who offered minimal hands-on care of Rachel and Bruce. Rachel was an impotent girl and young teenager who chafed at rules and restrictions. She liked the idea of the greater social freedom she had at her mother's house, where she could stay up as late as she wanted talking with and texting friends. But, she quickly learned she did not like her mother's expectation that she should do a lot for herself to ensure she was fed and had clean laundry. The reality of living with Briana was a clear motivator for Rachel to return to the more con-sistent caregiving home of her dad, even if it meant having more rules. Rachel discov-ered she was more comforted by her dad's rules after living with no rules at Briana's house.

Bruce was an omnipotent boy who didn't want to hurt either parent's feelings, espe-cially his impotent mother's. He tried for a long time to sacrifice himself to his mother's desire to have him half the time, until he could no longer do this without becoming suicidal. He felt such tremendous guilt over not being able to go along with what Briana wanted from him, that at age 13, he thought he was a bad son who deserved to die by his own hand.

Many joint custody cases do not fare this well in the legal system. Some do bet-ter. But, we found that due to the roles children and parents assume, evenly shared

parenting unduly burdens the children in favor of convenience to one or both par-
ents. We did not find the courts' assumptions accurate that parents are equal in their
parenting roles, in the absence of severe physical, sexual, or emotional abuse. Parents
are different, and one usually parents far better than the other.

Return to Single Life

The final divorce decree provides significant relief to both spouses, as it ends the exchange of counter charges and accusations. AS UNPLEASANT AS THE COURT EXPERIENCE IS, WE COMPEL BOTH SPOUSES TO PARTICIPATE IN THESE LEGAL LAST RITES TO THE RELATIONSHIP. DURING THE PROLONGED EMOTIONAL CATHARSIS OF THE LEGAL PROCEEDINGS, AN IMPOTENT EXTRACTS FINAL DEMANDS AND AN OMNIPOTENT DEFENDS AND JUSTIFIES HER BEHAVIOR TO THE REFEREE JUDGE OR MEDIATOR. Once the exhausting battle finishes, both people are free to seek financial and emotional recovery. Both can then resume their social lives as single people.

The majority of divorced singles plan to remarry, and most do. The youngest are the most likely. In the return to single living, ex-spouses do not find the same dating scene of their younger years. Earlier in life, the priorities were on preparing for work and marriage, and the mating dance involved most of their peers.

The newly divorced often find themselves isolated by their misfortune and alienated from their old married friends in their former social group. Divorce creates discomfort among many close friends, who may realize their own marriages have certain vulnerabilities. Former married friends tend to sympathize with one spouse in the divorce and to reject the other. The recently divorced are setting up a new lifestyle at the same time their old support group is less available. The scars of the failed marriage are still healing. By and large, we found divorced people lose the exuberance and optimism of their youth and become more wary, aware that their very best efforts in life may not be good enough to ensure success in relationships.

Repeating Earlier Failures

Many who are recently divorced seek professional counseling for the first time. We want help sorting out the causes of the divorce, as well as dealing with our distressing emotions and symptoms—anxiety, depression, or substance abuse. This step can help us discover our own contributions to relationship difficulties and what qualities we should look for in a new mate to avoid repeated failures. However, only a fraction of the millions of newly single divorced people seek psychological treatment.

MOST UNATTACHED DIVORCED PEOPLE GRADUALLY RETURN TO DATING, USING THE SAME CRITERIA IN CHOOSING A MATE AS THEY DID IN THEIR PREVIOUS UNSUCCESSFUL MARRIAGE. MOST OF US HAVE NO REAL OPTIONS IN MATE CHOICE BECAUSE OUR EARLY EMOTIONAL CONDITIONING IS OUR GUIDE.

In a rather common scenario, omnipotents may leave one impotent and commit themselves to younger impotents. This choice means they are likely to double their failure rate. Or, concerned friends arrange dates that seldom lead to beneficial or lasting relationships. In short, without professional counseling, the newly single find themselves in extremely complex and perplexing situations.

ANOTHER PITFALL IN DATING AGAIN IS THAT ALMOST ALL HETEROSEXUAL DIVORCED PEOPLE SHARE THE MISPERCEPTION THAT ALL MEMBERS OF THE OPPOSITE SEX ARE IDENTICAL TO PAST SPOUSES. When we generalize that we are typical members of our own sex and that ex-spouses characterize all members of the opposite sex, we are engaged in projection. It is difficult for us when resuming dating to recognize that we most often find *only one specific type of person* attractive. We are unaware that we reject other types of people when we look for those to date. This means that most often omnipotents do not seek out other omnipotents to date, nor do impotents seek out other impotents.

Lesley

At 52 years old, Lesley complained of poor energy and sleep and a hopeless belief that "there are no good men anymore, anywhere." She had divorced four times and had five children, two still living at home with her. Recently, she began a romantic relationship with another woman, but she was unhappy with how it was unfolding. "I thought I'd try women since I'd struck out with men," she explained.

In our work together, we discovered Lesley was always looking for a man who would rescue, care for, and indulge her, and "treat me like a queen," she said. In other words, she sought omnipotent men for relationships. She wanted tangibles of great monetary worth—jewelry, clothes, houses, and vacations. Two husbands went bankrupt trying to satisfy her desires. Lesley believed they failed to satisfy her, not that she expected too much in her marriages. When married, she behaved inertly—never holding a job, refusing to cook, run the households, or raise the children while her husbands worked at their jobs. She hired out all chores to housekeepers and nannies. She rarely was at home when her husbands came home from work, preferring to spend evenings on a gambling boat with female friends.

The marriages ended when she either got fed up with her husbands' inability to please her or her husbands became so worn out from her demands that they initiated a divorce. Interestingly, her attempt at having a romantic relationship with a woman failed to work out for the same reason: she expected total indulgence from her woman partner.

During her therapy, with increasing understanding of who she was and how she was emotionally conditioned, Lesley was able to expect more from and of herself in romantic encounters. These relationships went better once she stopped seeking omnipotents to do everything for her and instead put out more effort. Lesley was an impotent, but once she learned about her impotent role she was able to make changes in herself and avoided behaving and thinking so helplessly.

SINGLE DIVORCED PEOPLE FACE THEIR RETURN TO THE DATING SCENE WITH LITTLE SELF-AWARENESS AND LITTLE KNOWLEDGE OF HOW TO EVALUATE THE PEOPLE THEY DATE, OR WHAT QUALITIES THEY SHOULD LOOK FOR IN A PROSPECTIVE MATE. We found that omnipotents *anxiously* meet each new prospect for a serious relationship. As is their lifelong conditioning, they feel pressured by wondering what each new person may expect of them and whether they can perform to those expectations.

Omnipotents feel an immediate emotional and physical magnetism to some people. Toward other people, they feel lackluster and have little interest. The latter reaction may feel like dating a sibling. Naturally, omnipotents pursue the relationships that excite them most and remind them of enthralled times in their teenage years. When dating, omnipotents do what they have done since early childhood. They become hyperalert and filled with anticipatory anxiety. Their "guts," as well as their conscious intentions, lead them to connect again with impotents. When another omnipotent presents as a possible date, this may dampen their zeal because omnipotents often bristle at and back off from other caregiving people. Typically, omnipotents feel fraternal toward one another but do not deliberately choose one another to marry or for long-term relationships—either before or after a divorce.

Some omnipotents have minimal interest in remarriage. Often this is because they put themselves down so much and become enraged at themselves for their failure to hold their prior marriages together. Their failure to keep their marriage intact can create permanent repercussions for them. Such intense omnipotents become cynical about marriage and seek to avoid another failure. They live alone and adopt a strategy of rigorous self-sufficiency. They withdraw from the world and assume an austere post-marriage lifestyle, denying themselves luxuries or quality possessions they would have given their impotent spouse when married.

Omnipotents may date as if they are still interested in finding a new partner. However, they may hurriedly break off any inviting relationship before it becomes "serious." This is how they avoid exposing themselves to another devastating self-devaluation, which would take place if they had another failed marriage.

Impotents experience an opposite internal reaction from omnipotents. When dating, impotents easily recognize when they are in the presence of omnipotent, submissive people who will respond to their every desire. This recognition sets off the combined emotional and gut reaction that we interpret as affection and sexual attraction. Since impotents quickly recognize the presence of omnipotents, they have a reflex to cling to the omnipotents for the sake of security.

Impotents may date other impotents as an interesting interlude, but this will not create the heightened magnetic attraction of dating omnipotents. When meeting one another, two impotents may take the opportunity for indulgent and self-absorbed discussions of common experiences and interests. But, for an enduring long-term or serious relationship, impotents require the treasury of unending support only offered by omnipotents.

The dramatic passion generated by the mutual attraction of impotents and omnipotents includes sexual "chemistry." **IN OMNIPOTENT-OMNIPOTENT OR IMPOTENT-IMPOTENT DATING, THERE SOMETIMES IS INITIAL SEXUAL DYSFUNCTION IN ONE OR BOTH PARTNERS. WHEN THIS HAPPENS, BOTH PEOPLE ACCEPT THIS AS PROOF OF INCOMPATIBILITY, AND THEY END THE RELATIONSHIP.**

Impotents do not always find life without omnipotents as difficult as they thought it would be. We discovered that impotents do not miss individual omnipotents so much as the *services* they supplied. Impotents often perceived their former omnipotent partners as such a nuisance and inconvenience that many impotents go on to enjoy single life free of the need to tolerate others.

These impotents may arrange their living space as a personalized habitat where no intruders are allowed and only rarely entertain guests. Occasionally, they may have some social life with carefully selected omnipotent friends. This satisfies their need for emotional support. They use the remainder of their time for self-indulgent pursuits such as hobbies and travel. Impotents have little interest in future marriage when they adjust to their single lives in this way. Only exceptional situations could tempt impotents to leave such cozy isolation.

In postdivorce dating, both omnipotents and impotents show more selectiveness than in their younger years, since they know that there are other options besides marriage. And, they are aware some divorced friends go for years without committed relationships or the desire to be remarried. They see that such friends appear to be satisfied with their single lives.

A sobering concern when considering remarriage is combining households and parenting stepchildren. In addition, financial obligations from the first marriage may pose steep barriers to considering yet another marriage. Children's reactions to prospective stepparents also pose a further impediment to remarriage. For example, omnipotent parents may allow their impotent children to dictate decisions regarding who they should remarry.

Depending on the length of the first marriage, its ghosts can resist exorcism for a long time. Many divorced omnipotents remain more obligated to the commitments of the former marriage than to their own welfare, or to a new relationship. Divorced people seriously hamper any new relationship if they do not ensure it takes top priority over the old one.

Remarriage Accidents

Despite emotional conditioning to seek a spouse with the opposite role, a small percentage of remarriages are omnipotent-omnipotent or impotent-impotent pairs. This leads to much confusion in the new spouses as to how this relationship can be so different from their first marriages. We found that omnipotent-omnipotent relationships offer the most stability and longevity. The couple intently engages in caring for one another and is also very socially involved. In these marriages each person commits himself to the other for mutual care. Such pairings lead to closer personal relationships as well as a different concept of love than in their previous marriages.

An impotent-impotent relationship lacks stability and instead proceeds in a pattern of mutual indulgence and a high degree of volatility. These marriages follow little structure or responsibility to one another. Both impotent spouses feel free of the necessity to tolerate the serious, hardworking omnipotent mate each had in their previous marriages. For an impotent-impotent marriage to function, many other people must be recruited to provide support and structure when difficulties arise for those couples, such as former spouses, relatives, friends, or coworkers.

If it were not for the difficulty of diminishing our emotional conditioning, choosing a partner for a subsequent marriage would be much simpler. We might hope that omnipotents would find other omnipotents attractive, for they can be innovative, talented, and caring. But, since omnipotents unconsciously shift to a standard of *perfection* when associating with each other, they then project this expectation onto one another. This means that both omnipotents become hypercritical of one another, often becoming overbearing taskmasters, and hold one another to impossible standards and feats. Most often one omnipotent is intolerant of the other omnipotent wanting or needing anything. This is the same intolerance an omnipotent has for her own needs. It is all a projection. We discussed these less common relationships in Chapter 7.

Similarly, impotent individuals, also confined by their emotional conditioning, have fewer options in seeking a new mate. They might find many attractive companions among their fellow impotents, but they cannot get along. Impotents expect to be treated with an exclusive and continuous special attention that satisfies their every whim. When they are with one another, the two impotents clash over who is to dominate the other and who gets what they want from the other partner. Their self-absorption cannot tolerate a long-term relationship with a mate who is just as demanding and relentless in promoting his own self-interests. They put one another down and lose mutual interest. Interestingly, impotents can be very aware of the impulsivity, egocentricity, and demands of other impotents yet remain oblivious to their own identical traits. We also discussed these relationships in Chapter 7.

IT WOULD BE DESIRABLE FOR NEWLY DIVORCED SINGLES TO APPRECIATE AND CHOOSE DIFFERENT OPTIONS IN DATING AGAIN, BUT FEW ARE ABLE TO OVERCOME THEIR OWN LIMITATIONS DUE TO EMOTIONAL CONDITIONING. THE POWER AND TUG OF EMOTIONAL CONDITIONING IS NEVER MORE APPARENT THAN IN THE EFFORT TO FIND A MATE FOR REMARRIAGE.

Since an omnipotent struggles to avoid relationships in which he receives care and support, he isolates himself from others and forces himself to look after his own welfare. He may discover that he does a poor job of caring for himself. An impotent seeks an environment of total indulgence in his single life. However, he often has difficulty in functioning without the structure and organization supplied by omnipotents.

"My Divorce Just Happened—I Had No Control over It."

When we reflect about divorce and remarriage, many of us decide the circumstances leading to our divorce were outside our control. We think the events took place around us rather than resulting *from our own actions*. We feel powerless to control our own lives but compelled to repeat those decisions that have already created unhappiness and misfortune. We believe that the feeling of helplessness in managing our own lives may be vague, conscious awareness of the presence of our emotionally conditioned behaviors. As conditioned people, our options are limited to specific role responses, although we may vaguely sense other options are available for making decisions for ourselves.

OUR FIXED REACTIONS AS EMOTIONALLY CONDITIONED PEOPLE ARE REPETITIVE, DEHUMANIZED, AND STEREOTYPICAL. EVEN WHEN WE HAVE DESTRUCTIVE RESULTS, WE REPEAT THE SAME BEHAVIORS. ONLY IN RETROSPECT DO WE WONDER WHY WE SO CONSISTENTLY MADE WRONG DECISIONS—NOT JUST WRONG HALF OF THE TIME, BUT ALMOST ALL THE TIME. ONCE INSTILLED, OUR EMOTIONAL CONDITIONING APPEARS TO PROFOUNDLY INFLUENCE OUR THINKING, BEHAVING, AND EMOTIONS. WE CANNOT OVERESTIMATE THE STRENGTH, PERSISTENCE, AND RESILIENCE OF EMOTIONAL CONDITIONING IN CREATING DIFFICULTIES FOR DIVORCED PEOPLE.

WHAT YOU DISCOVERED IN THIS CHAPTER

- During divorce and afterward, each spouse acts in the same roles as they did when married.

- Impotents often receive tremendous sympathy during divorce from everyone—friends, relatives, the departing spouse—while omnipotents get little support.

- Shared custody creates problems for many children since their parents' individual parenting styles can be so different.

- Divorced people have little understanding of what went wrong during their marriage, little self-awareness of their role in the marriage breakup, and little knowledge of how to evaluate a prospective mate for dating and remarriage.

Questions to Ask Yourself

Before you begin the final chapters on deconditioning, give some thought to these questions.

- What do you notice about the way you think about your relationships? Are you suspicious or trusting? Zero-sum or win-win? Are you fatalistic, or do you believe you can achieve what you set out to do? Self-centered or focused on other people? Idealistic or realistic?
- Do you feel secure in the way you see yourself—your physical appearance, the sound of your voice, and how you fit into relationships?
- Is your mind incessantly busy?
- Are you obsessed with resolving problems?
- Are you preoccupied with satisfying others and trying to achieve perfection?
- Are you overly sensitive to minor inconveniences?
- Do those around you repeatedly disappoint you?
- What conditions create happiness for you?
- What situations create unhappiness for you?
- Do you find self-observation easy or difficult?
- How do you like the way your life is going?
- Is your life enjoyable?
- Do you anticipate the future with optimism?
- Do you feel comfortable in your relationships and the way you handle them?
- Do you feel free to express yourself around the important people in your life?
- Are you often surprised and concerned at your fantasies and feelings about the people in your life?
- Do you feel you are managing your life well?
- Do you feel your life comes rushing at you and seems outside your control?

PART 3

Solutions: Psychotherapy and Deconditioning

CHAPTER TEN

Emotional Illness and Therapy: The Deconditioning Process

No Such Thing as Normal

Psychotherapists describe people who have personality disorders as those who may function fairly well in society but have unconscious difficulties that produce conflicts in their interpersonal relationships. The percentage of the population with personality disorders varies widely from one study to another. Generally, we believe that a quarter to a third of the population will experience an emotional illness at some stressful point in life, and roughly 10 percent will develop a personality disorder. The majority of people—those who have not been diagnosed with a mental illness, emotional illness, or personality difficulty—were classified as "normal."

HOWEVER, OUR EXPERIENCE AND OBSERVATIONS OVER OUR COMBINED **80** YEARS AS PSYCHIATRISTS LED US TO BELIEVE THIS CLASSIFICATION IS GROSSLY MISTAKEN. WE REALIZED THAT A LARGE POOL OF "NORMAL" PEOPLE DOES NOT EXIST. All of the accumulated evidence we gathered from years of intense work with almost 2,000 people in the normal group confirms that many, if not all, of us appear to undergo emotional conditioning. As a result, most people react to personal encounters in life in an inappropriate and conditioned way to some degree. It seems we make this error about normality because we assume that people who haven't sought help for emotional difficulties are less disturbed than those who seek treatment.

Personality disorders were thought to be a serious issue because, until recently, people's personalities were considered unchangeable. More accurately, we can say that the personality can be in a state of constant, albeit gradual, change. This change can be positive or negative. Dr. Martin and I observed that with increasing age, most of our patients' emotional conditioning strengthened due to constant positive reinforcement in their relationships. This means we are continually reinforced to *stay* in our conditioned roles.

When a new patient begins psychotherapy, he or she is usually labeled as ill, and the remainder of the family is viewed as normal. However, therapists often find that others in the family may prove more emotionally disturbed than their patients. In our experience, people who seek help in psychotherapy tend to be distraught, curious, and more *concerned* than their unhealthy family members are.

Two or more people create the problems in any relationship, but only one may come for treatment. At times we encountered uncooperative adults or children who refused to participate in treatment. We handled this difficulty by counseling the "normal" participant(s) whose unconscious contribution perpetuated the problems. When we helped our more able and willing patients to change their conditioned responses, that meant their more troubled family members would also alter their destructive behaviors. Sometimes I used this approach in my practice as a child psychiatrist by treating the parent(s) instead of the child.

Here is a case example.

Morgan

Morgan, 27 years old, lived in a housing project as a single parent with her three children. Her son Andy was five years old and had two sisters. Morgan brought Andy to see me because he was bossy and unruly at home and in kindergarten. He hit, yelled, pinched, and bit classmates and his sisters whenever he was told no or could not immediately have his way. He was once admitted to a psychiatric hospital and took medications. Andy also could not get along with other children in the housing project. Morgan feared she might have to hospitalize him again. When she told Andy this, he would improve his behavior for a short time.

I saw Andy once in my office. He examined all the toys I had and briefly played with some of them. Then he announced he was bored and asked why I didn't have any "better toys to play with?" I tried to engage him further, but he escalated with demands for me to produce better toys, and then he wanted to leave my office and end the session. I also made home and school visits, but I could not get him to engage with me. He refused to return for any further appointments. I proposed to Morgan that I work with her instead of Andy, and she agreed.

Morgan told me that she was the youngest of three girls. Her mother had been a hairdresser and her father a policeman. She and her sisters stayed with their grandparents after school while their parents worked. Dad was the disciplinarian and quick to punish his children over the smallest thing. Mom was calmer but deferred to whatever dad wanted. Mom was a hard worker who took care of everything for her daughters.

Morgan had no difficulties with her own daughters, saying they behaved well and the six-year-old did well in school. After working together, we discovered that Morgan expected more reasonable behaviors from her daughters than she did Andy. She had always pampered and babied Andy, giving him anything he wanted and intervening so he never had to struggle with anything from zipping up his jacket to brushing his teeth. She also took him to Goodwill twice a week to pick out toys he desired. Whatever accounted for the different way she related to her daughters and to her son might be the clue to helping Morgan help Andy.

Morgan went on to tell me she had always felt sorry for Andy, because he was growing up without a father and that he seemed so helpless to her. She revealed this was the same way she felt about her dad, that he seemed domineering and needed to have things his way. "Is there anyone else you felt was fragile, helpless, and needy in the family?" I asked. Through copious tears, Morgan told me of her little brother, who died when she was seven and he was three. She was very close to him and spent a lot of time caring for him as a baby and toddler—changing his diapers, playing games, fixing bottles and snacks, and reading him stories. She always felt he needed a lot of help from her and that he was fragile. He died in a fire after playing with matches from a Christmas present she had made for her parents as a school project.

Commentary

Morgan and I discovered that she had linked Andy in her mind with her deceased little brother. We realized that her grief for and her guilt over feeling responsible for the death of her little brother accentuated her conditioning Andy as an impotent who needed to be cared for and spoiled. Only after Morgan dealt with her grief was she able to begin changing her expectations of Andy and see him as more capable and less fragile. At first this was not easy. Andy chafed at having reasonable conduct expected of him, and Morgan struggled as to whether it was okay for her to expect reasonable behavior from Andy. When Morgan became able to lessen her omnipotent role, Andy became less impotent, more cooperative, and better behaved, and did not always demand his way with Morgan, his sisters, and schoolmates.

Emotional Illness May First Seem Like Physical Illness

Psychotherapists often make a diagnosis of emotional illness by exclusion—that is, after all other causes have been ruled out. Our patients may reach a point in life where they have impaired functioning—they can't sleep, can't eat, or overeat, don't bathe regularly, or can't go to work. They may have one symptom or many and may be unsure of the cause. They may feel anxious, depressed (feelings of sadness and worthlessness), phobic (unreasonably fearful), obsessive (have recurrent thoughts they cannot control), or have intermittent anger. They might experience constant stress, fatigue, insomnia, intestinal complaints, and countless other symptoms. They often relate the symptoms to a physical cause and, in an attempt to uncover a definite physical problem, undergo extended medical examinations.

ONE OF THE MOST DIFFICULT DIAGNOSES CONFRONTING PHYSICIANS IS DISTIN-
GUISHING PHYSICAL ILLNESSES FROM EMOTIONAL DYSFUNCTIONS, AS THE LATTER CAN
MIMIC MANY TYPES OF PHYSICAL PROBLEMS. Because emotional illnesses arise
from unconscious concerns that we are unaware of, this makes for difficulty in determining the cause. Most people who seek treatment deny all
possibility of emotional conflict, citing a happy marriage, no unusual financial pressures, children who are doing well in school, and other positive
life circumstances. The very idea of having an emotional disorder is unac-
ceptable because we relate it to having a mental illness. We discussed these
differences between mental and emotional illnesses in Chapter 1.

The Origin of Emotional Illness Lies in Relationship Problems

A person with an emotional illness may not know why he or she is
symptomatic, due to the unconscious basis of the illness. She may be seen
first by her primary care physician, who tries to rule out physical illnesses
but cannot go much further. If a patient's emotional condition goes into
remission with rest, medication, or brief hospitalization, she may not continue the search for the reasons underlying the emotional illness. But if
rest, medication, or hospitalizations do not help or she is curious about
the cause, she may decide to try dynamic psychotherapy.
ANY INSIGHTS WE GAIN THROUGH SUCCESSFUL PSYCHOTHERAPY OPEN UP NEW
OPTIONS FOR US IN MANAGING THE PROBLEMS OF OUR EMOTIONAL ILLNESS. DEEPER
SELF-KNOWLEDGE ELIMINATES THE SYMPTOMS AND HELPS PREVENT RECURRENCES. INEV-
ITABLY, EMOTIONAL CONDITIONS *WILL* RECUR IF WE DO NOT CHANGE THE WAYS WE
RELATE TO OTHERS. CONTRARY TO POPULAR BELIEF, EMOTIONAL PROBLEMS DO NOT
ARISE PRIMARILY FROM TANGIBLE LIFE DIFFICULTIES. EMOTIONAL ILLNESSES USUALLY
ARISE FROM CONFLICTS AND SUPPORT IMBALANCES IN INTERPERSONAL RELATIONSHIPS.
Emotional illnesses result when our coping abilities are overwhelmed
by the accumulating difficulties with other significant people in our lives.
We may be partly conscious or aware of our conflicts, but the main causes
are usually beyond our awareness. We are accustomed to dealing with
people in our characteristic way and see no reason why we should be inca-
pacitated now when we weren't before. Because we are ailing and dealing
with others in the only way we have been taught, we are oblivious to alternative approaches. We are unaware of which of our relationships are path-
ological. In addition, we are unconscious of how we participate in our
relationships, how we attempt to deal with our problems, and why they
can exceed our coping abilities.
Dynamic psychotherapy provides a unique opportunity for us to observe
our ways of thinking from a wholly different perspective. A therapist

focuses on the unknown and hidden factors motivating us, such as the patterns of omnipotent thinking compared with impotent thinking. That's a striking demonstration of the diverse ways the mind can be programmed to deal with other people and problems.

In the eras preceding modern psychiatric treatment in the 20th century, many emotional illnesses, including severe depressions, either improved considerably or went into complete remission after a period of months up to two years. What caused the improvement? Was it herbal treatments, potions or today's medications, spas, prayers, or a change in scene?

Simply removing us from our family environment may temporarily relieve significant pressures and conflicts. All of these familiar measures, from medication to rest and removal, may provide sufficient relief to enable us to regain our customary way of functioning. Unfortunately, this does not assure our future stability. We are unlikely to receive a lasting benefit unless we identify the fundamental problem and deal with it. If we don't, our problems may become more ingrained and intractable. The good news is that if we avail ourselves of dynamic psychotherapy and use "deconditioning" treatments as soon as we recognize emotional difficulties, we could, in many cases, prevent future emotional breakdowns and avoid hospitalizations.

Prevention

In an ideal world, we would prevent emotional disorders by beginning with parents. Tradition has guided our child raising rather than a realistic awareness of what determines personality and emotional stability, and many couples have no clear plan for how they want to bring up their children.

The second most desirable time to offer a program of emotional wellness would be in elementary school when children's personality development is becoming well established and future difficulties are not yet set in stone. We could gradually shift from treatment to prevention to head off serious problems. The traditional approach of only seeking treatment once serious problems become obvious and bothersome is not working well. A smarter approach would be to focus on prevention in the early years.

When diagnosing and treating emotional illnesses, psychotherapists focus less on brain dysfunctions and more on emotional states. We can both lessen and even cure many emotional problems with this approach. Most dynamic psychotherapy focuses on the 90 percent of us who likely have no defect in brain anatomy or physiology but who may have distortions in our emotional ways of relating to others that create serious burdens.

Deconditioning Therapy

Psychotherapists can help people in therapy create basic changes in their personalities. These changes enable patients to recognize the inappropriate and destructive results of their emotional conditioning and to change their rigid patterns of behaving and relating to others. But many psychotherapists have found that some severely conditioned personality disorders, such as sociopaths, cannot benefit from treatment.

We therapists must abandon the traditional approach of only addressing superficial symptoms if we want to deal with the very foundation of emotional difficulties. If patients decide to undertake psychotherapy, they will need to make changes in their basic personalities. This is the only way to make permanent changes. Dr. Martin and I found this true in all emotional illnesses, from major emotional illnesses to the most minor emotional distress. Our unconscious personality difficulties remain even after our conscious symptoms are better. We therapists must help our patients identify and change their unconscious emotional conditioning if we want to help them have lasting improvement.

Both Dr. Martin and I were able to use therapy to decondition our patients' emotionally conditioned roles. Many patients with a history of unsuccessful treatment came to us for therapy. Some came because modern psychoactive medications did not help them or helped them only a little. Others came to therapy because they wanted to dig deeper and avoid repeating patterns in their relationships that led to distress.

We found that the most successful patients are omnipotents. They are hardworking and tenacious, and deal better with the slow process of acquiring self-understanding. As children they learned to delay gratification. This attribute comes in handy for dealing with the longer time span in dynamic psychotherapy before getting better. Impotents, if able to control their impulsivity and come to sessions regularly, are also able to knuckle down and learn about their early lives of overindulgence and their proclivity for demanding that others always cater to their helplessness. Impotent patients are as fascinated by how they got to be who they are as are omnipotents.

ONCE EMOTIONALLY CONDITIONED PEOPLE BECOME DECONDITIONED THROUGH PSYCHOTHERAPY—WHEN THEY LEARN TO RECOGNIZE THE OPPOSITE ROLE THEY'VE NEVER BEEN AWARE OF AND THE RIGID WAYS THEY PARTICIPATE IN RELATIONSHIPS— THEY OFTEN LOOK BACK IN WONDER AT HOW THEY COULD HAVE BEEN SO OBLIVIOUS. They are also surprised that those close to them cannot see what is going on, even when they point out the roles they each play.

This all makes more sense when we become aware of society's heavy use of rationalizations to explain imbalances in relationships. In the emotional conditioning process, we learn how to justify our behaviors when they are at odds with rational thought and common sense. Omnipotents justify their actions through attitudes of self-sacrifice. Impotents rationalize their self-indulgent expectations by myriad excuses for their helplessness. Families supply these rationalizations to future generations beginning in childhood.

Treatment that overcomes such conditioning requires a skilled therapist and many months of work, since reversing the conditioning process unfolds in the same gradual way and within an intense human relationship, just as the original emotional conditioning did. Each patient needs motivation and willingness to invest time and money in self-discovery. You will find there is nothing easy about the process of returning to a minimally conditioned state. It is not an undertaking for the fainthearted, but it should not be reserved just for those with severe emotional problems. Correcting emotional conditioning would have even more impact for those of us who were always thought of as normal, since we could bring these new understandings to our family, social, and professional relationships.

In years past, most psychotherapists thought that only people who had experienced painful personal problems in relationships were sufficiently motivated to undertake psychotherapy. We thought that a person would only accept treatment after he had endured repeated failures and knew his own methods would inevitably fail again.

However, many in-training psychotherapists sought therapy because they knew self-understanding is essential to understanding their patients in depth and to being aware of the subtle interplay between their patients and themselves. Most of these professionals undergoing treatment did not have trauma from repeated problems. The results of treating such professionals showed that marked benefits could be achieved for relatively "healthy" and "normal" people as patients. Here is a case example.

Successful Treatment of an Omnipotent Personality
Tom

Tom, 24 years old, sought psychotherapy because he was a social work student pursuing a master's degree. One of his supervisors suggested he try counseling to see what it was like, as it might be helpful for his training as a therapist. From the outset of his sessions, he said he was not particularly worried about anything in his personal life.

He had been married a little over a year. His wife, Beverly, a nurse, was pregnant and they felt happy. He seemed eager to learn about how counseling felt as a patient rather than as the counselor. He said he grew up in a "normal average" middle-class

family. His mother was a librarian, and his father owned a nursery. He had two siblings, an older sister, and a younger brother. He met his wife in college, and they dated
five years. He described her as "spunky, outgoing, and never without an opinion." He
described himself as a "regular guy." When asked to elaborate, he said he was shyer
than his wife and more hesitant to speak his mind than she was. He said he always got
along with "everybody."

As we discussed him and his childhood, he became more relaxed and forthcoming. He gave more details on his family. Mom was the one he went to talk things over
with. She was pretty but never wore makeup or stylish clothes, almost like she wanted
to "blend in, not stand out and be insignificant," Tom said. He added, "Mom is soft-
spoken and rarely angry, and she organizes everyone and keeps the household running
even though she works full-time in the city library as chief librarian." Tom recalled
that she comforted him when he had bike accidents, read him stories at bedtime, and
made luscious pancakes every Saturday. She was the go-to person for questions about
schoolwork, dating, and transportation needs.

"Did she ever have fun?" Tom hesitated, "Sometimes on family vacations, she
would sit on the beach in a lounge chair and just look at the waves for hours, not saying anything." Other times she went with Tom's dad out of town on business trips
and he "guessed" she was having fun but didn't know for sure. I encouraged him to
ask her.

"Dad was a workaholic," Tom volunteered. Often, he was out of town for work,
buying nursery stock. When he was home, he played golf at least twice a week in good
weather. Tom said he was always a little nervous around him but didn't know why. As
we discussed this more Tom said, "I always felt like I might say the wrong thing around
him and make him angry or upset him. He could come down hard on me."

Tom recalled times his dad belittled him, once over striking out in a T-ball game
when he was six, with dad saying he was "a loser." Another time he yelled at Tom for
making an A in English, saying it was a "waste of time to get a good grade in something so unimportant." Many examples tumbled out of Tom's memory from all ages.
Tom noted he always concealed his feelings, especially from his father. He also said
he felt he should always be happy with others and never be ill tempered.

"How was your dad involved with you?" Tom replied that he coached some of his
sports teams, and he always begged Tom to play golf with him. Tom didn't like golf
and got out of it as often as he could. He never understood why his dad wanted him
to go along. Dad also asked several golfing buddies to accompany them, never spoke
to Tom, and mostly ignored him when they were out on the course. "Dad loved to
hug us all, but I tried to avoid his hugs because he always made it so painful—like he
enjoyed giving us pain," Tom recalled.

How did mom and dad interact? Dad called most of the shots with her—from what
he wanted her to cook, to how he wanted his clothes washed, to deciding where the
family would go on vacations, to having her take care of the bills and also providing
entertainment for his business clients.

Tom recalled a time his mother won a gift certificate to a fancy department store.
"She bought a gorgeous cocktail dress, put it on to model for dad and the three of us.
I had never seen her wear anything so simple yet so elegant. She looked great, but
dad told her it made her stand out and be too noticeable and ostentatious. He didn't
want his business clients to see her in it and get distracted. He made her take it back

to the store. Mom pretty much did everything dad wanted her to and not vice versa," Tom mused.

In our continued work, Tom learned he was more like his mother, and his wife was more like his father. Tom functioned as the omnipotent in his marriage while Beverly functioned impotently. Tom only became excruciatingly aware of this two years after their son, Evan, was born.

At first, Beverly threw herself into being a mother. She was very attentive to Evan, breastfed him for 18 months, took him on outings, played with him, recorded all his milestones, and took tons of photos and videos. She was always the one to get up at night and tend Evan, who was an easygoing baby developing normally.

When Evan was just shy of being two, he began to be a typical two-year-old, using the "no" word and being more uncooperative with refusing food, sleep, and activities he had liked before. Beverly became extremely angry at this behavior. She yelled at him, called him names, and stormed out of the room, leaving him in tears at her eruptions. Her willfulness fought against Evan's. When he witnessed these episodes, Tom was aghast. He decided Beverly had to be in combat with Evan so she could "win" and call all the shots. "She had no tolerance for Evan's learning independence," Tom told me.

Tom fulfilled his omnipotent role by trying to interpret reality for Beverly. He explained normal child development to her. He begged her to stop her behaviors, but she could not. Evan sought out Tom when he was home, but Beverly still spent all day with Evan. Tom somehow thought he could save Evan and his marriage but found he was walking on eggshells emotionally. He became anxious and depressed that he was unable to "fix" the situation. His omnipotent role failed him. He noticed Evan had lost his former spunky, happy demeanor. Tom tried to get Beverly to see a therapist with him, but she refused. Reluctantly, he filed for divorce.

Fortunately, Tom remained in therapy through his divorce. He continued to learn about himself and his relationship with Beverly and why the characteristics that originally attracted him to her was the undoing of their marriage. Although Tom had the same rough time with getting divorced that omnipotents have, he learned to fight for his and Evan's needs. He and Beverly reached agreement on joint custody with Tom spending about half-time caring for Evan. Beverly had returned to being a full-time nurse, and Evan went to day care. Tom knew Beverly's time with Evan would be minimal, but he still worried about the effects on Evan.

Over the years, as the conflict subsided, Evan asked to spend more time with Tom, under the auspices of "dad helping me with ball practice and homework." Beverly had no interest in ball sports and not much interest in helping Evan with homework, so she agreed. Eventually Evan moved in with Tom and saw Beverly regularly for two- or three-day visits when Evan could work it out with her. Evan thrived with this arrangement.

By four years after the divorce, Tom had discovered a great deal about his own makeup. His self-understanding helped him in dating and in choosing a different type of woman to remarry. Evan also adored his new stepmother, and Tom adored his new eight-year-old stepdaughter. They had some rough spots in blending their families but together tackled the problems in a reasonable fashion. Tom believed his own therapy helped him with his relationships and also made him a better therapist.

Next we move on to a case example of treatment of an impotent personality.

Successful Treatment of an Impotent Personality
Alicia

Alicia was 52 years old. She sought help for depression and increased alcohol use. She was married with four children, three in their twenties and the youngest who had left for college three months earlier. She was a full-time mother and homemaker who never had a job outside the home. Her husband worked full-time as a government official holding an executive job.

She was a petite, demur woman with a college degree in anthropology. She had become despondent since her youngest daughter started college, just three months ago. It was not that she was an empty nester, she explained. She was not missing the children, and she had plenty of volunteer activities to do. It was that her children didn't "mind" her anymore. By this she meant she could no longer control them—or their whereabouts, who they associated with, what they did socially, and so on. Alicia said she loved being a mother. She said it was the only job she was cut out for. She relished planning her children's activities, wardrobes, sports, and extracurricular activities and social engagements.

During her first therapy session, she wanted to know if I had children and if so, how many and their ages. One practice in psychotherapy is that therapists do not answer personal questions. Instead, we try to find out why the information is sought and what this helps us discover about patients, their problems, and the ways they relate with other people. I did not answer her questions but probed further why the information was important to her.

At first, Alicia said it was because she did not want a therapist who lacked personal knowledge of raising children. But, as I gently questioned further, it became clear there was more to it. Alicia became angry and said, "I'll find out the answer some other way, you know. I'm used to getting my way eventually." The "why" she wanted the information suddenly became less important than her attitude of expecting me to give her the information she wanted and her expectation that she should have her way. Perhaps this was the same attitude Alicia had in some of her relationships.

As she grew up, she felt she had lots of "responsibility" for her four younger siblings and expectations to keep them in line. But, I later discovered that instead she commandeered her siblings to do activities she wanted. She believed she had been a "shy" but very happy child. She said her parents were "wonderful" and gave her everything she ever wanted. They never disappointed her in any way. Her father was a happy, outgoing man, and her mother was also very happy but a bit more reserved. Her mother was always home with Alicia and her siblings while dad worked for an insurance company.

As we continued our work Alicia's shy, soft-spoken demeanor quickly evaporated. She quickly showed anger with and animosity at her children for not being cooperative with her and under her thumb. I asked her what she expected now of her children. She told me of her expectations that they should check in with her by phone or text at least twice a day and that they should tell her where they are, and who they are with, what they are doing, and what their plans are for the evening.

She had been tracking with her phone GPS each child as to their whereabouts when they started college until each one of them shut it off. This greatly enraged her. She believed her expectations were entirely reasonable. She wanted to control whom they dated or befriended and wanted to hear their personal and job gossip.

As we explored further, I learned her father had insisted on knowing all these same things about her from early elementary school age through her adult life until he died. She and he fought a lot over his intrusions, beginning when she was a teenager. Her mother had not been so intrusive or nosy. Alicia reluctantly revealed she had acted in this same way with her younger brothers and sisters, being bossy and intrusive.

Over time Alicia said she felt sorry for herself because her children were "so neglectful of her." We continued to examine whether these expectations of her children were reasonable and where she learned such expectations. Gradually, Alicia appreciated she learned many of these ideas from her father. The thought began to take hold that, when looked at from her children's perspectives (and from her perspective as a teen with her father), maybe she was being unreasonable in wanting them to do just what she expected.

Over time Alicia intruded less into her children's lives and instead asked them how she could help them rather than ask for her needs to be met by having them do what she wanted. She was only able to do this as we explored how she picked up this habit of relating from her father.

A side effect of Alicia's three years of work in psychotherapy was that her relationship also improved with her husband. She had not realized that she called most of the shots in her marriage and that this distanced him from her. As she began to change with the children, she also began to ask him for his ideas and opinions. At first, he was taken aback but gradually became more forthcoming as Alicia listened to him. She saw improvements in their marriage.

Commentary

Alicia had thrown herself wholeheartedly into her role as mother, but we discovered she assumed an impotent role with her children. She expected them to cater to her desires to be nosy and intrusive about their personal lives in a manner that was unreasonable for their ages and circumstances. She discovered this role was similar to that of her impotent father. Her omnipotent mother, who let Alicia be bossy with and controlling of her younger siblings, also reinforced her role growing up. Alicia assumed the same impotent role with her husband. She was only able to make changes for the better in how she related to her children and her husband once she received some deconditioning therapy that helped her discover, unravel, and change her conditioned impotent role.

What the Deconditioned Person Looks Like

AFTER PSYCHOTHERAPY AND AS A DECONDITIONED PERSON, YOU NO LONGER PERCEIVE EITHER YOURSELF OR OTHERS AS ONE-DIMENSIONAL ACTORS PLAYING DEHUMANIZED ROLES. NOW YOU APPROACH EVERY PERSON AS THEY ARE, IN REALITY, *AT THAT MOMENT.* You are able to accomplish this through closely observing yourself and others. You achieve this through reality testing—comparing your thoughts, feelings, and perceptions to the real world to see if they are accurate—and by consciously refusing to engage in the mindless reflex behaviors of emotionally conditioned interactions. Now, when you react in an unconditioned way, you no longer allow yourself to be inconsiderate or unreasonable with others or accept their unreasonable treatment of you.

The changes you undergo by emotional deconditioning are all conscious and willing alterations. You still can revert to emotionally conditioned responses if you want. This is one option, whereas before it *had* been the *only* option. However, your choosing a conditioned response again is an unlikely choice. For you to retreat into an emotionally conditioned role would be a return to a pretense that you have finally discarded because it was illusory, unrealistic, and led to problems.

Even if you wanted to erase completely your emotionally conditioned personality, you cannot. However, you can change your thinking during dynamic psychotherapy. Now you can use your ability to think logically, an ability that had been previously subordinated to your emotionally conditioned responses, to manage your relationships. When you eliminate your reflex, stereotyped conditioned responses, you become aware of all the options that were not accessible before. Freeing your mind of its repetitious, unimaginative patterns allows you the full scope of your intellectual and creative potential.

Dr. Martin and I do not claim that "deconditioning" guarantees an ideal life. In our experience, emotionally deconditioned people in our society are rare. For decades we have heard our patients describe feeling that they are misfits, but happier misfits.

As an emotionally deconditioned person, you do *think* a great deal and no longer accept others' perceptions without question. You now depend on your own personal final judgments, carefully balancing what you owe others and what is due to you. You listen to everyone's judgments and opinions, and evaluate your own and others' perceptions. You respect opinions that are well conceived but arrive at your own conclusions. You base your decisions on evidence rather than by emotional persuasion.

As a deconditioned person, you become aware that you *can* revert to emotionally conditioned responses, but very rarely do you elect to do so, since this requires abandoning reality for the illusions derived from the role you're playing. Your life situations become more comprehensible and stable, and the world is a larger, more interesting, and more important place, when you can appreciate your own human qualities rather than pursue a stereotyped role.

What You Discovered in This Chapter

- We found there is no such thing as a "normal" person.
- Emotional illness is often difficult to distinguish from physical illness and results when we are overwhelmed by difficulties with managing our significant relationships.
- Without understanding the relationship problems in our lives, we are subject to emotional breakdowns.
- The ideal for preventing emotional disorders is to begin with parents of very young children as well as to reach children in elementary school.
- Successful treatment of emotional illness is possible with psychotherapy that involves a process of deconditioning for both omnipotents and impotents.
- The best way to achieve self-understanding is to observe the workings of your own mind.
- Emotionally deconditioned people think and behave autonomously, and are able to see themselves and others as they really are, rather than remaining stuck in a stereotyped role.

What You Can Do to Decrease Living on Automatic

What Have You Discovered About You?

By now we hope you have been able to grasp how we can be emotionally conditioned early in life into two distinct roles. We hope you are familiar with the skewed outlook on life that conditioning gives us—poor judgment, short-circuiting and creating different styles of thinking, alienation from others, stereotyping, symbiosis, and experiencing emotions differently. We hope you grasp why we all have difficulties communicating with people we most desire to be able to talk with and understand. Lastly, we hope you appreciate the connection between emotional conditioning and developing emotional illnesses. We have supplied reasons why you may want to better observe yourself, understand your own emotionally conditioned role, and realize what deconditioning you might need.

This final chapter includes case examples and suggested strategies you can begin applying in your own life. We hope you have enjoyed reflecting on the *Questions to Ask Yourself* found throughout this book and that you will continue to engage in self-discovery.

Self-knowledge influences every interaction we have with people in our relationships. We cannot truly understand others until we develop a deeper understanding of ourselves. Once we develop a measure of self-understanding, we find that we are better at understanding others, are able to respond with sensitivity to people in varying moods, and can learn to appreciate the reasoning for others' seemingly odd behaviors.

We do not acquire self-understanding through reading or sharing the intellectual experience of those who have successfully done so. THE BEST

APPROACH TO SELF-UNDERSTANDING IS AN INTELLIGENT INWARD STUDY OF OUR-SELVES RATHER THAN RELYING ON AN EXTERNAL SOURCE.

But, without prior experience in self-observation, an immediate problem arises: How can we develop the ability to self-observe rather than react reflexively according to our emotionally conditioned roles? We can practice by observing people we encounter every day, taking note of their actions, thoughts expressed, attitudes, emotions, peculiarities, and so on and, more importantly, *our own reactions to each person*. We must also *ask questions* about others' thoughts, emotions, and behaviors to clarify what *they* are thinking, feeling, and why they behave as they do. This avoids the pitfall of assuming another person is thinking and feeling as you are. There is nothing simple in this essential first step of learning to observe and ask questions.

First, work on seeing yourself more realistically. Assess whether you automatically fulfill a role and, if so, to what extent and with whom do you do this. Make a list of your thoughts about yourself, and observe your behaviors with others close to you. Next, identify the roles of those in these closest relationships—spouse, siblings, children, parents, and friends.

Another suggestion is observe every interaction you have with someone close to you. Write it down in a notebook if you want. Record what the encounter was like, who said or did what, how you felt during the interaction, and what emotions the other person showed. Afterward, as you look at your notes, think about the content of your interaction. What happened? Do you call the shots with some people? Do you go along indiscriminately with others? Are you helpful to some people and dismissive of others without any apparent reason?

ONCE YOU IDENTIFY YOUR EMOTIONALLY CONDITIONED ROLES IN YOUR VITAL RELATIONSHIPS, YOU CAN BEGIN TO MAKE CHANGES. REMEMBER, THIS IS NOT EASY AND WILL REQUIRE CONTINUED EFFORT OVER A LONG TIME, BUT IT IS WORTH THE EFFORT. Begin by making observations over time about *every interaction* you have with another person. Observe yourself and the other person simultaneously. It may be difficult but not impossible. If you rely on manipulation, scheming, and demanding behavior in your interactions, first observe when you do this. Then try the opposite of what you usually do. Do the *unnatural* but unconditioned behavior. For example, try asking a straightforward question without demanding or manipulating.

On the other hand, if you routinely fail to speak up for your own viewpoint and defer to another person, observe when you do this. Then do your *unnatural* but unconditioned behavior. Try saying, "My opinion about that is such and such." Do this regardless of what the other person's response is likely to be. Since there are two people in every relationship, your job, if you are an omnipotent, is to *think more about you*. On the other hand, if you are an impotent, you already think too much about your own view-point and desires, so your deconditioning job is *to think more about others first*. Initially this takes a lot of practice and will feel unnatural to you. But we have found that most of our patients can accomplish this and can change their reactions to others and develop more reasonable relationships as a result.

When you are interacting, attempt to introduce your *thinking* skills rather than just reacting or responding based on your emotions and what you feel. Learn to *slow down* your automatic responses. When you sense a purely automatic emotional reaction, say, "Let me think about what you are say-ing or asking. I'll let you know my thoughts about this later."

Next, think about the circumstances of each interaction you have. Who gives? Who receives? What is reasonable for the circumstance at that par-ticular time, in that particular situation, and for the people involved?

As you practice these skills, you might ask for help from your family and close friends. Ask them to give you their thoughts on how they see you behaving in your relationships. However, since your friends and family are also likely to be emotionally conditioned, you may get some distorted opinions. But you can compare what they say about you with what you observe about yourself and also *about them*. And, most importantly, you can ask them for real-life examples of their observations of you. This will help you discern whether they see you as you are or whether they are pro-jecting something about them onto you.

We suggest that you remind yourself daily to use your intellect and not just act on your emotions, question your and others' behaviors, aim to achieve balance in your relationships, and create your own good judgment about yourself, others, and your current circumstances. Here are some examples.

People No Longer Living on Automatic
Tamika and Isaiah

Tamika and Isaiah are measuring the family room for the dimensions to buy a new carpet. Their intellects alone are involved with taking and recording the measurements. Tamika has been thinking that a neutral carpet color, like beige, would go with the many other colors in the room. She mentioned this choice a few days ago to Isaiah, and he said whatever she thought would be fine. She writes down the dimensions and is ready to walk out the door to the carpet store. Suddenly, Isaiah yells at her from another room as she has one foot out the door, "Don't buy one of those light carpet colors like beige or tan. I think a dark color, like brown or gray, would be better. Okay?"

At this point, because of their close relationship as husband and wife, Tamika and Isaiah are in a situation in which emotional conditioning will kick in and, if they are not careful, cause them to respond automatically. How has Tamika been emotionally conditioned? And, how about Isaiah's conditioning? What roles are they in with one another? If Tamika is an omnipotent and Isaiah an impotent, Tamika's role will be to give in to her husband's wishes. If Tamika is an impotent and her husband an omnipotent, Tamika will want her color choice to prevail, and she will expect Isaiah to defer to her on the carpet's color.

If they want to work around their automatic responses, they will do something different. Tamika will not leave for the carpet store but will go to Isaiah and calmly ask without any attitude or emotion, but just curiosity, "A few days ago you suggested beige or tan would be fine, and now you don't think either of these colors is best. What are your new thoughts?"

And, if Isaiah wants to avoid a purely emotional response he might say, "I've thought about it some more. It seems to me that darker colors will show dirt less. Since we have a lot of foot traffic from outdoors through the family room, I thought it would look better and require less frequent vacuuming and shampooing to have a darker color."

Now Tamika has some additional intellectual information, from Isaiah's point of view, to ponder. She might decide Isaiah has a reasonable point and change the carpet color choice. "That's a good point. I hadn't thought of that. I see what you are saying. Thanks for your input." Or, Tamika might say, "Let me think about what you've said and I'll let you know." She then thinks over what he has said instead of immediately responding emotionally. Or, she might discuss further with Isaiah why she prefers the lighter colors—that they would brighten the room or go better with the decor. But the engagement stays on point in a nonemotional realm, and they respectfully ask for input and listen to one another.

As an alternative scenario, suppose Isaiah responds purely emotionally that he has no reason for his color choice. He just wants the color he wants. Then Tamika must decide, is his response based on reason or is it just emotional? If she decides he is being solely emotional and not reasonable, she can tell him, "If you can't give me any reasonable explanation that has to do with the carpet color, I am going to choose beige or tan for the reasons I have already given you."

Doug and Brenda

Doug likes to talk to his best friend by phone once a week. They chat for about an hour. Almost always, Brenda, his wife, interrupts his call about 10 minutes into their conversation with a request that she needs help right now with finding a book she wants to give a friend the next time she sees her or some similar nonurgent request.

Doug wants to avoid these interruptions, so he decides to think about this situation before he acts or reacts. And, since this situation repeats, he knows he needs to discuss his concerns with Brenda. Is this a reasonable request Brenda makes? She wants Doug to hang up with his best friend now to find her book now. This is a request for Doug to shift his attention from something he enjoys to something that immediately satisfies Brenda. There is no urgency in this situation. Brenda is not asking him to get off the phone because there is a fire in the house. Would it be unreasonable for Doug to wait to answer Brenda's request until after he gets off the phone? Would it be unreasonable for Brenda to wait?

What would happen if he said yes? He would end the call and go find her book. He would give up something he enjoys to cater to Brenda's want. How would he feel? He might be angry, resigned, or sad that he did not do the fun thing he wanted. What *would happen if he said no? Then Brenda might be angry, pout, be belligerent, or just leave him alone. But, he might be glad he talked to his friend. He might also feel guilty he didn't please Brenda.*

How would you respond if you were Doug?

How would you respond if you were Brenda?

Doug will do himself a world of good if he goes through this examination and analysis of the situation before he acts. It would also help him if he goes over the situation beforehand with Brenda.

These new ways of participating in relationships and of communicating require making an effort to use your mind and brain rather than having an emotional knee-jerk reaction. Putting this into action takes practice and at first will seem difficult and unnatural. Fulfilling your emotionally conditioned role feels so natural. *If you want to quit living on automatic, try out the unnatural in your closest relationships.*

Once you become practiced in doing this for yourself, if you are a parent, you can help your children learn these skills. Introduce the behaviors and ways of thinking you want to expect from your children that are contrary to and inconsistent with their already established roles in the family. Expect more self-responsibility and empathy but less impulsivity and self-centeredness from your impotent children. Expect your omnipotent children to decrease their focus on others' happiness, have more fun and carefree play, show caring for themselves, and be less regimented. Expect and teach your children how to look at the immediate circumstances in relationships and see what each person reasonably needs. Help them understand flexibility in interactions, not fixed responses according to roles. Here are some examples.

Travis

Travis is 8 years old. His sister Emily is 11. Recently Emily broke both arms falling off a swing. She is in casts up to her armpits and requires help with everything. She has chores of making her bed, getting out trash, and folding the laundry. Now she cannot do chores. Their parents are scrambling to keep up with just caring for Emily—feeding, bathing, dressing, and toileting—and with her chores. Emily has been in an omnipotent role in the family and Travis in an impotent role.

Dad, after some self-deconditioning, has the idea that, in this situation, expecting help from Travis is reasonable. This is an unusual idea because no one expects effort from Travis. Everyone expects him to "play." They only expect him to dress, undress, and brush his teeth. Getting him to bathe or do homework is a struggle.

Dad tells Travis he wants him to take over some of Emily's chores, make her bed, and take out the trash. Travis says he does not want to. Dad has a conversation with him. He begins by asking Travis what he is thinking about when asked to do Emily's chores.

Travis gives an emotional response, "I don't like chores. It is too hard. I want to play, not do chores."

Dad engages him further to make him think. "What should we do while Emily cannot do her own chores?"

"You and mom do them," Travis says angrily and begins to pout.

Dad says, "We already have a lot to do taking care of Emily in other ways. We need help, and you are the other person in the family who can help out. What if you had broken arms and needed help with everything. Who would help you?"

"Probably you, mom, and Emily," says Travis.

"That's right," says dad. "When people we love need help we find a way to help them, depending on our situations. So what can you do to help out, Travis?"

"I think I can make her bed and do the trash but I don't like it," Travis replies. Dad then says, "You don't have to like it. You just have to do it to help Emily."

Astrid

Astrid is a 17-year-old high school senior. A boy at another school asked her to an event at his school. She does not know him well. They've interacted twice at a regional academic team competition. She is unsure whether to accept his invitation, so she talks the situation over with her mom.

Mom: *What do you know about him?*

Astrid: *Not much. But he is cute. His clothes are wrinkled a lot and he seems geeky. Other girls who know him say he is quiet and not much fun.*

Mom: *What is important is not what others say but what you observe and what your opinion is. What are the possible decisions that you can make in this situation?*

Astrid: *I go or I don't.*

Mom: *And what are the possible results for each of the decisions you see?*

Astrid: *I go and have a good time, or I have a lousy time or I just turn him down, and do something else.*

Mom: *Is there anything else you'd prefer to do that evening?*

Astrid: *So far I don't have any other plans.*

Mom: *If you decide to go, why would you do it?*

Astrid: *Well, I wouldn't want to hurt his feelings by turning him down.*

Mom: *What about your feelings? What would you get out of it?*

Astrid: *I'd get to wear a new dress, which would make me happy. And maybe I'd meet some people at his school or, I might be bored.*

Mom: *So, what would you or could you do if you get bored?*

Astrid: *Just talk to people, I guess, or get some food.*

Mom: *And how would that be?*

Astrid: *Okay, 'cause then I'd know what he is like. I guess I'd get to know him better.*

Mom: *And, what about you? Is there anything you might learn about you?*

Astrid: *Well, I might learn more about how to be around people I don't know—strangers. I might get more comfortable with how to meet and talk to them.*

Mom: *And, what would be the best and worst parts of not going?*

Astrid: *I might do something better with my friends or I might be sorry for not going if I learned it was fun and that he's a great guy. Okay, mom, I think I know what I'm going to do. I'll go with him and see what he's like, and if I have a good time with him or, if not, maybe I'll meet someone new I like better.*

Mom: *I think that's well thought out. After all, the only way to know a person is to spend time with him. Another thought I had would be to ask him to meet with before you make your final decision. Just say you'd like to get acquainted since you don't know one another well.*

In both of the above situations parents help their children look at decision making more intellectually to develop rational judgment and balance in relationships and avoid emotional reactions. Parents can also discuss these issues after the fact. Dad can ask Travis what it has been like for him helping out Emily and what did he discover about himself. Mom can ask Astrid what she learned about herself and the boy at his school event and how she later saw her decision. And, would she make the same decision again? Why or why not?

Five Steps to Free Yourself from Living on Automatic

After reading this book, we hope that you have a better idea of who you are and what your close relationships are like. Now it's time to think about how to put this knowledge to use when you interact with others. Here are five steps to help you break free from your emotional conditioning and avoid automatic responses (Table 11.1).

1. Observe and think about *when and under what circumstances* your emotional responses take place. Are they with your spouse, children, parents, coworkers? In what sorts of situations do they occur?

2. Observe and think about *what will bring out* the emotionally conditioned behaviors, thoughts, and emotions in you and the other person? Do your spouse or children *want something from you*? Do you feel the *need to have your coworkers' attention* when you arrive at work each day? Are you tempted to think, feel, or behave the same old way with them?

3. Think about your *method of stopping* your emotionally conditioned reactions, be it your behaviors, thoughts, or emotions. If you anxiously dread arriving home each day, anticipating numerous and simultaneous requests from your children, how will you lessen your dread and start *thinking* about what you need to do? Any strategy that will slow down your response gives you time to think. You might try writing down your strategies, speaking them to yourself, and rehearsing. Making and taking extra time is being a good friend to you.

4. You need a way *to remind yourself to think* about your present situation instead of reacting with your conditioned emotional response. Ask yourself, what is reasonable to do in this situation? What are the different possibilities I can think about? Make contingency plans. Do I tell all my children to wait 15 minutes before they ask me anything so I can change out of my work clothes and lie down for 5 minutes? Do I tell only the oldest children to wait but allow my youngest to make requests? Do I tell all my children to leave me alone and ask their other parent?

5. *Take action* to communicate or reveal your decision after you have thought about the situation, gathered information, and decided on a path for yourself. Tell your children, spouse, coworker, what you think or have decided to do and why. You might rehearse your actions for your frequent interactions in which you function automatically, reacting instead of evaluating, questioning, and thinking. Feel free to invent your own method to find an approach that works for you.

Table 11.1   Five Steps to Free Yourself from Living on Automatic

1. Think about the circumstances and situations that cause you to react emotionally. Who triggers these automatic responses? When and where are these reactions likely to occur?
2. Review the situations, behaviors, and thoughts you have that cause you to react emotionally.
3. Plan a *method* you can use *to stop* your emotionally conditioned reactions.
4. Prepare for how you will *remind yourself to think* rather than *quickly react.*
5. List the ways you can *take action to communicate* your decisions that use thought instead of emotions.

Would People Welcome "Deconditioning"?

If we accept as valid the idea of emotional conditioning, would we find the idea of deconditioning appealing so that we might become more sensitive in our relationships? Would we like the idea of abandoning our dehumanized roles and manner of relating to other people?

If you are a parent, would you want to help your children learn how to become more stable emotionally? Would you like to enable them to avoid predictable or disastrous choices dictated by emotional conditioning in their approach to work, marriage, and friendships? Would you willingly take deconditioning courses to break the chain of emotionally programming your children?

If you are a business leader, would you explore the possibility of deconditioning to improve your managerial skills, upgrade your judgment, and be able to discriminate between conscientious employees and those who create problems? Could we improve our government by training politicians, leaders, and the judiciary to understand their own emotional conditioning before making decisions with momentous consequences?

We all need answers to these questions. Such answers would not ensure a utopia but only a baptism into reality. But, discovering how to live in reality benefits us all as it makes possible transformation of our relationships and ourselves.

We value corroboration of our findings by other psychotherapists, but will be most gratified if this book provides a stimulus to our readers to seek further self-understanding and learn to override involuntary and robotic emotional, behavioral, and thought responses.

With all these new discoveries you can now choose to be on a path to greater self-understanding and master your automatic emotional responses to other people. We hope that you continue to enjoy your voyage of self-exploration, lessen problems from "living on automatic," and savor and delight in an expanded personal world where you can truly be yourself.

WHAT YOU DISCOVERED IN THIS CHAPTER

- The best approach to self-understanding is an intelligent study of yourself.
- Observing, questioning, and thinking are the keys to "deconditioning" on your own and avoiding living on automatic.
- Set a goal to observe yourself and others simultaneously in your interactions.
- Both omnipotents and impotents find deconditioning difficult. Initially, it may make us anxious and insecure. However, practicing these skills offers great benefits, deepens our understanding of others and ourselves, and has the potential to transform our relationships.

Notes

Chapter 2

1. Sigmund Freud used the terminology *infantile omnipotence* and *omnipotence of thought*, the latter characteristic of the obsessive neurotic, in *Totem and Taboo: Resemblance Between the Psychic Lives of Savages and Neurotics,* trans. by A. A. Brill (New York: Moffat, Yard and Co., 1918). However, Freud's definition does not apply to what Dr. Martin discovered or to how he uses the term *omnipotent* as a role arising from emotional conditioning.

Chapter 4

1. Wayne E. Oates, PhD, created the term *workaholic* in *Confessions of a Workaholic: The Facts About Work Addiction* (New York: World Publishing Company, 1971).

Chapter 9

1. Richard A. Gardner, MD, created the term *parental alienation syndrome* in his book *The Parental Alienation Syndrome: A Guide for Mental Health and Legal Professionals* (Cresskill, NJ: Creative Therapeutics, 1998).

Suggested Reading and Viewing

Fiction

A Passage to India by E. M. Forster
Of Mice and Men by John Steinbeck
The Winter of Our Discontent by John Steinbeck
Tender Is the Night by F. Scott Fitzgerald
White Oleander by Janet Fitch
The Adults by Alison Espach
Enchantment: A Novel by Daphne Merkin
Coffee Will Make You Black by April Sinclair
The Fifth Child by Doris Lessing
A Child Called It: One Child's Courage to Survive by Dave Pelzer
Freedom: A Novel by Jonathan Franzen
The Prince of Tides by Pat Conroy
The Chosen by Chaim Potok
The Odyssey by Homer
The Aeneid by Virgil
Tartuffe by Moliere
Candide by Voltaire
King Lear by William Shakespeare
Macbeth by William Shakespeare
The Taming of the Shrew by William Shakespeare
Othello by William Shakespeare
The Pillars of the Earth: A Novel by Ken Follett
Flight Behavior: A Novel by Barbara Kingsolver
The Adventures of Huckleberry Finn by Mark Twain
Go Tell It on the Mountain by James Baldwin
A Grief Observed by C. S. Lewis
The Bell Jar by Sylvia Plath
Women by Susan Sontag and Annie Leibovitz

The Feminine Mystique by Betty Friedan
In Cold Blood by Truman Capote
Little Fires Everywhere by Celeste Ng

Nonfiction

The Bible
First Father, First Daughter: A Memoir by Maureen Reagan
Savage Beauty: The Life of Edna St. Vincent Millay by Nancy Milford
The Far Side of Paradise: A Biography of F. Scott Fitzgerald by Arthur Mizener
My Father at 100 by Ron Reagan
Confessions of a Workaholic: The Facts About Work Addiction by Wayne E. Oates
The Year of Magical Thinking by Joan Didion
Civilization and Its Discontents by Sigmund Freud
The Seven Storey Mountain: An Autobiography of Faith by Thomas Merton
If This Is a Man by Primo Levi
Black Boy: A Record of Childhood and Youth by Richard Wright
The Death of Santini by Pat Conroy
The Virtue of Selfishness by Ayn Rand
Travels with Myself and Another by Martha Gellhorn
Tough Choices by Carly Fiorina
Links about Ivan Pavlov:
http://www.learning-theories.com/classical-conditioning-pavlov.html
http://en.wikipedia.org/wiki/Classical_conditioning
http://psychology.about.com/od/classicalconditioning/a/pavlovs-dogs.htm
http://www.muskingum.edu/~psych/psycweb/history/pavlov.htm
Links about Konrad Lorenz:
http://www.simplypsychology.org/attachment.html
http://www.wikipedia.org/wiki/konrad_Lorenz
http://www.britannica.com/EBchecked/topic/348157/konrad-lorenz
Links about John B. Watson:
http://www.wikipedia.org/wiki/John_B._Watson
http://www.brynmawr.edu/psychology/rwozniak/watson.html
Links about B. F. Skinner:
www.bfskinner.org
http://www.nndb.com/people/297/000022231
http://www.theoryfundamentals.com/skinner.htm

Viewing (Film, Television, Theater)

Fear and Loathing in Las Vegas
Ordinary People
Hustle and Flow

Hud
Remains of the Day
The Door in the Floor
Gran Torino
Blue Jasmine
Sling Blade
When Harry Met Sally
The Hundred-Foot Journey
A Walk in the Woods
Fences
Prince of Tides
Florence Foster Jenkins
Amadeus
Darkest Hour
The Crown
The Jewel in the Crown
The Human Stain
Sully
Beasts of the Southern Wild
The Way, Way Back
Disconnect
Café Society
Fruitvale Station
Mississippi Grind
Indignation
J. Edgar
The King's Speech
Maudie
Maggie's Plan
A Separation
What Maisie Knew
American Sniper
I, Tonya
Lady Bird

Index

Page numbers followed by *t* indicate tables.

ADHD, 68

Adolescent impotents, 70–71; attraction to omnipotents, 70–71; college experience of, 71; high school experience of, 71; parental appeasement of, 70; risk-taking behavior of, 70

Adolescent omnipotents, 52–53; depression and suicide risk in, 53; modeling of omnipotent parent, 52; peer pressure and, 53; protection of impotent parent, 52

Adultery. *See* Extramarital affairs

Adult impotents, 71–72; charisma and manipulation, 71; commanding role in family, 72; disability or helplessness of, 72; leisure activities of, 54

Adult omnipotents, 53–55; civic and volunteer activities of, 55; competitiveness of, 54–55; marriage and family roles of, 54; overcommitment of, 54; as workaholics, 54

Aggression, impotents and, 66–67

Aging: impotents and, 72–73; omnipotents and, 55–56

Anger: emotional illness and, 153; impotent display of, 66, 67, 68;

omnipotent restraint and concealment, 48, 58

Anxiety, 9–11, 153; contradictory messages and, 8; impotents and, 67, 75; marriage and, 108, 141; need to control, 9; omnipotents and, 20, 35, 47–49

Assessment of others: failure, and miscommunication, 81–82; new method for, 38–39

Assuming others think like us, 81, 96–97

Assumptions, as substitute for observations, 85–86

Attention span, of impotents, 65, 68

Attitude, omnipotent *vs.* impotent, 40*t*

Attraction: extramarital, as warning sign, 122; omnipotent–impotent, 19, 70–71, 106–108, 116–117, 143–144

Authentic selves, role-playing *vs.*, 16

Authority, impotent defiance of, 69, 70, 71

Automatic, living on: case examples of changing, 166–170; deconditioning from, 164–172; deconditioning therapy for, 156–162; depersonalization and, 30–31; freeing self from, five steps for,

Automatic, living on (*cont.*)
170–171, 171*t*; impaired judgment
and, 31–33; knee-jerk reactions, 17,
33, 38, 168; need to control anxiety
and, 9; roles and role-playing,
15–28; self-discovery *vs.*, 164–170;
self-observation *vs.*, 165–166;
short-circuited thinking and,
29–30; stereotyping and, 33–34;
teaching children to recognize and
avoid, 168–170; trying out
unnatural role *vs.*, 165–166, 168

Birth, conditioning before, 23–24,
45, 64
Birth order, 64; and impotents, 64;
and omnipotents, 45
Busy-ness of mind, 100–101

Child and strange dog scenario,
97–98
Childhood: emotional conditioning
in, 5–8, 25–26; legacy of
experiences, 10; parental teaching
on avoiding automatic living,
168–170; personality formation in,
8, 15; roles assigned by parents in,
23–25, 45, 64; roles learned in,
18–22; unconscious emotional
messages from parents, 6–8, 15.
See also Preschoolers, impotent;
Preschoolers, omnipotent; School-
age impotents; School-age
omnipotents
Civic work, omnipotents and, 55
Cleanliness, of omnipotents, 47
Cohabitation, 132
Commitment mode, omnipotent *vs.*
impotent, 40*t*
Communication. *See*
Miscommunication
Competition, between impotent
parent and impotent child, 66
Competitiveness, of omnipotents, 49,
54–55

Conflicts, in marriage, 116–131; case
examples of, 109–111, 122–129;
over extramarital affairs, 117–123;
over finances, 125–126; over
parenting, 126–127; role-based,
108–112; over sex, 116–117, 118;
over substance abuse, 124, 127–129
Conscience: of impotents, 40*t*, 68–69;
of omnipotents, 40*t*, 49
Context: automatic, reflexive action
vs., 9; roles and role-playing *vs.*, 20.
See also Reality
Continuum of emotional
conditioning, 26
Coparenting, 132, 137
Culture, and role-playing, 16
Custody: battles over, 137–141; case
example of, 139–141; children's
difficulties with parental roles,
138–141; evaluations and
mediation, 136

Dating: after divorce, 141–145;
omnipotent–impotent attraction,
19, 70–71, 106–108, 143–144;
rehearsing for marriage, 107–108
Deconditioning, 164–172; freeing self
from automatic living, five steps for,
170–171, 171*t*; parental teaching of
children, 168–170; self-observation
for, 165–166; trying out unnatural
role, 165–166, 168; willingness and
welcoming, 171–172
Deconditioning therapy, 156–162;
case examples of, 157–161; for
impotents, 160–161; life after,
161–162; for omnipotents, 156,
157–160
Defining words differently, and
miscommunication, 81, 98–99
Dehumanization, 21, 29
Denial of needs and wants,
omnipotent, 20, 47, 58
Dependency, state of: impotent
dependence and passivity, 20, 21,

40*t*, 95, 99; omnipotent position of service and control, 20, 40*t*, 50, 54, 58, 89

Depersonalization, 30–31

Depression, 9–11, 153, 155; contradictory messages and, 8; marriage and, 108, 141; omnipotent role and, 48, 49, 53, 128

Devalued omnipotent, 47–48, 55, 118, 133, 143

Disability, of impotents, 72

Divorce, 132–147; case examples of, 134; custody battles in, 137–141; custody evaluations and mediation in, 136; effects on children, 135–136; as impetus for counseling, 141; impotent child and, 135–138; joint custody and children's difficulties with parental roles, 138–141; as last resort, 133; legal proceedings in, 134–135, 141; omnipotent child and, 43–44, 50–51, 137–138; parental alienation syndrome in, 137; rates of, 104; reaction of friends, 134, 141; remarriage after, 141, 144, 145–146; repeating earlier failures after, 141–145; return to single life, 141; roles continuing in, 133–134; self-understanding *vs.* roles in, 146; stigma of, 104, 132

Double standards, 81, 95–96

Drugs. *See* Substance abuse

Effects of emotional conditioning, 29–38, 30*t*; creation of symbiosis, 34–35; depersonalization, 30–31; impaired judgment, 31–33; perception and interpretation of emotions, 36–38; reducing others to stereotype, 33–34; short-circuited thinking, 29–30; thinking styles, 35–36

Elite social groups, in school, 69

Emotion, perception and interpretation of, 36–38

Emotional conditioning, 13–28; assessment of others, 38–39; child-to-child variation in, 26; common patterns in, 15–17; continuum of, 26; deconditioning therapy for, 156–162; dehumanization in, 21, 29; depersonalization in, 30–31; discoveries about, 27*t*; early childhood, 5–8, 25–26; effects of, 29–38, 30*t*; examples of, 25–26; first observations of, 13–15; freeing self from, five steps for, 170–171; impaired judgment in, 31–33; individuality *vs.*, 25; labels in, desire to reject, 22; perception and interpretation of emotions in, 36–38; process of, 22–28; recognition and awareness of, 26–28, 37, 165–166; reducing others to stereotype in, 33–34; roles and role-playing in, 15–28; self-reinforcement of, 43; short-circuited thinking in, 29–30; symbiosis creation in, 34–35; thinking styles in, 35–36

Emotional illnesses, 9–11; conflict and, 9; contradictory messages and, 8; diagnosis by exclusion, 153; emotional overload and, 10; examples of, 10; label, *vs.* normal, 151–153; in marriage, 123–125; mental illnesses *vs.*, 10–11; origin in relationship problems, 154–155; physical manifestations of, 10, 153–154; prevention of, 155; psychotherapy for, 11, 151–163; recovery from, 11; stigma of, 11; understanding origin of, 11

Emotionally conditioned thinking, 35

Emotional maladjustment, recognition and awareness of, 26–28

Emotional overload, 10

Emotional support: demands for, 40*t*; extramarital affairs and flow of, 120; in marriage, omnipotent vs. impotent, 111–112

Emotional wellness programs, 155

Emotion-skewed thinking, and miscommunication, 81, 82–84

Extramarital affairs, 117–123; case example of, 122–123; flow of emotional support in, 120; havoc created by, 121–122; ignoring or accepting, 119, 120; impotent having, 119; impotent reaction to spouse's, 119, 121–122; marriage prolonged by, 119, 122–123; nature and ubiquity of, 117–120; omnipotent having, 118–119, 120; omnipotent reaction to spouse's, 121; rigid roles as cause of, 120; threesome equilibrium in, 120

"Falling in love," 98, 106, 108

Family: omnipotent and impotent roles in, 16–28; toll of emotional illnesses in, 10. *See also* Parent(s)

Fastidiousness, of omnipotents, 47

Financial conflict, in marriage, 125–126

First-born children, as omnipotents, 45

Freedom from automatic living, 170–171, 171*t*

Freud, Sigmund, 82

Gardner, Richard, 137

Gender, and roles, 16–17

Good babies, omnipotents as, 45–47

Grandiosity, in impotent role, 33

Gratification, for impotents, 65–66, 75

Group assignments, in school, 68

Helicopter parenting, 22

Helplessness, of impotents, 72

Hero, omnipotent as, 20

Hobbies, omnipotents and, 54

Hyperawareness, omnipotent role and, 20

Ideal world, behavior and relationships in, 8–9

Ideas of others, openness to, 81, 99–100

Illness: emotional (*see* Emotional illnesses); physical, as manifestation of emotional illnesses, 10, 153–154; physical, omnipotent denial of, 20, 55

Imagination, 82–84; impotent use of, 84; omnipotent use of, 84

Impotents, 16–28, 19–22, 60–77; adolescent, 70–71; adult, 71–72; aging and, 72–73; attention span of, 65, 68; attraction to omnipotents, 19, 70–71, 106–108, 116–117, 143–144; behaviors, emotions, and thoughts of, 19–22; belief in omnipotence, 17, 75; busy-ness of mind, 101; case examples of, 60–64, 73–75; characteristics of, 40*t*; conscience of, 40*t*, 68–69; custody battles and, 137–141; deconditioning therapy for, 160–161; defiance of authority, 69, 70, 71; dependency and passivity of, 20, 21, 40*t*, 95, 99; depersonalization by, 30–31; desire to reject label, 22; divorce and, 133–134, 143–144; emotion-skewed thinking of, 83–84; finances of, 125–126; identifying and distinguishing, 39, 40*t*; imagination of, 84; impaired judgment of, 31–33; impotent child and impotent parent, 60, 65, 66; impotent child and omnipotent parent, 21, 60, 135–136, 137; impotent parent and omnipotent child, 20, 47–48, 50–51, 52, 137; impulsivity of, 36, 68–69, 70, 94; infancy of, 64–66; insatiable, 48,

83, 89, 119; love definition of, 99; magical thinking of, 87–89; marriage to another impotent, 113–115, 114t, 145–146; marriage to omnipotent, 19, 54, 57, 105–112, 114t; observations of, inadequate, 84–87; openness to others' ideas, lack of, 99–100; parental assignment of role, 23–25, 64; perception and interpretation of emotion, 36–38; personality summary, 75; preschool, 66–67; projection by, 90–93; rationalizations of, 94; reducing others to stereotype, 33; school-age, 49, 67–70; sex for, 116–117, 118; short-circuited thinking of, 29–30; sibling relationships of, 60; substance abuse of, 70, 128; symbiosis creation by, 34–35; thinking processes of, 21–22, 32; treating people differently, 95–96

Impulsivity, of impotents, 36, 68–69, 70, 94

Individuality: emotional conditioning vs., 25; role-playing vs., 16, 18

Infancy: emotional conditioning in, 5–6; of impotents, 64–66; of omnipotents, 45–47; role assignment in, 23–25

Insatiable impotent, 48, 83, 89, 118, 119

Intimacy, roles interfering with, 30–31

Introspection, lack of, 85–86

Joint custody, 137–141

Knee-jerk reactions, 17, 33, 38, 168

Labels: desire to reject, 22; normal vs. emotionally ill, 151–153

Learning problems, 68

Logical reasoning, emotional conditioning vs., 19–20, 33, 83

Love, 105–107; defining, 98–99, 105–106; "falling in love," 98, 106, 108; high regard as basis, 106; meaning to impotents, 99; meaning to omnipotents, 98; omnipotent–impotent attraction, 19, 70–71, 106–108, 116–117, 143–144

Magical thinking: definition of, 87; and miscommunication, 81, 87–89

Manipulation: by impotents, 30, 67, 71; of omnipotents, 32

Marriage: alternatives to, 132; bad, enduring, 104–105; case examples of, 109–115; choosing partner, 104–105; conflicts in, 108–112, 116–131; culture and, 16; devalued omnipotent in, 118; discarding roles in, 105; emotional illnesses in, 123–125; emotional support in, omnipotent vs. impotent, 111–112; extramarital affairs in, 117–123; failed, 104, 132–133 (see also Divorce); financial issues in, 125–126; impotent–impotent partners, 113–115, 114t, 145–146; insatiable impotent in, 118; love and, 105–107; omnipotent–impotent attraction, 19, 70–71, 106–108, 116–117, 143–144; omnipotent–impotent partners, 19, 54, 57, 105–112, 114t; omnipotent–impotent relationship as human-made misconception, 107; omnipotent–omnipotent partners, 112–113, 114t, 145–146; parental model of, 105; parenting issues in, 126–127; reasonable priorities for, establishing, 107; rehearsing for, 107–108; roles in, 19, 104–115; sex in, 116–117, 118; small percentage of different, 112–115; substance abuse in, 124, 127–129; successful, defining, 105

Mental capacity, omnipotent *vs.*
   impotent, 40*t*
Mental illnesses, *vs.* emotional
   illnesses, 10–11
Mind: busy circuits of, 100–101;
   definition of, 82; theories of, 82–83
Miscommunication, 81–102;
   assuming others think like us and,
   81, 96–97; busy circuits of mind
   and, 100–101; chaos from, 81;
   defining words differently and, 81,
   98–99; double standard (treating
   people differently) and, 81, 95–96;
   emotion-skewed thinking and, 81,
   82–84; identifying and correcting,
   81; inadequate observation and, 81,
   84–87; lack of openness to others'
   ideas and, 81, 99–100; magical
   thinking and, 81, 87–89; projection
   and, 81, 89–93; rationalization and,
   81, 94; reasons for, 81, 82*t*; seeing
   things differently and, 97–98

Normal: deconditioning for "normal"
   patients, 157; mistaken
   classification of, 151–153;
   projection of own perception
   as, 91

Observations: inadequate, and
   miscommunication, 81, 84–87;
   learning through self-observation,
   165–166
Obsession, 153
Old age: of impotents, 72–73; of
   omnipotents, 55–56
Omnipotence, belief in, 19, 75
Omnipotents, 16–28, 19–22, 43–59;
   adolescent, 52–53; adult, 53–55;
   aging, 55–56; anxiety of, 20, 35,
   47–49; attraction to impotents,
   19, 70–71, 106–108, 116–117,
   143–144; behaviors, emotions, and
   thoughts of, 19–22; belief in

omnipotence, 17, 75; busy-ness of
   mind, 100–101; case examples of,
   43–44, 50–51, 56–58;
   characteristics of, 40*t*; conditioning
   before birth, 45; conscience of, 40*t,*
   49; custody battles and, 137–141;
   deconditioning therapy for, 156,
   157–160; denial of own wants and
   needs, 20, 47, 58; depersonalization
   by, 30; depression of, 48, 49, 53,
   128; desire to reject label, 22;
   devalued, 47–48, 55, 118, 133, 143;
   divorce and, 133–134, 143;
   emotion-skewed thinking of,
   83–84; finances of, 125–126;
   first-born children as, 45; general
   formula for, 51; hero role of, 20;
   identification with fellow
   omnipotents, 54–55; identifying
   and distinguishing, 39, 40*t*;
   imagination of, 84; impaired
   judgment of, 31–33; infancy of,
   45–47; love definition of, 98;
   magical thinking of, 87–89;
   marriage to another omnipotent,
   112–113, 114*t,* 145–146; marriage
   to impotent, 19, 54, 57, 105–112,
   114*t*; mission in life, 55;
   observations of, inadequate, 84–87;
   omnipotent child and impotent
   parent, 20, 47–48, 50–51, 52, 137;
   omnipotent child and omnipotent
   parent, 48, 52; omnipotent parent
   and impotent child, 21, 60,
   135–136, 137; openness to others'
   ideas, lack of, 99–100; parental
   assignment of role, 23–25, 45;
   perception and interpretation of
   emotion, 36–38; performance of
   children, 20, 49–50; personality
   summary for, 58; position of
   control and service, 20, 40*t*, 50,
   54, 58, 89; preschool, 47–48;
   problem-solving role of, 16, 19,

21, 35, 54; projection by, 90–93; psychotherapy sought by, 16, 19; rationalizations of, 94; reducing others to stereotype in, 33; school-age, 48–52; self-esteem of, 21, 40*t*, 51, 53–54, 108, 128; self-reliance of, 40*t*, 49, 58; seriousness of, 49, 53–54; sex for, 116–117, 118; short-circuited thinking of, 29–30; sibling relationships of, 60; substance abuse of, 127–128; suicide risk in, 32, 34, 51, 53, 124, 140; symbiosis creation by, 34; treating people differently, 95–96

Openness to others' ideas, lack of, 81, 99–100

Parent(s): impotent parent and impotent child, 60, 65, 66; impotent parent and omnipotent child, 20, 47–48, 50–51, 52, 137; infant caregiving, 5–6; marriage of, 105, 126–127; omnipotent–impotent combination of, 22–23; omnipotent parent and impotent child, 21, 60, 135–136, 137; omnipotent parent and omnipotent child, 48, 52; principles taught by, 7; projections of, 23–25, 89, 91; psychotherapy for, 152–153; roles assigned by, 23–25, 45, 64; teaching children to avoid automatic living, 168–170; teaching limited by personal knowledge, 7–8; unconscious emotional messages from, 6–8, 15

Parental alienation syndrome, 137

Parenting: attitudes toward, 23; helicopter, 22; limited participation of impotents in, 65; marital conflict over, 126–127; process of emotional conditioning in, 22–28; unique challenge of, 22

Pavlov, Ivan, 20, 36, 51

Peer pressure, and omnipotent adolescents, 53

Perfection, omnipotent quest for, 40*t*; adult, 55; anxiety over, 35; conscience and, 49; imperfection perceived as weakness, 32, 58; meeting needs of others as, 21, 50; relationship sabotage in, 30; school performance and, 49–50; suicide risk in, 32, 34, 51, 53, 124, 140; thinking style and, 35

Personality: childhood formation of, 8, 15; deconditioning and changes in, 156–162; enduring nature of, 8, 21; impotent, 60–77; omnipotent, 43–59; role as mold for, 18

Personality disorders, 151–153

Personal standards, 40*t*, 96–97

Phobia, 153

Physical manifestations, of emotional illnesses, 10, 153–154

Preschoolers, impotent, 66–67; aggressive acts of, 66–67; competition with impotent parent, 66; emotional displays of, 67; intimidation of parents, 67

Preschoolers, omnipotent, 47–48; denial of own needs and wants, 47; impotent parent and, 47–48; omnipotent parent and, 48; shattering realization of, 47

Problem solver: omnipotent as, 16, 19, 21, 35, 54; psychotherapy sought by, 16

Projection: case examples of, 92, 93; defining, 89–90; and miscommunication, 81, 89–93; most basic (own perception as normal), 91; omnipotent *vs.* impotent, 40*t*; parental, 23–25, 89, 91

Psychotherapy, 151–163; awakening observational powers in, 86; case examples of, 152–153, 157–161;

Psychotherapy (*cont.*)
  deconditioning in, 156–162;
  dynamic, 11, 23, 154–155;
  mistaken classification of normal
  in, 151–153; omnipotent role and,
  16, 19; parental, for family/child
  problems, 152–153; problem solver
  as initiator of, 16; relationship
  origin of emotional illnesses in,
  154–155; roles of patients in, 23;
  seeking, for emotional illnesses, 11;
  successful, insights gained in, 154

Rationalizations: deconditioning for
  overcoming, 158; and
  miscommunication, 81, 94
Reality: emotion-skewed thinking *vs.*,
  82–84; as erosive force, and
  marriage, 124–125; inadequate
  observations *vs.*, 84–87; magical
  thinking *vs.*, 87–89; projection *vs.*,
  89–93; rationalization *vs.*, 94;
  testing mode, omnipotent and
  impotent, 40*t*
Relationships: ideal world, 8–9;
  managing, role-playing and, 17;
  need to control anxiety and, 9;
  origin of emotional illnesses in,
  154–155; questions about, 4;
  unconscious patterns in, 5; well-
  being dependent on, 5. *See also*
  specific relationships and topics
Remarriage, after divorce, 141, 144,
  145–146
Retirement: impotents and, 72–73;
  omnipotents and, 56
Risk-taking behavior, of impotents, 70
Roles and role-playing, 15–28;
  assessment of others, 38–39; belief
  in omnipotence, 17; case example
  of, 18; culture and, 16;
  depersonalization in, 30–31;
  discarding, in successful marriage,
  105; freeing self from, five steps for,

  170–171, 171*t*; fulfilling potential
  vs., 15; gender and, 16–17;
  identifying and distinguishing, 39,
  40*t*; impaired judgment in, 31–33;
  individuality *vs.*, 16, 18;
  inevitability of, 19–22; labels in,
  desire to reject, 22; learning in
  childhood, 18–22; managing
  relationships through, 17; marriage,
  19, 104–115; omnipotent and
  impotent, 16–28; parental
  assignment, 23–25, 45, 64; parental
  combinations, 22–23; patterns in,
  15–17; perception and
  interpretation of emotions in,
  36–38; reducing others to
  stereotype in, 33–34; satisfaction
  with, 15; short-circuited thinking
  in, 29–30; symbiosis creation in,
  34–35; teaching children to
  recognize and avoid, 168–170;
  thinking styles in, 35–36;
  unconscious cues of, 29, 51;
  unnatural, adopting, 165–166, 168.
  See also Impotents; Omnipotents

School-age impotents, 67–70; chosen
  interests *vs.* academic work, 67–68;
  delay in starting school, 67; elite
  social groups of, 69; entering
  school as traumatic time, 67;
  teacher attention for, 49, 67, 69
School-age omnipotents, 48–52;
  general formula for, 51; idealization
  of home, 49; success and
  performance of, 49–50; as teacher's
  pet, 51–52
Scope of interests, omnipotent *vs.*
  impotent, 40*t*
Seeing things differently, 97–98
Self-discovery, 164–170
Self-esteem: impotent, 40*t*; marriage
  and, 108–109, 124; omnipotent, 21,
  40*t*, 51, 53–54, 108, 128

Self-observation, 165–166
Self-reliance, of omnipotents, 40*t*, 49, 58
Self-understanding: acquiring, 164–170; awareness of emotional conditioning and, 26–28; deconditioning and, 156–162, 171–172; divorce and, 146; failure to learn, 4–5; need for, 15; observations for, 165–166; psychotherapy and, 154–155
Self-worth, omnipotent *vs.* impotent, 40*t*
Seriousness, of omnipotents, 49, 53–54
Sex: extramarital, 117–123; marital conflict over, 116–117; omnipotent–impotent attraction, 19, 70–71, 106–108, 116–117, 143–144
Shared custody, 137–141
Short-circuiting, of thinking, 29–30
Sibling relationships, 60, 84
Sibling rivalry, 84
Stereotype: deconditioning *vs.*, 162; inadequate observation and, 85–86; marriage/divorce and, 146; projection and, 90–93; reducing others to, 33–34; roles assignment and adherence in, 24, 34, 38
Stigma: of divorce, 104, 132; of emotional illnesses, 11
Substance abuse: impotents and, 70, 128; in marriage, 124, 127–129; omnipotents and, 127–128
Suicide risk, for omnipotents, 32, 34, 51, 53, 124, 140
Symbiosis, creation of, 34–35

Teachers: and impotents, 49, 67–70; and omnipotents, 49–52

Teacher's pet, 51–52
"Terrible twos," 65–66
Thinking: assuming others think like us, 81, 96–97; emotionally conditioned, 35; emotion-skewed, and miscommunication, 81, 82–84; impotent role and, 21–22, 32; magical, 81, 87–89; quality, omnipotent *vs.* impotent, 40*t*; short-circuiting, 29–30; styles of, 35–36; unconditioned, 35
Threesome equilibrium, extramarital affairs and, 120
Toddlers: impotent, 65–66; omnipotent, 46–47
Toilet training: of impotents, 66; of omnipotents, 47
Treating people differently (double standard), 81, 95–96

Unconditioned thinking, 35
Unconscious cues, of roles, 29, 51
Unconscious emotional messages, from parents, 6–8, 15
Unconscious patterns, 5
Unnatural role, adopting, 165–166, 168

Value system, omnipotent *vs.* impotent, 40*t*
Verbal communication, unconscious emotional messages *vs.*, 6–8
Volunteerism, of omnipotents, 55

Well-being, dependence on relationships, 5
Will, 82–83
Words, defining differently, 81, 98–99
Work life: of impotents, 72–73; of omnipotents, 53–56

About the Authors

Homer B. Martin, MD, practiced general (adult) psychiatry for 40 years in Louisville, Kentucky. He trained at the Sheppard and Enoch Pratt Hospital in Towson, Maryland, and practiced forensic psychiatry in Baltimore, Maryland. He was an assistant clinical professor of psychiatry and behavioral sciences at the University of Louisville School of Medicine and a member of the American Psychiatric Association and the Southern Medical Association. Before becoming a psychiatrist, he was a general practitioner. He passed away in 2007. Jane Martin, his wife, asked Christine B. L. Adams, MD, to complete this book and share their findings about emotional conditioning.

Christine B. L. Adams, MD, has been in the private practice of child, adolescent, and adult psychiatry for 40 years. During her career, she has been a forensic child psychiatrist and worked in academic and community mental health settings, for the Social Security Administration and for the Department of Defense. She has been an examiner for the American Board of Psychiatry and Neurology in both Child and Adult Psychiatry and received the National Psychiatric Endowment Fund Award. She is a Distinguished Life Fellow of the American Academy of Child and Adolescent Psychiatry and Life Member of the American Psychiatric Association. Her website is DoctorChristineAdams.com.